BIOGRAPHICAL ENCYCLOPEDIA OF
20th-Century
World Leaders

BIOGRAPHICAL ENCYCLOPEDIA OF
20th-Century
World Leaders

Volume 5

Rusk – Zia-ul-Haq

Editor
John Powell
Pennsylvania State University, Erie

Marshall Cavendish
New York • London • Toronto • Sydney

Marshall Cavendish Corporation
99 White Plains Road
Tarrytown, New York 10591-9001

© 2000 Marshall Cavendish Corporation
Printed in the United States of America
09 08 07 06 05 04 03 02 01 00   5 4 3 2 1

Library of Congress Cataloging-in-Publication Data

Biographical encyclopedia of 20th-century world leaders / John Powell
p. cm.
   v. cm.
   Includes bibliographical references and index.
   1. Heads of state Biography Encyclopedias. 2. Statesmen Biography Encyclopedias. 3. Biography 20th century Encyclopedias. I. Powell, John, 1954-   . II. Title:
Biographical encyclopedia of twentieth-century world leaders
   ISBN 0-7614-7129-4 (set)
   ISBN 0-7614-7134-0 (vol. 5)
   D412.B56   1999
   920'.009'04—dc21

                                        99-34462
                                        CIP

∞ This paper meets the requirements of ANSI/NISO Z39.48-1992 (R1997)
Permanence of Paper for Publications and Documents in Libraries and Archives

CONTENTS

Key to Pronunciation

As an aid to users of the *Biographical Encyclopedia of 20th-Century World Leaders*, guides to pronunciation for all profiled leaders have been provided with the first mention of the name in each entry. These guides are rendered in an easy-to-use phonetic manner. Stressed syllables are indicated by capital letters.

Letters of the English language, particularly vowels, are pronounced in different ways depending on the context. Below are letters and combinations of letters used in the phonetic guides to represent various sounds, along with examples of words in which those sounds appear and corresponding guides for their pronunciation.

Symbols	Pronounced As In	Spelled Phonetically
a	answer, laugh	AN-sihr, laf
ah	father, hospital	FAH-thur, HAHS-pih-tul
aw	awful, caught	AW-ful, kawt
ay	blaze, fade, waiter	blayz, fayd, WAYT-ur
ch	beach, chimp	beech, chihmp
eh	bed, head, said	behd, hehd, sehd
ee	believe, leader	bee-LEEV, LEED-ur
ew	boot, loose	bewt, lews
g	beg, disguise, get	behg, dihs-GIZ, geht
i	buy, height, surprise	bi, hit, sur-PRIZ
ih	bitter, pill	bih-TUR, pihl
j	digit, edge, jet	DIH-jiht, ehj, jeht
k	cat, kitten, hex	kat, KIH-tehn, hehks
o	cotton, hot	CO-tuhn, hot
oh	below, coat, note	bee-LOH, coht, noht
oo	good, look	good, look
ow	couch, how	kowch, how
oy	boy, coin	boy, koyn
s	cellar, save, scent	SEL-ur, sayv, sehnt
sh	issue, shop	IH-shew, shop
uh	about, enough	uh-BOWT, ee-NUHF
ur	earth, letter	urth, LEH-tur
y	useful, young	YEWS-ful, yuhng
z	business, zest	BIHZ-ness, zest
zh	vision	VIH-zhuhn

BIOGRAPHICAL ENCYCLOPEDIA OF
20th-Century
World Leaders

Dean Rusk

Born: February 9, 1909; Cherokee County, Georgia
Died: December 20, 1994; Athens, Georgia

U.S. secretary of state (1961-1969)

David Dean Rusk (DAY-vihd DEEN RUHSK) was the son of Robert Hugh, an ordained Presbyterian minister, and Frances Elizabeth (Clotfelter) Rusk, a former schoolteacher. After graduating from Davidson College in 1931, Rusk won a Rhodes scholarship to attend St. John's College at Oxford University, England. He graduated with the M.A. degree in 1934. Rusk returned to the United States to teach at Mills College in Oakland, California, where he later became dean

Dean Rusk *(Library of Congress)*

of the faculty. In 1937 he married Virginia Wynifred Foisie of Seattle, Washington, and they had three children, David Patrick, Richard Geary and Margaret Elizabeth. He studied law at the University of California at Berkeley from 1937 to 1940. In 1940 he joined the U.S. Army.

Early Years

Rusk began his army career as an infantry reserve captain. Subsequently, he was assigned to work as head of the British Empire section of military intelligence. In 1943 Rusk went overseas to the China-Burma-India theater of operations where he became deputy chief of staff to General Joseph Stilwell.

After leaving the service in 1946, Rusk worked for the Department of State for six years in several high-level positions that concerned Far Eastern affairs (including the Korean War), U.N. affairs, and the establishment of the state of Israel. In 1952 he left the State Department to succeed Chester I. Barnard as president of the Rockefeller Foundation. He still occupied this position on December 12, 1960, when President John F. Kennedy appointed Rusk secretary of state.

Secretary of State

Rusk first served under a president intensely concerned with foreign affairs. As secretary of state, Rusk's role was to operate under the directions of the president. The first months of his appointment were faced with crises: a war in Laos, an abortive U.S.-backed invasion of Cuba, and the closing of the border between East and West Berlin. In 1963 Rusk helped to conclude the Limited Test Ban Treaty.

After President Kennedy's assassination in 1963, Lyndon B. Johnson retained Rusk in office.

The Rockefeller Foundation

The Rockefeller Foundation, chartered on May 14, 1913, by the New York State legislature, was established by John D. Rockefeller, Sr., for the well-being of people throughout the world. The foundation's strategies have always centered on the following core concepts: the conquest of hunger, population control, improvement of health care, the resolution of international conflict, education in developing countries, equal opportunity, environmental quality, and cultural development. An independent board of unsalaried trustees meets quarterly to award grants and to set guidelines and policy. Trustees are drawn from scholarly, scientific, and professional areas.

A president administers the foundation with the assistance of a staff, which consists of members of a variety of professional disciplines.

The president of the Rockefeller Foundation is the official spokesperson for the foundation, so careful consideration is given to the selection of a president. Dean Rusk, who left the foundation in 1960 to become secretary of state, was one of its best-known presidents. He served from 1952 to 1960 and oversaw the distribution of approximately $250 million for various projects, including aid to Asia, Africa, and Latin America. The first non-American to head the foundation, Gordon Conway, was appointed in 1997.

U.S. forces in Vietnam in 1964, early in the escalation that President Lyndon Johnson ordered and Secretary of State Dean Rusk suported. *(U.S. Marine Corps)*

Rusk became the spokesperson for the president's Vietnam War policy at congressional hearings. He supported the initiatives that led to the first Vietnam peace talks in May, 1968. Other developments that involved Rusk were the U.S. intervention in the Dominican Republic in 1965 and the withdrawal of France from military participation in the North Atlantic Treaty Organization (NATO) in 1966.

Scholar

Rusk left government in 1969 and returned to his home state of Georgia. He taught international law at the University of Georgia until 1984. Dean Rusk left a mark on the Department of State as well as a mark on the world. A visionary in terms of national issues, Rusk encouraged minorities and women to enter the foreign service. A visionary in terms of world leadership, Rusk paved the way to future arms control negotiations. Rusk served the United States with loyalty and integrity during one of the country's most turbulent decades.

Bibliography

Cohen, Warren I. *Dean Rusk*. Totowa, N.J.: Cooper Square Publications, 1980.
Rusk, Dean. *As I Saw It*. New York: Norton, 1990.
Schoenbaum, Thomas. *Waging Peace and War: Dean Rusk in the Truman, Kennedy, and Johnson Years*. New York: Simon and Schuster, 1988.

Karan A. Berryman

Carlos Saavedra Lamas

Born: November 1, 1878; Buenos Aires, Argentina
Died: May 5, 1959; Buenos Aires, Argentina

Foreign minister of Argentina (1932-1938), winner of 1936 Nobel Peace Prize

Carlos Saavedra Lamas (KAHR-lohs sah-ah-VAY-thrah LAH-mahs) was an Argentine diplomat who was awarded the Nobel Peace Prize in 1936 for his role in negotiating the end of the Chaco War, fought between Bolivia and Paraguay during the early 1930's. Saavedra Lamas was born in Buenos Aires and educated in the law. He began his career as a university professor and eventually went into politics. One of Saavedra Lamas's most influential academic works attacked interventionist policies, especially the type of intervention in other countries' affairs that was practiced by the United States. His work significantly influenced his later political theory. He was elected as a member of Parliament before the age of thirty, and by 1917 he had been appointed the Argentinean minister of justice and public education.

Foreign Affairs

In 1928, Saavedra Lamas became the president of the International Labor Congress in Geneva, Switzerland. During his tenure as president, he studied the Geneva institutions in detail, thus preparing him for his role in international politics. In February, 1932, he became Argentina's foreign minister. Saavedra Lamas served as minister of foreign affairs from 1932 to 1938. During this time, he also served as the president of the Pan-American Conference in Buenos Aires in 1936. In 1933, he persuaded the Argentine government to resume working with the League of Nations. He served as president of the League of Nations Assembly in 1936.

The Chaco War broke out in 1932, and Saavedra Lamas attempted to coordinate peace efforts from the beginning. Between the months of October, 1933, and June, 1934, the United States, Italy, and fourteen Latin American nations signed an antiwar treaty prepared by Saavedra Lamas. The treaty was used as the basis and blueprint for ending the war. He organized and presided over the international mediation committee of Brazil, Chile, Peru, Uruguay, and the United States, which secured the armistice between Bolivia and Paraguay on June 12, 1935.

Peacemaker and Scholar

The Nobel Peace Prize was awarded to Saavedra Lamas in 1936 for the antiwar pact that he

Carlos Saavedra Lamas *(The Nobel Foundation)*

The Chaco War

The Chaco War, which occurred during the years 1932-1935, was a conflict between Bolivia and Paraguay over a sparsely populated region between the two countries called the Chaco Boreal. Bolivia wanted an oil pipeline to the ocean through the disputed region. The Bolivian army held the initial advantage in 1932 when the war began. By 1935, however, the Paraguayans had gained control of the area, primarily through knowledge of the terrain. Argentine statesman

Carlos Saavedra Lamas played an instrumental role in the Chaco Peace Conference, which included representatives of Argentina, Brazil, Chile, Peru, Uruguay, and the United States. The fighting stopped in 1935, and a peace treaty was signed in Buenos Aires on July 21, 1938. Paraguay received 75 percent of the disputed region, and Bolivia received the rest, including a route to the Paraguay River and a port. Almost 100,000 men lost their lives in the war.

composed in his first year as Argentine foreign minister. He continued to work to secure ratification of the pact, proving himself to be a visionary statesman and leader. Saavedra Lamas continued to be instrumental in treaty negotiations. They resulted in a permanent Argentine-Paraguayan peace agreement, signed on July 21, 1938. Saavedra Lamas wrote several influential books on international law, peacekeeping, economics, and education. He continued his academic work after he stepped down as foreign minister. He served as rector of the University of Buenos Aires from 1942 to 1943. He also taught courses at the National University of La Plata.

Bibliography

Aaseng, Nathan. *The Peace Seekers: The Nobel Peace Prize (Nobel Prize Winners)*. New York: Lerner, 1989.

Farcau, Bruce. *Chaco War: Bolivia and Paraguay, 1932-1935*. Westport, Conn.: Praeger, 1996.

Holl, Karl, and Anne C. Kjelling. *The Nobel Peace Prize and the Laureates: The Meaning and Acceptance of the Nobel Peace Prize in the Prize Winner's Countries*. New York: Peter Lang, 1994.

Meyer, Edith Patterson. *In Search of Peace: The Winners of the Nobel Peace Prize, 1901-1975*. Nashville, Tenn.: Abingdon, 1978.

Karan Berryman-Pittman

Anwar el-Sadat

Born: December 25, 1918; Mit Abul-Kum, Egypt
Died: October 6, 1981; Cairo, Egypt

President of Egypt (1970-1981), winner of 1978 Nobel Peace Prize

Muhammad Anwar el-Sadat (moo-HAH-mahd AHN-wahr ehl-sah-DAHT) was born in a small village in the Nile Delta of Egypt, where he lived with his grandmother until 1925. In that year, the British, who controlled Egypt, ordered the Egyptian army to withdraw from the Sudan. Sadat's father returned from the Sudan to Egypt and brought the family to live in Cairo. As a child and young man, Sadat developed a strong conviction that the British should be driven out of Egypt.

Early Military Career

In 1936, Sadat entered Egypt's Royal Military Academy. During this time, according to some reports, Sadat was involved with the extreme nationalist organization Young Egypt. He also apparently had close connections to a radical Islamic group, the Muslim Brethren.

Sadat graduated from the military academy in February of 1938. In 1939, he became one of the founding members of a secret organization of army officers, known as the Free Officers' Organization, that sought to drive the British from Egypt. In 1941, Sadat was involved in a plot to form an alliance with Nazi German forces. Sadat and a number of other anti-British officers were arrested in 1942 and imprisoned. Following the war, Sadat was apparently involved in the assassination of pro-British former Egyptian finance minister Amin Osman in 1946. From 1946 to 1948, Sadat was in prison awaiting trial for the assassination of Osman, but he was released without conviction.

Support for Nasser

In late 1949, eleven members of the Free Officers' Organization came together to form the Revolutionary Command Council to plan to re-place the corrupt government of King Faruq. The eleven included Lieutenant Colonel Anwar el-Sadat and Lieutenant Colonel Gamal Abdel Nasser. Nasser was elected chairman of the council and Sadat, who had known Nasser since they were together at the military academy, became his loyal follower.

The economic situation in Egypt had worsened since the end of World War II, and opposition to the monarchy was growing among the military and police. In January of 1952, British troops killed about seventy rebellious policemen in Ismailia, and rioting broke out in Cairo. On

Anwar el-Sadat *(AP/Wide World Photos)*

Egyptian president Anwar el-Sadat (left) meeting with Palestinian Liberation Organization leader Yasir Arafat in Cairo in 1972. *(Camera Press Ltd./Archive Photos)*

July 23, 1952, Nasser and his Free Officers seized power.

General Muhammed Naguib became the first president and prime minister of the new republic, but Nasser replaced Naguib as prime minister in 1954. In 1956, with Sadat's support, Nasser was elected president and led Egypt until his death fourteen years later. Sadat served in a number of high offices under Nasser and twice served as Nasser's vice president, from 1964 to 1966 and from 1969 to 1970.

Presidency

Gamal Abdel Nasser died on September 28, 1970. Vice President Sadat became acting president and then was elected to the office on October 15. Although Sadat initially continued to maintain close relations with the Soviet Union, he moved the country away from reliance on the Soviets and toward closer relations with the United States. In 1972, Sadat expelled most Soviet advisers and technicians from Egypt.

The Arab-Israeli War of 1973 (the Yom Kippur War) began when Egypt and Syria invaded Israel. Although the Israelis launched a successful counteroffensive, the Egyptian army did manage to

The Young Egypt Party

The Young Egypt Party grew out of an Egyptian nationalist group founded by a lawyer named Ahmad Husayn in 1933. Young Egypt, or Misr al-Fatat became popular among students in many of the country's large cities. These students formed a paramilitary movement, known as the Green Shirts, associated with Young Egypt. In 1938, Young Egypt became a political party. It published the newspaper *Misr al-fatat*, which called for the establishment of a strong central government, the creation of an Egyptian empire, the nationalization of foreign companies, and the development of Egyptian industry.

The Young Egypt Party called for Egypt to be a leader in reviving Arabic and Islamic social values. These goals appealed to young nationalist officers and the party achieved a strong following in the military. In 1940, the party changed its name to the Nationalist Islamic Party. The creed proclaimed by the party at the time of the name change forbade followers to speak any language but Arabic, to purchase goods from stores that did not have Arabic signs, to buy goods from anyone but Egyptians, or to wear any clothes not produced in Egypt.

The 1971 Treaty of Friendship

During the presidency of Gamal Abdel Nasser, the Soviet Union became the major supplier of foreign aid and military assistance to Egypt. Toward the end of Nasser's life, he began to grow dissatisfied with Soviet support. When Anwar el-Sadat assumed the presidency in 1970, Sadat continued to move away from the Soviet Union and to seek other alliances. On September 1, 1971, Egypt entered into a federation with Libya and Syria. One of the outspoken opponents of the federation had been Egyptian vice president Ali Sabry, known as the most pro-Soviet member of the Egyptian government. In early May, Sadat had dismissed Sabry and then put Sabry and ninety others on trial for conspiracy against the government.

Sabry's dismissal disturbed the leaders of the Soviet Union. Soviet president Nikolai Podgorny led a delegation to Egypt to meet with Sadat. Sadat managed to convince the Soviets of Egypt's continued loyalty. On May 27, 1971, the Soviet Union and Egypt signed a fifteen-year Treaty of Friendship. Nevertheless, Sadat's dissatisfaction with Soviet support for Egypt's conflict with Israel led to the expulsion of thousands of Soviet advisers and technicians in 1972, This move definitively changed the direction of Egyptian foreign policy.

retake some of the land on the Sinai Peninsula that had been lost to Israel during the previous war in 1967. This limited success contributed to Sadat's prestige and provided him with a sufficiently strong position to seek peace with Israel.

Treaty with Israel

On November 19, 1977, Sadat traveled to Israel and appeared before the Israeli parliament, the Knesset, to propose a plan for achieving peace. The diplomatic negotiations between Egypt and Israel led to the joint award of the Nobel Peace Prize to Sadat and Israeli prime minister Menachem Begin in 1978. Their two nations signed the first peace treaty between Israel and an Arab nation on March 26, 1979. The treaty with Israel was opposed by many in Egypt and the rest of the Arab world. Egypt was also troubled by a worsening economy in the years following the peace treaty, and internal opposition to Sadat grew. Sadat responded with repression. In 1981, while he was reviewing a parade honoring the 1973 Arab-Israeli War, Sadat was assassinated by Muslim extremists.

Anwar el-Sadat on a 1977 visit to Israel, seated (third from right) between former Israeli prime minister Golda Meir and former Israeli defense minister Shimon Peres. Speaking at left is former Israeli prime minister Yitzhak Rabin. Sadat's visit launched peace negotiations that led to a historic 1979 treaty. *(AP/Wide World Photos)*

In Western nations, Anwar el-Sadat is regarded as a peacemaker. His treaty with the Nazis during World War II is generally overlooked or regarded as a tactical alliance to oppose British colonialism. Many people in Arab nations, however, look upon Sadat as a man who betrayed Arab unity against the common Israeli enemy. Regardless of one's perspective on Sadat, there is no question that he brought about a major change in the political life of Egypt and the Muslim world. He shifted Egypt from a pro-Soviet to a pro-Western position and weakened the solid anti-Israeli bloc of African and Middle Eastern Muslim nations.

Bibliography

Finklestone, Joseph. *Anwar Sadat: Visionary Who Dared*. Portland, Oreg. Frank Cass, 1996.

Hirst, David, and Irene Beeson. *Sadat*. London: Faber & Faber, 1981.

Israeli, Rafael. *Man of Defiance: A Political Biography of Anwar Sadat*. Totowa, N.J.: Barnes & Noble, 1986.

Sadat, Anwar el-. *In Search of Identity: An Autobiography*. New York: Harper & Row, 1977.

Sadat, Camelia. *My Father and I*. New York: Macmillan, 1985.

Sadat, Jihan. *A Woman of Egypt*. New York: Simon & Schuster, 1987.

Carl L. Bankston III

Andrei Sakharov

Born: May 21, 1921; Moscow, U.S.S.R.
Died: December 14, 1989; Moscow, U.S.S.R.

Soviet scientist and dissident, winner of 1975 Nobel Peace Prize

Andrei Dmitrievich Sakharov (uhn-DRYAY-ih duh-MYEE-tryih-yeh-vyihch sah-KAH-rof), son of a well-known physicist, spent his early years in Moscow surrounded by his family. After graduating from high school with honors in 1938, Sakharov enrolled in the physics department of Moscow University. After graduating with honors in 1942, Sakharov worked in a munitions factory, where he developed several inventions and wrote his first scientific papers.

Early Scientific Career

In 1945 Sakharov became a graduate student at the P. N. Lebedev Physical Institute of the Academy of Sciences of the Soviet Union, where he was taught by theoretical physicist Igor E. Tamm, a Nobel laureate. In 1948 Sakharov joined Tamm's research team working on a thermonuclear weapon. Beginning in 1950, Sakharov worked with Tamm on the first research concerning controlled thermonuclear reactions. Sakharov was elected a member of the Academy of Sciences in 1953, and through 1962 he continued to work on thermonuclear weapons and controlled reactions, first in Moscow and then in a secret location.

Developing Sociopolitical Views

Sakharov, while developing thermonuclear weapons, became aware of the long-term dangers to animal and plant life that the weapons posed, and the moral implications of this knowledge. In the latter half of the 1950's, Sakharov began to push for the limiting or banning of nuclear testing, creating conflict between him and several Soviet officials, including Nikita Khrushchev. Sakharov actively campaigned for the 1963 Moscow Treaty (the Limited Test Ban Treaty) that banned the testing of nuclear weapons in the atmosphere, in space, and under water.

Beginning in 1966-1967, Sakharov became an outspoken advocate for the victims of political oppression. In 1968 he published an essay entitled "Thoughts on Progress, Peaceful Coexistence, and Intellectual Freedom," which gained worldwide recognition. The essay contained an appeal to the international community to reject all forms of confrontation between nations, to cooperate in efforts to end world hunger, to support the science community's efforts to solve eco-

Andrei Sakharov *(The Nobel Foundation)*

Soviet scientist and dissident Andrei Sakharov and his wife, Elena, in exile in Gorky. *(Archive Photos)*

by the end of 1968 and banned Sakharov from any further secret scientific work. Nevertheless, Sakharov continued to study science until his death, focusing primarily on cosmology and particle physics.

The Nobel Peace Prize

By 1970 the defense of human rights had begun to occupy more of Sakharov's time. During 1970 he was a founding member of the Human Rights Committee, an organization that adopted petitions on many human rights issues. Sakharov spoke frequently about nuclear disarmament, and freedom of association, movement, and information. Sakharov also protested against unjust arrest and

logical problems, to work for the implementation of the Declaration of Human Rights, to support the democratization of society, and to encourage intellectual freedom. The Soviet government, although initially silent, had denounced the essay exile, capital punishment, forcible psychiatric hospitalization of dissidents, religious persecution, and discrimination in education. Sakharov struggled for freedom of emigration for the Soviet Union's national minorities and was deeply

Controlled Thermonuclear Reaction

Andrei Sakharov, physicist and human rights activist, joined Nobel laureate Igor E. Tamm's research team working on a thermonuclear weapon for the Soviet Union in 1948. While conducting this research, Sakharov proposed that the controlled thermonuclear reactions could be used to produce fissionable materials for use as fuel in atomic power plants. In 1952 Sakharov began research on and eventually developed magnetoplosive generators, which are used to turn the energy from a chemical or nuclear explosion into the energy of a magnetic field. The magnetic field controls the thermonuclear reaction, allowing fissionable materials for peaceful uses to be produced without mass destruction. Over time Sakharov observed the devastating effects of nuclear testing and weapons on plants and animals. He became an outspoken activist for the limiting or banning of nuclear testing and weapons. He was an advocate of the 1963 Moscow Treaty (the Nuclear Test-Ban Treaty), which banned nuclear weapons testing in the atmosphere, space, and water.

Sakharov's Exile in Gorky

In December of 1979, the Soviet Union sent troops into Afghanistan. A special secret-police unit executed President Hafizullah Amin, while Babrak Karmal formed a new government. The Soviet troops and Karmal's supporters began fighting Afghan guerrillas opposed to Soviet intervention and Karmal's rule. The struggle resulted in high civilian casualties and four million Afghan refugees. Andrei Sakharov, Soviet physicist and human rights activist, condemned the Soviet Union's intervention in interviews with foreign journalists. As a result, in January, 1980, the Soviet government stripped Sakharov of his government awards and extralegally exiled him to the city of Gorky. In Gorky Sakharov and his wife Elena Bonner were kept under strict surveillance and in isolation from family and friends. Several times government officials stole personal objects and papers, including articles, letters, and notes, from the Sakharovs' apartment. Mikhail S. Gorbachev ended the Sakharovs' exile in 1986.

concerned about the conditions of South Vietnamese refugees, the delivery of food relief to Cambodia, and the repression endured by Polish workers involved in the Solidarity movement and by Czechoslovakian political dissidents. In order to help victims of political oppression, Sakharov sent letters and appeals to Soviet and Western agencies, scientists, organizations, and politicians. Sakharov also frequently attended trials, traveled to refugee camps and places of exile, and participated in hunger strikes. Because of these actions, Sakharov and his family and friends were increasingly monitored and often harassed by the Soviet government.

Although Sakharov was given awards by several international human rights organizations for his human rights work, the greatest recognition of Sakharov's activism came in 1975, when he was awarded the Nobel Peace Prize. The Soviet government did not allow Sakharov to travel to Norway to receive the prize, but they did allow his wife, Elena Bonner, to go and to accept for him. On December 10-11, 1975, Bonner accepted the Nobel Peace Prize for Sakharov and delivered a lecture prepared by him for the occasion titled "Peace, Progress, and Human Rights." While honored at the recognition of his work, Sakharov was happiest that the Peace Prize established the validity within the international community of the human rights movement in Soviet Union.

Andrei Sakharov writing in his Moscow apartment in 1986 after being allowed to return from exile. (Reuters/Robert Evans/Archive Photos)

Exile and Beyond

In January of 1980, Sakharov condemned in interviews for foreign newspapers the Soviet Union's December, 1979, invasion of Afghanistan. As a result, the Supreme Soviet passed a decree on January 8, 1980, revoking Sakharov's government awards. On January 22 they exiled him to Gorky. In Gorky Sakharov and Bonner, who was allowed to accompany him, were kept under strict surveillance and in virtual isolation. In 1986 Mikhail S. Gorbachev allowed Sakharov and Bonner to return to Moscow.

Back in Moscow, Sakharov quickly discovered that he could be a leader in the *perestroika* process that Gorbachev had instituted. Sakharov pressed for the release of political prisoners and nuclear disarmament, and Gorbachev complied, freeing several hundred dissidents and negotiating with the United States on the elimination of intermediate-range missiles in Europe.

Sakharov was invited to participate in Congress. While he declined the position of People's Deputy, Sakharov did participate in the drafting of the new constitution and was elected to the five-member Interregional Group of Deputies. In 1989, Sakharov, dismayed at Gorbachev's slowness in instituting reforms, called on the people of the Soviet Union to stop work for two hours on December 11, and he encouraged the Interregional Group of Deputies to declare itself a formal opposition to Gorbachev's government. In his last public address, Sakharov reiterated the importance of a formal, loyal opposition and urged those working for reform to persist. Afterward, Sakharov returned home, where he was found dead by his wife a few hours later. The Soviet Union responded to Sakharov's death with four days of national mourning, during which thousands of people paid tribute to the memory of the brilliant, compassionate scientist and human rights activist.

Bibliography

Babyonshev, Alexander, ed. *On Sakharov*. Translated by Guy Daniels. New York: Vintage Books, 1982.

Lozansky, Edward, ed. *Andrei Sakharov and Peace*. New York: Avon Books, 1985.

Sakharov, Andrei. *Memoirs*. Translated by Richard Lourie. New York: Alfred A. Knopf, 1990.

_____. *Moscow and Beyond: 1986 to 1989*. Translated by Antonina Bous. New York: Alfred A. Knopf, 1990.

Erin K. McClain

António de Oliveira Salazar

Born: April 28, 1889; Vimiero, near Santa Comba Dão, Beira Alta province, Portugal
Died: July 27, 1970; Lisbon, Portugal

Authoritarian premier of Portugal (1932-1968)

António de Oliveira Salazar (ahn-TOH-nyew thee oh-lee-VAY-ee-rah sah-lah-ZAHR) was the son of a peasant estate manager and a shopkeeper. He became a professor of finance and economics and then one of the founders of Portugal's New State dictatorship. He dominated the most durable authoritarian system in twentieth-century Western Europe until shortly before his death.

Early Career

Salazar spent most of his early life as a student and later as a teacher in a secondary school before becoming a professor at Coimbra University's law school. The serious Salazar at one point considered the priesthood but instead began his studies at Coimbra in 1910. Salazar received among the highest grades of his generation of students. He received his doctoral degree in finance and economics in 1918. When the republican government offered him an invitation to become finance minister in 1918, Salazar declined on the basis of inexperience. He preferred campus life at Coimbra, where he published studies on the troubled finances of the First Republic and became involved in Catholic organizations. He entered political life in 1921 as a Catholic deputy in the turbulent legislature of the First Republic, but he resigned after witnessing only one session. Salazar continued to teach at the university until 1928.

When the military overthrew the First Republic in 1926, Salazar entered the federal government for the first time. Once again he was offered the post of finance minister, this time by the Portuguese military. He accepted but he resigned when he discovered the chaos within the regime and when his demands for personal authority were rejected. The military failed to maintain fiscal and financial discipline, however, and

Salazar eventually received personal control over all budgetary matters in April, 1928.

Once he implemented financial reforms, Salazar received an appointment as minister of colonies in 1930. At that point he gathered sufficient prestige and authority to become a civilian dictator. His power became official when he was named prime minister in July, 1932.

The Salazar Regime

From 1928 to 1944, Salazar and his government enjoyed wide popularity. Able to provide order, Salazar put many to work by means of a wide variety of public works projects. Moreover, he

António de Oliveira Salazar *(Popperfoto/Archive Photos)*

1371

During World War II British leaders negotiated with António de Oliveira Salazar's Portuguese government to establish a base in the Azores from which to combat German submarines. Here American planes and destroyers force a damaged German U-boat to the surface. *(Library of Congress)*

made it clear that the Catholic Church would be protected and promoted. The Spanish Civil War (1936-1939) shook Salazar's plans to stabilize the economy and strengthen financial programs. Salazar backed Francisco Franco's rebel movement strongly in the Spanish Civil War, even contributing a group of volunteers who fought against the Spanish Republic. To his dying day, Franco kept a photograph of Salazar on his desk. As Salazar monopolized power in Lisbon, he assumed even more key cabinet posts. In the early days, Salazar dominated day-to-day administration, although this level of

The New State

The "New State"—in Portuguese, *Estado Novo*—was the name given to the ideology of António de Oliveira Salazar's government. It emphasized Portuguese nationalism through Catholicism, conservative fiscal management, and rebuilding the empire. The Great Depression of the 1930's forced Portugal to become more self-reliant internally as well as to seek new markets abroad. Middle-class civilians who admired the fascist outlook of Germany and Italy dominated Salazar's cabinets. There was never a single party that dominated politics. Particularly famous was Salazar's slogan, "Nothing against the Nation, All for the Nation." Economic corporatism enabled employees and employers to resolve disputes by "national" solutions. A huge bureaucracy provided employment, so much of the middle class remained loyal. The secret police was given extensive powers, including the use of torture and concentration camps.

A 1940 concordat restored many of the Catholic Church's past privileges. For example, priests were allowed to teach in the schools, and divorce was forbidden to people who were married in a Catholic Church. Salazar's regime stopped any anti-Catholic writing and permitted religious orders to operate schools and charitable works.

The fiscal and economic developments were generally improvements. Salazar always balanced the budget, but his governments never had great revenues. In the early days of the *Estado Novo*, Salazar enjoyed a certain popularity because taxes were less regressive than before and many people were employed in a fairly ambitious public works program. Highways, bridges, dams, and irrigation works appeared in great number.

The Angolan Revolt

Angola, in southwestern Africa, was a Portuguese colony (until 1951) and then a Portuguese province (until 1975). Although all inhabitants of Angola had been made full citizens of Portugal in 1961, a powerful revolution eventually ended Portuguese rule in 1975. The Movimento Popular de Libertacao de Angola (MPLA) was headed by Henrique Galvao, a former adviser to Salazar. The MPLA fought hard, and hundreds died in massacres in the bloody war. The Portuguese army could not stamp out the insurrection despite the eventual presence of 100,000 troops in Angola by 1968. Basing its power on assemblies and direct committees, the MPLA appealed to Angolan desires for decentralized popular participation in government. Although the MPLA triumphed in 1975, it faced further struggles, having to fight intervention by the U.S. Central Intelligence Agency and by South Africa.

control diminished as the dictator delegated wider power to others after 1945. During his thirty-six-year tenure as premier, Salazar manipulated the key cabinet appointments.

A lifelong bachelor who once boasted that he would never depart Lisbon, even to care for his aging mother, Salazar never married. Instead he lived with a beloved housekeeper from Coimbra and adopted two daughters.

World War II

Portugal declared neutrality during the beginning stages of World War II but could not avoid minimal involvement. When the conflict affected the Atlantic—because of German submarines and British attempts to combat them—the Portuguese Azores, Madeira, and Cape Verde Islands became important. In Asia, Japan had for some years been overrunning other European colonies but left the Portuguese colony of Macao alone; eventually Japan did seize Portuguese Timor. Meanwhile, Portugal enjoyed a certain level of pros-

Portuguese premier António de Oliveira Salazar in 1956, speaking at the twentieth anniversary of the Portuguese Legion. *(National Archives)*

perity. Refugees from Axis-occupied nations often sought to enter Britain, the United States, or Brazil, and the best route lay through Portugal. Some came well provided, and a few chose to stay in the country.

Moreover, Portugal purchased a large quantity of Nazi gold through Swiss bankers, more than any other European neutral power. Many of the gold ingots that arrived in Lisbon had been stolen by the Nazis from Holland and Belgium. The Portuguese government was adamant in its claim that the gold had been obtained from Switzerland in good faith. The government refused to approve the gold's return.

Salazar foresaw an Allied victory sooner than any other European statesman except Britain's Winston Churchill. He realized that the United States would eventually enter the war. Once the United States entered the war in December, 1941, U.S. president Franklin D. Roosevelt wanted a base in the Azores from which to combat German submarines. At U.S. urging, Britain opened negotiations for these bases, which both countries used effectively in defeating the German submarines.

The Final Years

After World War II, Salazar survived international attacks upon his semifascist past by emphasizing his anticommunist credentials. This tactic enabled Portugal to join the North Atlantic Treaty Organization (NATO) and obtain Marshall Plan funding. The government's ongoing emphasis on building and maintaining the infrastructure meant that the traditional weakness of

Portuguese education continued. The number of primary schools, for example, had increased from only seven thousand in 1927 to a paltry ten thousand by 1950. An estimated 45 percent of the country was still illiterate in 1950. Meanwhile, higher education under Salazar's government actually declined; fear, harassment, and faculty purges created an unstimulating atmosphere.

The government's basic failure to develop Portuguese society and distribute economic rewards in a rational way resulted in high levels of emigration after World War II. Many Portuguese went to Brazil, the United States, Canada, and Western Europe in great numbers as migrant workers. Paris soon had the second largest concentration of Portuguese people in the world. In 1966, 120,000 people left the country, breaking past records. Workers within Portugal received no welfare benefits or pensions. At that time ten families owned 168 firms and controlled 53 percent of the national wealth.

Bibliography

Delgado, Humberto. *The Memoirs of General Delgado*. Edited by Iva Delgado. London: Cassell, 1964.

Figueiredo, Antonio. *Portugal: Fifty Years of Dictatorship*. London: Penguin, 1975.

Kay, Hugh. *Salazar and Modern Portugal*. New York: Hawthorne, 1970.

Pinto, António Costa. *Salazar's Dictatorship and European Fascism: Problems of Interpretation*. New York: Columbia University Press, 1995.

Douglas W. Richmond

Augusto César Sandino

Born: May 18, 1895; Niquinohomo, Nicaragua
Died: February 21, 1934; Managua, Nicaragua

Nicaraguan guerrilla leader

Augusto César Sandino (ow-GEW-stoh THAY-sahr sahn-DEE-noh) was born to a coffee grower and a servant girl in the highlands of Nicaragua. After spending his early life in poverty, he trained to be a produce merchant. In search of new opportunities, he left Nicaragua and traveled to Honduras and Guatemala. Eventually, he settled in Mexico to work in the oil industry. In Mexico, Sandino learned the basics of liberalism, radical nationalism, and social revolution—ideas that would greatly affect both his future and that of his homeland. In 1926, Sandino returned to Nicaragua and soon joined the effort to force U.S. troops from his country.

American Occupation

Initially, Sandino was not opposed to the United States itself, but he was against the American troops sent to Nicaragua in 1912 to support a series of pro-United States Conservative leaders. Sandino joined lower-class peasants and merchants in backing the nationalist Liberals against the Conservative government, which was supported by the upper classes and by U.S. economic interests. Following his return to Nicaragua in 1926, Sandino's revolutionary radicalism made Liberal leaders nervous. He formed his own guerrilla force among peasants, Indians, and miners. In 1926, Sandino led an army of eight hundred Sandinistas (followers of Sandino) in a war against the Conservatives and their American backers.

When the United States stepped in to negotiate a settlement of the conflict in 1927, Sandino led his army into the mountains, where they began a hit-and-run guerrilla war against the Americans. For nearly six years, Sandino led a struggle against the U.S. occupying forces.

Sandino's Assassination

As the American war against the Sandinistas dragged on, the U.S. public grew increasingly opposed to the conflict. The United States decided to withdraw the Marines and replace them with the Nicaraguan National Guard. The guard was established, trained, and equipped by the United States and led by Anastasio Somoza García. The United States completed its withdrawal of troops in 1932. As he had promised to do, once the Americans had left Nicaragua, Sandino joined negotiations for peace with the government of President Juan Bautista Sacasa in January, 1933. Sandino swore loyalty to the Sacasa government and even offered to protect the president from the

Augusto César Sandino *(Library of Congress)*

1375

U.S. Marines with a rebel flag captured from Sandino's forces in 1932. *(National Archives)*

National Guard. After the settlement of the war, Sandino returned to the countryside.

In February, 1934, Sandino returned to the Nicaragua capital, Managua, to help finalize the peace talks. On February 21, 1934, as he and two Sandinista officers were leaving the farewell dinner at the end of the meetings, National Guard troops arrested the three and took them to an airfield, where they were shot. Somoza later admitted full responsibility for masterminding the executions but claimed that he did so with the authorization of the American ambassador, Arthur Bliss Lane. Lane denied involvement in the murders.

Second Sandinista Movement

The memory of Sandino led to the establishment of the *Frente Sandinista de Liberación Nacional* (FSLN) in 1961, when three major guerrilla groups chose to pool their resources. The FSLN brought together various groups' interpretation of what Sandino himself had fought for: Marxism, liberalism, and social Christianity. The FSLN began fighting against the U.S.-supported regime of Anastasio Somoza Debayle, finally emerging victorious in 1979 after the execution of Samoza. The United States interpreted this takeover as the beginning of Soviet Communist expansion in the Americas. The United States therefore began to provide support for the anti-Sandinista rebels called the Contras during the presidency of Ronald Reagan.

Bibliography

Macaulay, Neill. *The Sandino Affair*. Chicago: Quadrangle Books, 1967.

Selser, Gregorio. *Sandino*. New York: Monthly Review Press, 1981.

Walker, Thomas. *Nicaragua: The Land of Sandino*. Boulder, Colo.: Westview Press, 1991.

Matthew A. Redinger

An American Outlaw

Augusto César Sandino's success in using a small, relatively poorly armed guerrilla army to fight the Western Hemisphere's greatest power to a standstill made him an outlaw in the United States. The U.S. press depicted Sandino as a bandit and a gangster. However, while he was internationally hated, the Nicaraguan people and other Latin American peasants hailed Sandino as one of the most popular patriots. Sandino worked in the countryside to help peasants establish self-sufficient agricultural cooperatives. He inspired nationalist anti-imperialist movements throughout Latin America; for this and his collectivist land policies, the American press and government portrayed him as an advocate of Soviet-inspired communism.

Eisaku Satō

Born: March 27, 1901; Tabuse, Yamaguchi Prefecture, Japan
Died: June 2, 1975; Tokyo, Japan

Prime minister of Japan (1964-1972), winner of 1974 Nobel Peace Prize

Eisaku Satō (ay-sah-kew sah-toh) was the adopted son of Satō Matsusuke, and his mother impressed upon her sons a sense of obligation to serve Japan. After graduation from the law school of Tokyo University in 1924, Satō entered the Ministry of Railways, which sent him to study in Europe and the United States from 1934 to 1937. Immediately following World War II, he was named general director of the Railway Administration and was soon promoted to vice minister of transportation, the highest rank for a civil servant in Japan.

Political Career

After Japan's defeat in World War II, it was occupied by the victorious Allies. Under the occupation, the government purged large numbers of prominent prewar politicians, which provided room for new people to participate in parliamentary politics. Recognizing Satō's ability to handle troublesome new labor unions, Prime Minister Shigeru Yoshida appointed him as chief cabinet secretary in 1948. Satō soon won a seat in the Japanese parliament, the Diet. Between 1950 and 1954, Satō served in many government positions, including secretary general of the Liberal Party, minister of postal services and telecommunications, and minister of construction. In 1954, Yoshida rescued Satō from accusations that he had received political bribes from shipbuilding executives.

Having built a strong personal following, Satō helped his brother, Nobusuke Kishi, become prime minister in 1957 and served in the cabinet as minister of finance until 1960. From 1960 to 1962, Satō was the minister of international trade and industry, and from 1963 to 1964, he held positions as minister of state in charge of science

and technology and in charge of the eighteenth Olympic Games, held in Japan. In 1964, Satō was defeated by Hayato Ikeda in a bitter struggle to become prime minister. However, stricken with cancer, Ikeda retired in 1965, and Satō succeeded him to the premiership of Japan by acclamation.

Prime Minister

As prime minister, Satō faced a crisis in the universities as well as continuing problems in Japanese-U.S. relations. To deal with campus disorders and riots, Satō passed a bill that would allow the Ministry of Education to take over any

Eisaku Satō *(Library of Congress)*

1377

The United States-Japan Security Treaty

The United States-Japan Security Treaty, originally signed in 1951 and first revised in 1960, guaranteed that the United States could continue to use its military bases in Japan in order to protect Taiwan and South Korea. Through the efforts of Japanese prime minister Eisaku Satō, the Security Treaty was amended in 1971 to bring Okinawa and the other Ryukyu Islands that were captured by the United States during World War II back under Japanese sovereignty in 1972. The United States retained the use of its military installations on Okinawa after 1972, provided that it did not keep nuclear weapons on Okinawa and did not send military forces into combat from Japanese territory without the consent of Japan. Another revision to the treaty in 1996 stated that the United States would eventually return to Okinawa 20 percent of the land held by the U.S. military.

Japanese prime minister Eisaku Satō bidding farewell to U.S. president Lyndon B. Johnson after talks at the White House in 1967. *(Arnold Sachs/CNP/Archive Photos)*

university where disruption persisted for more than nine months. Japan's continued economic growth and Satō's hard line on student disorders made him a popular prime minister.

Because of Satō's negotiations with the United States in 1967, the Bonin Islands were returned to Japan in 1968. In November of 1969, Satō flew to the United States to conclude negotiations for the return of Okinawa to Japanese sovereignty by 1972. Upon returning to Japan, Satō won a resounding victory in the general elections held in December, 1969. After the United States returned the southern Ryukyu Islands, including Okinawa, to Japan in May, 1972, Satō resigned in July at the age of seventy-one. For his policies on nonproliferation of nuclear weapons, Satō became the first Asian to receive the Nobel Peace Prize, sharing it with Sean MacBride in 1974.

Japanese Legend

Under Satō's direction, Japan developed its immense economic strength, which enhanced its political power in the international community. Satō was instrumental in negotiating a revision of the United States-Japan Security Treaty that returned Okinawa to Japan in 1972. He also made major contributions to world peace by opposing nuclear arms, bringing Japan into a pact on the nonproliferation of nuclear arms, and conducting a peaceful foreign policy.

Bibliography

Hellmann, Donald C. *Japanese Foreign Policy and Domestic Politics*. Berkeley: University of California Press, 1969.

Reischauer, Edwin O. *Japan: The Story of a Nation*. New York: Knopf, 1989.

Thayer, Nathaniel B. *How the Conservatives Rule Japan*. Princeton, N.J.: Princeton University Press, 1969.

Alvin K. Benson

Jeanne Mathilde Sauvé

Born: April 26, 1922; Prud'homme, Saskatchewan, Canada
Died: January 26, 1993; Montreal, Quebec, Canada

Canadian political figure, first woman governor-general of Canada (1984-1990)

Jeanne Mathilde Sauvé (ZHUHN mah-TIHL-deh soh-VAY) was the fifth child of Anna and Charles Benoît. Her carpenter father moved the family to Ottawa, where Jeanne attended the French-language Notre Dame du Rosaire, winning first-class honors (in the English provincial examinations) in 1940 and a university scholarship. When her father refused to let her attend the University of Ottawa, she took a full-time job as translator for the Department of National Defence and earned her B.A. by taking evening courses. She also worked for the Jeunesse Étudiante Catholique (JEC, young Catholic student) movement and managed to convince her parents to allow her to accept a job at its Montreal headquarters. In 1948 she married Maurice Sauvé (their son, Jean-François, was born in 1959) and

Jeanne Mathilde Sauvé *(UPI/Corbis-Bettmann)*

launched a highly successful broadcasting and journalistic career.

Youth Leader, Broadcaster, and Journalist

Sauvé's outstanding organizational, communication, and negotiating skills were first developed through her work as national president (1942-1947) of the JEC. She visited schools, colleges, and churches across the country, speaking about religious, social, and political reform. She enjoyed intellectual discussions with like-minded colleagues such as Maurice Sauvé, Gérard Pelletier, Pierre Juneau, Marc Lalonde, and Claude Ryan, all of whom would figure prominently in public affairs. She accompanied her husband to London, where he completed his doctorate in economics. Later she served as director of the Youth Secretariat of the United Nations Educational, Scientific, and Cultural Organization (UNESCO) in Paris. She studied French civilization at the Sorbonne. Her cosmopolitanism conflicted with the provincialism of French Quebecers, who tended to see the federal government and English Canadians as perpetual enemies. Her liberal thinking was influenced by her husband, an advocate of workers' rights who served in the Confederation of National Trade Unions before becoming a cabinet minister for Lester B. Pearson.

Sauvé became a public personality in the early 1950's. Her appearances on *Femina*, a public-affairs radio program, opened the door to television. Her first stint on live television in December, 1952, was disastrous: In the course of a lesson on sewing boys' short pants, her machine jammed and she lost track of the script. However, subsequent appearances on popular discussion shows on the French-language network pro-

Jeunesse Étudiante Catholique

The Jeunesse Étudiante Catholique (JEC, young Catholic student) movement was begun in the 1920's by a Belgian priest named Joseph Cardijn. It was an offshoot of Cardijn's original organization for Catholic working people. Cardijn believed that the Catholic Church was too dogmatic. He envisioned a movement that would be led by lay people, with the assistance of clergy. His program for the movement was based on a three-step process: *voir, uger, agir,* which translates as look (or see), judge, and act. This program was intended to encourage young people to bring Christian principles into their daily lives in an active way. In 1931 Father Henry Roy started the first Quebec branch of the JEC. In Canada the activist, localized approach of the JEC attracted many members, including Jeanne Sauvé, who would later be in the vanguard of provincial and federal reform.

moted her image as a forward-thinking liberal, as did her own talk show, *Opinions.* Sauvé's broadcasting career lasted from 1952 to 1963.

Cabinet Minister

Sauvé was one of three Quebec women elected to Parliament in 1972. She became the only woman in Pierre Trudeau's cabinet and the third woman in Canadian history to be a federal minister. She was minister of state for science and technology before becoming minister of environment in 1974. Her biggest concerns were St. Lawrence River pollution and the threat posed to humans and wildlife by highly toxic polychlorinated biphenyl compounds (PCBs). In 1975, she became head of the Department of Communications, urging more Canadian content in broadcasting, tighter advertising codes, and technological advancements. As speaker of the House of Commons (1980-1984), she took measures to reduce waste of taxpayers' money even while opening the first day-care center on Parliament Hill.

First Female Governor-General

As governor-general, the queen's representative (1984-1990), she reformed the office's administration and promoted tolerance and national unity. She made official visits to every province, as well as to the Yukon and Northwest Territories, and was Canada's official host to the queen, the pope, U.S. president Ronald Reagan, foreign ambassadors, and thousands of other guests.

Jeanne Sauvé's patriotism sometimes stirred controversy. She angered Quebec nationalists by stating that Quebecers could advance more effectively through personal effort and reform than by separatism. Her foes criticized her farewell speech as governor-general because of its political tone, but she believed in a multicultural, bilingual country.

Bibliography

Greenwood, Barbara. *Jeanne Sauvé.* Markham, Ontario: Fitzhenry & Whiteside, 1989.

Woods, Shirley E. *Her Excellency Jeanne Sauvé.* Toronto: Macmillan, 1986.

Keith Garebian

Gerhard Schröder

Born: April 7, 1944; Mossenberg, Germany

Chancellor of Germany (elected 1998)

Gerhard Fritz Kurt Schröder (GAYR-hahrt FRIHTZ KEWRT SHROO-dur) was the son of a common laborer and a cleaning woman. He never knew his father, who was killed while serving in the German army during World War II. His mother worked as a cleaning woman to support her five children. Upon completing primary and working-class secondary education, Schröder went to work as a retail sales clerk. Between 1962 and 1966 he completed a college preparatory course through adult education. From 1966 to 1971 he studied law at Göttingen University; from 1972 to 1976 he interned in legal work. In 1976 he was admitted to the bar, and he briefly practiced law. He married four times.

Membership in the Social Democratic Party

Schröder had joined the Social Democratic Party as early as 1963. He worked actively in the radical Young Socialist movement, sponsored by the Social Democratic Party as a means of bringing new leaders up from the ranks. Schröder's associates were passionate theoreticians with strong Marxist beliefs. Schröder himself, though professing to believe in Marxism, seemed more interested in the organizational development of the Young Socialists. He served as nationwide chairman of the organization between 1978 and 1980.

In 1980, forced out of the Young Socialists because he had reached the age limit of thirty-five, Schröder acquired a seat in the Bundestag, the national legislature of Germany. He achieved some notoriety by not wearing a tie during his first speech there. During the 1980's, Schröder rose gradually within the party, eventually becoming a member of the presidium, the party leadership, in 1989.

Gerhard Schröder surrounded by photographers in September, 1998, shortly after being elected German chancellor. *(Reuters/Jerry Lampen/ Archive Photos)*

Minister-President of Lower Saxony

In 1986 Schröder shifted his focus to state politics, becoming chairman of the Social Democratic group in the Lower Saxony state legislature. After one unsuccessful attempt at the position, he was elected minister-resident, the equivalent of governor, of the state of Lower Saxony in 1990. In order to have a majority in the legislature, the Social Democrats had to ally with the Green Party, the environmental party, and for four years Schröder headed an administration shared with the Greens. This led the state government to sponsor numerous environmental actions that required the borrowing of substantial sums of money.

From 1994 to 1998, however, the Social Democrats were strong enough in the state legislature for Schröder to reign supreme in Lower Saxony. Schröder devoted much of his effort to trying to retain existing businesses, especially the largest employer in the state, Volkswagen. In September, 1998, Schröder became the Social Democratic candidate for chancellor of Germany, a post he assumed in September, 1998. Schröder took over the chancellorship from Christian Democratic Union leader Helmut Kohl, who had been chancellor for sixteen years.

Chancellor of Germany

The German government headed by Chancellor Schröder planned to focus on Germany's major problem, a high level of unemployment. In 1998 it stood at 12 percent nationally and was even higher in depressed regions such as eastern Germany (the former communist East Germany) and Schröder's home state of Lower Saxony. Schröder's government also promised initiatives to increase the number of apprenticeships. In deference to its allies in the governing coalition,

German chancellor Gerhard Schröder before addressing the National Press Club in Washington, D.C., in 1998. *(Reuters/Mark Wilson/Archive Photos)*

The German Election of 1998

In the election held on September 27, 1998, 40.9 percent of German voters chose the Social Democrats, Gerhard Schröder's party, giving them 298 seats in the 656-seat legislature. The Christian Democratic/Christian Social alliance won 245 seats, with 35.2 percent of the vote. The Greens captured 6.7 percent of the vote and 47 seats. Three smaller parties also passed the 5 percent threshold to secure representation in the legislature. While the defeat of Chancellor Helmut Kohl of the Christian Democratic Union had been predicted by the polls, the margin of the Social Democrats' victory surprised some observers. Kohl had been in office for sixteen years and had become something of an institution in German politics. By creating a coalition with the Greens, Schröder and the Social Democrats assured themselves of a voting majority in the legislature. With the principal ministries in the hands of Social Democrats, the party also assured itself of dominance. The only important ministry ceded to the Greens was the foreign ministry; Green leader Joschka Fischer became foreign minister. About 82 percent of the qualified voters cast ballots in this election, 3 percent more than in the preceding election in 1994.

the Greens, the Schröder government announced plans to phase out nuclear plants in Germany and to ease access to German citizenship.

Bibliography

Braunthal, Gerard. *The German Social Democrats Since 1969*. 2d ed. Boulder, Colo.: Westview Press, 1994.

_____. "The 1998 German Election: Gerhard Schröder and the Politics of the New Middle." *German Politics and Society* 50 (Spring, 1999).

Kramer, Jane. "The Once and Future Chancellor." *The New Yorker*, September 14, 1998, 58-71.

Livingston, Robert G., ed. *West German Political Parties: CDU, CSU, FDP, SPD, the Greens*. Washington, D.C.: American Institute for Contemporary Politics, The Johns Hopkins University, 1986.

Nancy M. Gordon

James Henry Scullin

Born: September 18, 1876; Trawalla, Victoria, Australia
Died: January 28, 1953; Melbourne, Victoria, Australia

Prime minister of Australia (1929-1931)

James Henry Scullin (JAYMZ HEHN-ree SKUH-lihn) was the son of an Australian railway employee. Scullin took night courses in commerce and economics after he completed primary school, and in 1903 he opened a small grocery store in Ballarat. At that time he also joined the local branch of the Labour Party. Considered a champion debater at a young age, Scullin became an organizer with the Australian Workers' Union. He entered the realm of politics and campaigned against Prime Minister Alfred Deakin for his seat in the 1906 election. After losing this election, Scullin campaigned again in 1910 for the seat of the Corangamite district and won. He lost his seat in 1913.

Parliament

After losing the 1913 election, Scullin moved into the field of journalism. As the editor of the *Ballarat Evening Echo*, the daily newspaper of the Labor Party, he continued to support the party's causes. In 1916, Scullin served as a Victorian delegate to the special federal conference that dealt with the issue of conscription during World War I (1914-1918). Much of Scullin's political theory was disseminated through the *Ballarat Evening Echo*, which continued to have a great influence on Australian politics through the war years. He attended the 1921 federal conference, at which he supported socialist objectives, controversial at the time.

In 1922, Scullin was reelected to Parliament. Impressed by his knowledge of finance and taxation, as well as by his speaking ability, his colleagues elected him leader of the Labor Party in 1928. Under Scullin's vision and leadership, the party regained the strength it had lost from a 1916 split in policy. One of his biggest disadvantages as party leader, and throughout the rest of his political career, was the loss of a kidney, which caused him to experience poor health.

Prime Minister

Scullin was elected prime minister in 1929. During his tenure in office, he faced some critical problems. These included the onset of the Great Depression, opposition control of the Senate, little cooperation from the Australia Commonwealth Bank, and a cabinet that included only two members who had experience as state officers.

James Henry Scullin *(Corbis/Bettmann-UPI)*

The Federal Parliamentary Labour Party

The Federal Parliamentary Labour Party became an aggressive political organization in Australia in the 1890's. The party favored egalitarianism and social reform. Australia's first government after becoming a commonwealth was formed by the Labour Party, with John C. Watson as prime minister. The party continued to exert influence in Australian politics. James Henry Scullin was one of its most influential leaders. The Labor Party (the spelling changed from "Labour" in the 1910's) position was consolidated in 1944 with forty-nine seats in the House. One of the later significant acts of the Labor Party was the creation of the Australian Whaling Commission in 1949. In 1958, the Labor Party reorganized under new leadership.

Scullin initiated measures to combat the Depression that included wage decreases, rationing, limitations on imports, and balancing the budget. These measures were successful in the beginning of his term. However, Scullin's treasurer, Edward Granville Theodore, was forced to resign from office in 1930 because of a Queensland mining scandal. When Theodore resigned, the cabinet split on support for financial policy. Scullin assumed the position of treasurer until Theodore's return to the cabinet in 1931. Scullin wanted to initiate a plan to expand credit. The plan ultimately divided the Labor Party and led to his defeat in the 1931 election.

Scullin was primarily defeated by the divisions within the Parliamentary Labor Party and by the absence of a Labor majority in the Senate. Scullin continued to lead the Labor opposition until September, 1935. At that time he resigned, and John Curtin was elected as his successor. Curtin offered Scullin a position in his government, but Scullin declined. He remained in Parliament and was often consulted by the political leaders of the day. Scullin retired from the Parliament in 1949.

Bibliography

Childe, V. Gordon. *How Labour Governs: A Study of Australia*. New York: Cambridge University Press, 1964.

Hawker, Geoffrey. *Politics and Policy in Australia*. St. Lucia, Queensland, Australia: University of Queensland Press, 1979.

Robertson, John. *J. H. Scullin: A Political Biography*. Nedlands, Australia: University of Western Australia Press, 1974.

Ward, Russel Braddock. *Concise History of Australia*. St. Lucia, Queensland, Australia: University of Queensland Press, 1992.

Wilson, Charles. *Australia, 1788-1988: The Creation of a Nation*. Totowa, N.J.: Barnes and Noble, 1988.

Karan Berryman-Pittman

Hans von Seeckt

Born: April 22, 1866; Schleswig, Prussia
Died: December 27, 1936; Berlin, Germany

Head of the German army between World Wars I and II (1920-1926)

Johannes "Hans" Friedrich Leopold von Seeckt (yoh-HAH-nehs "HAHNS" FREED-rihk LAY-oh-pohlt fon ZAYKT) was the son of a Prussian general, although most of his family was middle class, not aristocratic. After completing secondary school in the Protestant *Gymnasium* in Strassburg, he became a junior officer in the elite Prussian regiment known as the Emperor Alexander Grenadier Guards. In 1893 he married Dorothea Fabian from a leading Jewish family. She was the granddaughter of the liberal writer Ernst Moritz Arndt.

World War I and After

Seeckt had an active military career during World War I. After serving initially on the western front, he was appointed to the staff of General von Mackensen and is credited with planning the great German victory over the Russians at Gorlice in May, 1915. In 1916-1917 he served with the joint German-Austrian army and helped plan the sweeping victory of this force over Romania. In 1918 he was sent to Turkey, where he served as chief of staff of the Turkish armed forces until Turkey's surrender in September of 1918.

Back in Germany following the armistice of 1918, Seeckt established a reputation as a nonpolitical soldier in the confusion of demobilization of the imperial army. His reputation as a brilliant staff officer brought him appointment, by the provisional government of the German Republic, to the post of chief of the Troops Office, on December 24, 1919. In that capacity Seeckt presided over the gradual reduction of the German army, endearing himself to the political leaders of the German Republic by refusing to support a radical-right attempt to seize power in March, 1920, led by Friedrich Kapp. The loyalty of the overwhelming majority of German officers to Seeckt ensured that the Kapp putsch would collapse for lack of army support.

Head of the *Reichswehr*

In late March, 1920, Seeckt was appointed provisional chief of the German army, called the *Reichswehr*; his appointment was made permanent on June 5. From then until his dismissal in 1926, Seeckt presided over the shrinking of the German army to the 100,000-man force required by the 1919 Treaty of Versailles, despite the oppo-

Hans von Seeckt *(Corbis/Austrian Archives)*

Commander of the *Reichswehr*, 1920-1926

Hans von Seeckt was commander of the German army, the *Reichswehr*, during the early years of the German Republic (the Weimar Republic). He had to follow the restrictions imposed on Germany by the Allies in the Treaty of Versailles at the end of World War I. General von Seeckt created an entirely volunteer force with a high degree of professionalism. He succeeded in keeping the army out of the many antigovernment outbreaks, from both Right and Left, that occurred during these years. The most important was his isolation of the outbreak that occurred in Munich in November, 1923—the failed beer-hall putsch led by Adolf Hitler. Despite the sympathy that many officers felt for right-wing causes, the strict and unrelenting enforcement of discipline and obedience to orders from above kept the army out of politics during these years.

sition of conservative and Right radical forces. He earned the gratitude of the leaders of the Republic by the restraint he enforced on the German armed forces during the French invasion of the Ruhr in early 1923. He successfully engineered the suppression of revolts against the Republic both from the Left (in Saxony in September, 1923) and the Right (in Munich in November, 1923—the famous beer-hall putsch of Adolf Hitler).

Seeckt was determined to make the *Reichswehr* a nonpolitical army dedicated only to the defense of Germany. He adhered to the military limitations imposed on Germany in the Treaty of Versailles, although he countenanced military cooperation with the Soviet Union that enabled some German officers to gain experience in military branches forbidden by the treaty. He turned the *Reichswehr* into a highly professional and skilled force, that later formed the core of the German army turned loose on Europe by Adolf Hitler.

Forced out of office by his indiscretion in allowing a Hohenzollern prince to participate in some army maneuvers, Seeckt served in the *Reichstag*, the German legislature, from 1930 to 1932. In 1934-1935 he served in China as an adviser to Chiang Kai-shek. He was also the author of several books on military policy and international affairs.

Bibliography

Goerlitz, Walter. *The German General Staff*. Translated by Brian Battershaw. New York: Praeger, 1953.

Gordon, Harold J., Jr. *The Reichswehr and the German Republic, 1919-1926*. Princeton, N.J.: Princeton University Press, 1957.

Wheeler-Bennett, J. W. *The Nemesis of Power: The German Army in Politics, 1918-1945*. London: Macmillan, 1953.

Nancy M. Gordon

Léopold Senghor

Born: October 9, 1906; Joal, Senegal

Senegalese poet and first president of independent Senegal (1960-1980)

Léopold Sédar Senghor (lay-oh-POHLD say-DAHR san-GOHR) was born in the small Senegalese seaside village of Joal. Senegal was then a colony of France. His father, Diogoye, was a wealthy merchant. The Senghors were part of the Catholic minority in the largely Muslim Senegal. The young Léopold received his primary and secondary education at Catholic schools in Senegal and then began his university studies in Paris. While he was a student in Paris, he became friends with Georges Pompidou, who would later serve as the French president from 1969 to 1974, with Aimé Césaire from Martinique, and with Léon-Gontran Damas from Guyana. Like Senghor, Césaire and Damas would become well-known poets. Senghor earned a degree in linguistics and grammar. In 1935, he was the first black African to pass the French agrégation, a national competition used to select teachers for permanent positions in French high schools. He taught Latin and French for several years.

Early Career

Soon after his arrival in Paris in 1928, Senghor became acquainted with several black writers from many French-speaking countries. With his friend Aimé Césaire, he created a literary movement called *négritude*, which encouraged black French-speaking writers to express the cultural values of their countries in a positive and creative way. They did not want to be assimilated into French culture but rather to express their visions of the world in poetry that treated themes of universal interest. Senghor's success in the difficult agrégation competition in 1935 suggested that he could have a long academic career, but things turned out differently.

In 1939, World War II began, and Senghor was called back to active service in the French army. In June, 1940, the Nazis arrested him. He spent more than two years in Nazi prisoner of war camps. He helped other soldiers to escape from the Nazis. These two years of imprisonment changed Senghor. In 1942, he was released from prison because of his deteriorating health. He resumed teaching and joined the French Resistance. In 1945, Lamine Guèye, the representative from Dakar, Senegal, to the French legislature, persuaded Senghor to run for an opening in the district in which Joal is located. Senghor represented his district in Paris until Senegal obtained its independence in 1960. While a representative

Léopold Senghor *(Archive France/Archive Photos)*

Senegalese president and poet Léopold Senghor presenting a graphic arts award at the 1966 Dakar Festival Awards ceremony in New York. American poet Langston Hughes (right) is accepting the award for William Majors. *(National Archives)*

in Paris, he continued to publish his poems and strove to persuade successive French governments to grant more independence to Senegal and the other French African colonies. In 1958, Senghor persuaded the new French president, Charles de Gaulle, to create a French-African commonwealth and then to prepare a schedule for the colonies to obtain their independence. Senghor's exquisite tact and profound respect for French and Senegalese cultures created numerous friends and supporters, both in France and in Senegal.

The Presidential Years

When Senegal obtained its independence in 1960, Senghor was elected its first president, a position which he held for twenty years until he voluntarily retired from politics so that he could spend his remaining years writing poetry. Senghor thought that he would serve as the head of state while his prime minister, Mamadou Dia, would carry out the everyday responsibilities of governing the country. This idea proved to be a

The Aggregation Degree

Each year the French Ministry of Education organizes a national competition called the aggregation (in French, *agrégation*) to select people for permament teaching positions in French high schools. Those who pass this highly competitive examination are called *agrégés*. If, for example, the French Ministry of Education determines that it will need thirty new French teachers for the next academic year, only thirty candidates will become *agrégés* that year.

Only French citizens may take the *agrégation* examination. Since Léopold Senghor was born in Senegal, he was not a French citizen, but he requested and obtained French citizenship in

1932. Senghor passed the *agrégation* in French grammar in 1935 and was assigned to teach French and Latin in Tours, France. He was the first black African to become an *agrégé*. His success at the *agrégation* not only made it possible for him to teach in France but also opened many doors of opportunity. Influential French governmental officials and leaders in private industry generally believe that *agrégés* are among the brightest people in France and can perform admirably in fields well removed from teaching. Senghor firmly believed that he would never have been asked to run for political office in Senegal had he not been an *agrégé*.

Négritude

The term "négritude" (blackness) was first used in 1931 by Aimé Césaire, a French poet from Martinique whom Léopold Senghor had met that same year. Césaire, Senghor, and their mutual friend Léon-Gontran Damas, a poet from Guyana, created a literary movement which they called négritude. Together they launched a literary journal called La Revue du monde noir (the review of the black world). Its first issue, which was published in late 1931, acknowledged a large debt to the Harlem Renaissance in the United States and to the African American poet Langston Hughes in particular. Senghor, Césaire, and Damas wanted black French-speaking writers to express the positive and traditional values and experiences of their cultures in poems that would touch readers from all over the world.

serious error in judgment: Mamadou Dia tried to transform Senegal into a strictly socialist country, whereas Senghor favored a policy of balancing the general welfare of ordinary citizens with encouraging foreign companies to invest in Senegal in order to create jobs for Senegalese citizens.

In December, 1962, Dia tried to overthrow Senghor's govenment. The leaders of the armed forces supported Senghor, and the coup d'état failed. Dia and his coconspirators were arrested. Senghor assumed complete power himself. He protected Senegal from exploitation by foreign companies by preventing foreign countries from buying land in Senegal. He encouraged foreign investment in Senegal by assuring foreign companies that they could transfer their profits from Senegal as long as they hired an appropriate number of Senegalese citizens. His government also passed laws which specifically guaranteed the rights of foreign investors.

Senghor was a respected leader whom presidents of other African countries frequently asked to help resolve thorny diplomatic disagreements. Thanks to his wise governance, Senegal became a stable democracy that did not experience the turmoil of civil war or military dictatorship. In 1970, he re-created the position of prime minister and named Abdou Diouf to serve as his first prime minister since Mamadou Dia. During his twenty years as president, Senghor helped to create a solid educational system at all levels, implemented changes which encouraged economic development which was fair to all citizens, passed laws which protected the rights of the majority Muslims and the minority Christians, and organized festivals which brought to the public's attention the rich cultural diversity of black French-speaking countries. In late December, 1980, Senghor retired from politics and was succeeded as president of Senegal by Abdou Diouf.

Retirement Years

His retirement years brought both sorrow and honors to Senghor. Two of his children died in the early 1980's. In 1984, he became the first black African elected to the Académie française. He had become a revered figure in the French-speaking world.

Bibliography

Colvin, Lucie. Historical Dictionary of Senegal. Metuchen, N.J.: Scarecrow Press, 1981.

Markovitz, Irving. Léopld Sédar Senghor and the Politics of Négritude. New York: Atheneum, 1969.

Senghor, Léopold Sédar. Selected Poems. Translated by John Reed and Clive Wake. New York: Atheneum, 1964.

Edmund J. Campion

Eduard Shevardnadze

Born: January 25, 1928; Mamati, Georgia, U.S.S.R.

Soviet foreign minister (1985-1990, 1991), president of Georgia (took office 1995)

Eduard Amvrosiyevich Shevardnadze (ih-dew-AHRT ahm-VROW-see-yeh-vyihch shvayrd-NAHD-zeh) was born in the village of Mamati in the Lanchkhuti region of Georgia, which at the time was a constituent republic of the Soviet Union. Shevardnadze was the son of a schoolteacher, and he became involved with politics at a relatively early age. He joined the Komsomol (communist youth league) in 1948, becoming the first secretary of Georgia's Komsomol in 1957. Throughout the 1960's Shevardnadze became increasingly involved in Georgian government and politics, and in 1972 he became the first secretary

Eduard Shevardnadze *(National Archives)*

of the Central Committee of Georgia's Communist Party. In 1976 he moved from the Georgian Communist Party organization to the country-wide Soviet level, becoming a member of the Central Committee of the Communist Party of the Soviet Union (CPSU). Two years later he became a candidate member of the Politburo, the CPSU's highest policy-making body.

The Gorbachev Years

When Mikhail Gorbachev replaced Konstantin Chernenko as Soviet leader in 1985, he sought dramatic reforms of elements of the country's government, foreign policy, and official ideology. To facilitate this agenda and to solidify his power base, Gorbachev selected a number of reform-minded individuals to be placed in positions of governmental and party power. Shevardnadze was one of the first and most important of Gorbachev's appointments. Gorbachev made Shevardnadze a full member of the Politburo and appointed him to be the new Soviet foreign minister, replacing the aging Andrei Gromyko.

Shevardnadze became recognized as the second most important figure in the Soviet Union, after Gorbachev. He served as one of Gorbachev's closest advisers, accompanied Gorbachev on most of his state visits, acted as Gorbachev's spokesman on foreign policy and other issues, and held innumerable meetings with his counterparts in other countries. As foreign minister, Shevardnadze had primary responsibility for defining and implementing Gorbachev's New Thinking—a broadly-conceived initiative to promote international cooperation with the West (particularly the United States), thereby reducing military burdens on the Soviet bloc and earning various forms of aid from the Western powers. New Thinking eventually included major arms-control initiatives, a new permissiveness toward Soviet alliance partners in Eastern Europe, the phased withdrawal of Red Army troops from Afghanistan, and negotiations concerning the eventual reunification of Germany.

Warnings and Resignation

In the course of five years, Shevardnadze played a central role in the Soviet Union's retreat from its long-time role as leader of world communism. He helped to negotiate several unprecedented arms control treaties, fashioned the Soviet Union's response to the weakening (and breakup) of the Warsaw Pact, and negotiated the final settlement for the unification of Germany. Shortly after this last act, however, Shevardnadze resigned from his position as foreign minister. Shevardnadze's resignation was dramatic and unexpected. In a December, 1990, speech, he warned that the country was sliding toward a dictatorship, with nationalist and conservative "reactionaries" threatening the country from within. He could not continue to work under those circumstances, he said, and therefore resigned in protest.

Eduard Shevardnadze at a Warsaw Pact summit in 1990, serving as Soviet foreign minister. At left is Soviet president Mikhail Gorbachev. *(Reuters/ Leszek Wdowinski/Archive Photos)*

Shevardnadze's words were prescient, for the following August a group of conservatives and ultranationalists within the military and the government launched a coup against Gorbachev's leadership. The coup collapsed within three days, but it nonetheless fatally weakened elite support for the Soviet state. Shevardnadze returned to his post as foreign minister in late November, 1991, but scarcely a month later the Soviet Union disintegrated into its fifteen component republics.

Shevardnadze's 1990 Resignation

Eduard Shevardnadze announced his resignation as Soviet foreign minister on December 20, 1990. In his speech to the Soviet parliament, Shevardnadze warned that "reactionaries" were gaining power in Gorbachev's government. He claimed that the "democrats" who had earlier supported the country's reforms were nowhere to be seen and that "dictatorship" was looming. He decided to resign, he said, because "I cannot reconcile myself to what is happening in our country and the trials awaiting our people." It was unclear precisely what Shevardnadze expected to happen, but an attempted conservative coup in August, 1991, seemed to vindicate his warnings. Shevardnadze resumed his post as foreign minister shortly after the coup failed, only to lose that position when the Soviet Union collapsed a month later.

Ethnic Georgians

About five and a half million persons live in the Republic of Georgia. About 70 percent are ethnic Georgians, while 8.1 percent are ethnic Armenians, 6.3 percent ethnic Russian, 5.7 percent Azerbaijani, three percent Ossetian, and 1.8 percent Abkhazi. The ethnic Georgians, like most of the other ethnic groups in Georgia, have a history of being dominated by the Russians. With the collapse of the Soviet Union in 1991, many ethnic Georgians sought to reestablish their newly independent country as an independent homeland for their people. However, the presence of the other ethnic groups and the proximity of Russia prevented the immediate realization of that goal.

Georgian ethno-nationalism was championed by Zviad Gamsakhurdia, who was elected Georgia's president in May, 1991. He was overthrown in January, 1992, and afterward Georgia experienced numerous ethnic clashes, sometimes rising to the level of civil war. Separatist movements also emerged among Georgia's ethnic minorities, such as the Abkhazians, who tend to be concentrated in administrative subregions created by the old Soviet elites. The ethnic Georgians can trace their ancestry in the region back to the thirteenth century. So can other of the country's ethnic groups, however, a situation that creates intractable disputes over territory and autonomy.

Leader of Georgia

Like the other constituent republics of the Soviet Union, Georgia experienced a growing independence movement in 1991. Even before the formal dissolution of the Soviet Union, Georgia elected as its own president a Georgian nationalist, Zviad Gamsakhurdia, in May of 1991. Gamsakhurdia's nationalist policies, coupled with the power vacuum occasioned by the collapse of the Soviet government, spawned a complex series of political and military clashes in Georgia that erupted into civil war by the end of the year. Opposition forces drove Gamsakhurdia into exile in January, 1992, and Shevardnadze became the new Georgian leader in March.

As the president of the newly independent Georgian state, Shevardnadze was confronted by numerous crises and problems. Foremost was continuing resistance from Gamsakhurdia's supporters, who launched guerrilla attacks on the Shevardnadze government. Shevardnadze was forced reluctantly to seek assistance from the Russian army, which eventually led to the defeat of the

Georgian president Eduard Shevardnadze (left) with Russian president Boris Yeltsin in Moscow in 1996 following talks in the Kremlin. *(Reuters/ Grigory Dukor/Archive Photos)*

rebels. (Gamsakhurdia himself died in January, 1993.) Russia continued to have a large influence on Georgian politics after (and because of) that military assistance, and this earned Shevardnadze considerable animosity from many Georgian nationalists.

At the same time, Shevardnadze had to contend with separatist drives by several minority ethnic enclaves within Georgia. Although these had been largely quieted by the late 1990's, the possibility of ethnic violence continued to loom. Further, Georgia, like most former Soviet republics, was beset by financial crises throughout the 1990's. Shevardnadze's popularity frequently suffered as a result.

Successes and Failures

Despite his successes as Soviet foreign minister, Shevardnadze's ability to stabilize Georgia's economy, shore up its sovereignty, and quell its ethnic conflicts was not assured at the close of the decade. Overseeing the stabilization of a newly independent country proved to be much more difficult than overseeing the dismantling of an old empire. Nevertheless, Shevardnadze had clearly established his place as an especially capable leader who played a central role in one of the most critical times in history for Georgia, the Soviet empire, and the world.

Bibliography

Coleman, Fred. "A Soviet Bombshell: Shevardnadze Resigns, Blasting Gorbachev's Turn to the Right," *Newsweek*, December 31, 1990: 50-52.

Ekedahl, Carolyn McGiffert, and Melvin A. Goodman. *The Wars of Eduard Shevardnadze*. University Park: Pennsylvania State University Press, 1997.

Palazchenko, Pavel. *My Years with Gorbachev and Shevardnadze: The Memoir of a Soviet Interpreter*. University Park: Pennsylvania State University Press, 1997.

Shevardnadze, Eduard. *The Future Belongs to Freedom*. New York: Free Press, 1991.

Steve D. Boilard

Muhammad Siad Barre

Born: c. 1910; Shiilaabo, Ogaden, Abyssinian Somaliland (now Ethiopia)
Died: January 2, 1995; Lagos, Nigeria

Dictatorial ruler of Somalia, 1969-1991

Muhammad Siad Barre (moo-HAH-muhd see-AHD bah-RAY) was born in the Ogaden region of what is now Ethiopia to a father of the Marehan clan and a mother of the Ogadeni subclan. He had no formal education as a youth, but he learned English in British-administered Kenya while training for the police force. After Somalia's independence in 1960, he emerged as a prominent figure in the military, eventually assuming general command of the Somali National Army in 1965. In 1969, Somalia's government experienced considerable corruption and political instability, which culminated in the assassination of President Ali Shermarke. In the aftermath of this assassination, Siad Barre, with the backing of the military, seized control of the government, thus beginning twenty-two years of largely dictatorial rule.

Early Successes

At first, Somalis warmly supported Siad Barre's government. He put an end to the corruption and political instability that had plagued the country. His economic policies initially sparked a period of growth. He introduced an alphabet for the Somali language, traditionally an oral language, and he instituted a literacy campaign. He relied on the Soviet Union for military aid and strengthened the country's military. In 1970, barely a year after the coup, he announced a program of scientific socialism for Somalia. When famine struck in 1973, he resettled nomads and encouraged them, unsuccessfully, to develop a fishing industry. His socialist reforms, however, betrayed certain authoritarian tendencies, and Muslim critics of his regime were treated harshly. On the whole, however, the first several years of his regime were regarded as a time of general stability and progress.

The growth of Soviet influence in Somalia and of Somali nationalism was troubling for Somalia's neighbors. Their concern was soon to be justified. Siad Barre began supporting the Western Somali Liberation Front, which fought a guerrilla war against Ethiopia over control of the Ogaden region, Barre's birthplace.

The Ogaden War

In 1977, Siad Barre sent Somali troops across the border to reclaim the Ogaden region occupied

Muhammad Siad Barre *(Corbis/Kevin Fleming)*

Somalian rebels in a tank captured from Muhammad Siad Barre's soldiers in January, 1991, when increasing guerrilla warfare and divisions within the military forced Siad Barre to flee the country. *(AP/Wide World Photos)*

Italian Somaliland

The division of Somalia into different colonial territories explains in part the conflicts that have marked Somali political life. During the colonial era, Italy occupied and administered the southern portion of Somalia, while the British occupied Somaliland in the northwest. The French exercised control over Somali Isaq clans in Djibouti, while Britain administered the Northwest Frontier District in Kenya and Ethiopia occupied Somali-inhabited lands in the Ogaden region. Desires to unite these areas of Somalia have long been a part of Somali national consciousness.

Thus, when Muhammad Siad Barre sought to reclaim the Ogaden in 1977, he initially had the support of most Somalis. The defeat of Somali forces, however, sparked opposition. Moreover, the dominance of the former Italian Somalia in Somali political life, the location of the country's capital, Mogadishu, in the south, and the favoritism shown to southern Somali clans in the south by Siad Barre caused great resentments in the former British Somaliland, and contributed to its effort to proclaim independence in 1991.

The Politics of Language

The one lasting positive achievement of Muhammad Siad Barre in his twenty-two years of rule was his campaign to create a written component to the Somali language. For centuries Somalis communicated solely by oral means, in a language that was rich in poetry and tonal beauty. As long as Somalia remained a nomadic society of herders, there was no need for a written language. As Somali cities grew and the demands of modernization increased, however,

Siad Barre decided to call upon Somali scholars and linguists to create an alphabet and a written language to complement the oral tradition of the Somali language. This was seen as essential for maintaining and sustaining Somali nationalism while introducing literacy to the wider population. The campaign to establish the language and encourage education and literacy in it, is one of the few positive contributions Siad Barre made to his country.

by Ethiopia but long inhabited by Somali nomadic clans. At first the invasion was a popular move among Somalis. However, after Siad Barre expelled the Soviet Union, the latter threw its support fully behind Ethiopia and sent military aid, advisers, and Cuban troops to ensure Ethiopia's victory. By the spring of 1978, Somali troops had retreated from the Ogaden in defeat and disgrace. In subsequent years, millions of refugees spilled over the borders into Somalia, creating a humanitarian crisis. Many Somalis quietly blamed Siad Barre for blunders that led to these catastrophes, and the most disgruntled elements formed opposition groups in exile.

Siad Barre turned to the conservative Arab countries and the West to help him defend against possible Ethiopian attack. The United States and other anticommunist governments provided him with defensive military assistance and, during the refugee crisis of the early 1980's, large amounts of additional humanitarian assistance. This did not, however, eradicate popular resentment to Siad Barre's increasingly authoritarian policies and the favoritism he showed to members of his family's clans. Opposition groups became more bold, using Ethiopian territory to lauch sporadic attacks into Somalia. Fearing this emboldened opposition, Siad Barre made peace with Ethiopia's leader, Haile Mengistu

Mariam, and signed a mutual nonaggression pact with him, hoping that this would eliminate the opposition threat. Instead, it forced several Somali resistance groups, including the Somalia National Movement (SNM), to carry their war into Somalia itself.

The Siad Barre Regime Collapses

Siad Barre's troubles deepened in late 1988 as the SNM, heavily supported by the Isaq clan, provoked an open war of rebellion in northwest Somalia. He met this threat with brutal bombings of major cities in the region, including Hargeisa, the capital. Hundreds of thousands of Somalis fled into Ethiopia as refugees, while members of Siad Barre's military split along clan lines. Opposition forces, including the United Somali Congress, mounted guerrilla campaigns against Siad Barre's remaining forces during 1989 and 1990. By January, 1991, his regime was in a precarious state. Under threat of capture, Siad Barre fled from Mogadishu, first to Kenya and then to Nigeria, where he received political asylum and faded into obscurity. USC forces claimed control of Somalia, but forces loyal to Siad Barre continued to fight in the southern part of the country.

Legacy of Civil War and Famine

In the wake of Siad Barre's fall, Somalia descended into lengthy civil war among factions competing for control of the government. Although Siad Barre had little influence on his country after his flight in January of 1991, he bears considerable responsibility for the country's collapse in subsequent years. He reinforced clan identities during his regime, and in the post-Barre period clan-related disputes emerged in full force and with bloody consequence. The wars, coupled with bad weather in the south, led to a famine in which 300,000 Somalis died before the United States and the United Nations intervened in Operation Restore Hope to provide security for delivery of humanitarian aid. The U.N. operation failed to disarm the Somali factions, and U.N. personnel and U.S. troops were eventually forced to withdraw. Years of hardship followed, as political disputes hampered peace talks. Siad Barre is not solely responsible for these later developments, but his brutal, authoritarian, and repressive policies provoked them. Apart from his closest associates, few Somalis regard him as a ruler to be remembered with affection or admiration.

Bibliography

Ghalib, Jama Mohammed. *The Cost of Dictatorship: The Somali Experience.* New York: Lilian Barber, 1995.

Metz, Helen Chapin. *Somalia: A Country Study.* Washington, D.C.: U.S. Government Printing Office, 1993.

Samatar, Ahmed I. *The Somali Challenge: From Catastrophe to Renewal.* Boulder, Colo.: Lynne Rienner, 1995.

Robert F. Gorman

Norodom Sihanouk

Born: October 31, 1922; Phnom Penh, Cambodia

King of Cambodia (1941-1955, then from 1993), also at various times Cambodia's prime minister, head of state, and president

When Norodom Sambeth Preah Sihanouk (NOH-ro-duhm SAHM-beht PRAY-ah SEE-hah-nook) was born, his grandfather was King Sisowath Monivong of Cambodia, which was a colony of French Indochina. In 1941, when the king died, the French government prevailed on Sihanouk, then a high school student, to become the new king. For the rest of his life, he sought to outmaneuver opponents in order to wrest power in Cambodia away from those who would exploit the people. In a very real sense, he is the father of the modern Cambodian state.

Norodom Sihanouk *(National Archives)*

Sihanouk Seeks Independence for Cambodia

Japan took control of Cambodia in 1944. In 1945, when Tokyo offered Cambodia independence, Sihanouk agreed. After World War II, however, French colonial rule returned by force of arms. Sihanouk demanded independence. Paris responded by abolishing the absolute monarchy, though he was allowed to remain as king with nominal powers. In 1946 Sihanouk signed an agreement to rule an internally autonomous Cambodian state within the French Union.

France insisted on a democracy in Cambodia, and Sihanouk's opponents won the first election in 1946. As king, he attempted to crack down on dissidents. Establishing a pattern of dramatic moves to disarm his opponents, he went to Paris in 1952, threatening to abdicate if he failed to achieve independence for Cambodia. France granted his request in 1953, and Cambodian independence was confirmed in 1954 at the Geneva Conference on Indochina.

Sihanouk Struggles for Power

In 1955 Sihanouk again surprised his opponents by abdicating in favor of his father, Norodom Suramarit. Sihanouk sought to gain more public support at the grassroots level in the role of prince. His People's Socialist Community Party won by a landslide that year, although the election was rigged. Similar victories in 1958, 1962, and 1966 prompted many opponents eventually to go underground. In 1960, when the king died, Parliament named Sihanouk head of state, thus ending the monarchy.

During the era when the United States intervened in the Vietnamese civil war, Sihanouk insisted on Cambodian neutrality in the conflict in order to keep Cambodian sovereignty intact. He was a founding member of the nonaligned movement. However, North Vietnam used Cambodian territory to supply revolutionaries in South Vietnam, and the United States bombed the supply lines while secretly aiding Marshall Lon Nol, Sihanouk's defense minister. In 1970, while Prince Sihanouk was out of the country, Lon Nol staged a *coup d'état*. The prince then established a government in exile in Beijing along with his hitherto communist opponents, the Khmer Rouge. When the Khmer Rouge defeated the Lon Nol government in 1975, Sihanouk returned as head of state. In 1976, after a tour of the countryside, the prince protested policies of the Khmer Rouge by resigning his position; he was then placed under house arrest in the palace.

The Khmer Rouge, on coming to power, sought to seize territories ruled by Vietnam for centuries

Cambodian king Norodom Sihanouk returning to Phnom Penh, Cambodia, in 1996 after attending the funeral of François Mitterrand in France. *(Reuters/ Darren Whiteside/Archive Photos)*

but long claimed by Cambodian monarchs as a part of Cambodia. Believing that Hanoi's army was exhausted, the Khmer Rouge launched brutal border attacks inside Vietnam. In 1978 Hanoi decided to counterattack. Just before Vietnam's

Jayavarman VII, a Cambodian Icon

During the eleventh century, the kingdom of Angkor occupied large areas of what is now Cambodia, Laos, and Thailand. Then, in the early part of the twelfth century, Angkor suffered a defeat from the Champa Kingdom, which occupied part of what is now Vietnam. Jayavarman VII became king in 1181, and his conquests expanded the Angkor Empire to its largest reach, extending into the regions that later became Burma, Malaysia, and Vietnam. Jayavarman also converted from Hinduism to Buddhism and made Buddhism the national religion. He instituted a vast and frantically paced building pro-

gram, constructing many Buddhist temples, hospitals, and rest houses. He rebuilt the capital city of Angkor (also called Angkor Thom).

Jayavarman was little to known to historians until the twentieth century, when excavations revealed his importance. In Cambodian politics in the 1950's and 1960's, an era dominated by Norodom Sihanouk, Jayavarman VII became a national icon and hero. His name and image were used as symbols of Cambodian greatness and to evoke the concept of a state inspired by Buddhism to care for its people's physical and spiritual needs.

The People's Socialist Community

In 1955 Norodom Sihanouk abdicated as king in order to form the Sangkum Reaster Niyum (People's Socialist Community Party). The party won handily after ruthlessly harassing other parties and stuffing ballot boxes. Sihanouk's party, which won every subsequent election until the *coup d'état* of 1980 led by Defense Minister Lon Nol, had no particular ideology despite bearing "socialist" in its title.

armies reached the Cambodian capital of Phnom Penh, the prince flew to Beijing. Sihanouk then formed a new coalition government in exile, this time with both his right- and left-wing opponents, to oppose the newly formed government, the People's Republic of Kampuchea (PRK), which was composed of refugees from the Khmer Rouge who had military support from Vietnam.

Sihanouk as Peacemaker

Throughout the 1980's, Sihanouk sought a political formula to end Vietnam's presence in Cambodia, but he refused to deal with Vietnam. Vietnam indicated in 1979 that it wanted to leave Cambodia, provided that the Khmer Rouge would not return to power. In 1982 the prince proposed a peace plan, but nobody listened. In 1987, impressed with the new PRK peace plan, he went on leave as coalition head to discuss the plan with Hun Sen, the PRK premier. What emerged were a series of informal discussions to devise a peace treaty that would bring the warring factions into a unity government, preparatory to elections. In 1989, when Vietnamese troops were scheduled to withdraw unilaterally from Cambodia, Sihanouk supported the Khmer Rouge peace plan rather than a compromise draft, and a conference at Paris failed to come up with a peace agreement. In 1991, after the factions agreed to an arrangement brokered by Australia, a peace agreement was signed in Paris. Sihanouk soon returned to his country as the head of the transitional Supreme National Council.

In 1992 the United Nations Transitional Authority in Cambodia implemented the Paris accords by taking over the government of the country. In 1993 U.N.-supervised elections were held in Cambodia. Sihanouk's son Ranariddh won 45 percent of the votes. Hun Sen's party, which won 38 percent of the votes, was reluctant to yield power, and Sihanouk's son Chakrapong even threatened to establish a breakaway Cambodian state consisting of some of the eastern provinces. Although Sihanouk proposed to head a government in order to break the impasse, he backed down when the United Nations objected that such a move was contrary to the election results. The compromise was the formation of a coalition government with Ranariddh as first premier and Hun Sen as second premier. By the end of 1993, a new constitution was written and Sihanouk was proclaimed king. Sihanouk continued to mediate between the opposing factions in order to keep Cambodia at peace.

Bibliography

Cixous, Helene, Lollie Groth, and Judith Pike. *The Terrible but Unfinished Story of Norodom Sihanouk, King of Cambodia*. Lincoln: University of Nebraska Press, 1994.

Haas, Michael. *Genocide by Proxy: Cambodia Pawn on a Superpower Chessboard*. New York: Praeger, 1991.

Osborne, Milton. *Sihanouk: Prince of Light, Prince of Darkness*. Honolulu: University of Hawaii Press, 1994.

Michael Haas

William Joseph Slim

Born: August 6, 1891; Bishopston, near Bristol, England
Died: December 14, 1970; London, England

British military leader, commander of Burma campaign during World War II

William Joseph Slim (WIHL-yuhm JOH-sehf SLIHM), the son of a small businessman, was educated at King Edward's School, where he was in the Officer Training Corps. In World War I, he fought at Gallipoli as well as in France and the Middle East. After the war, he served with the Indian army. In 1926 he married Aileen Robertson. Slim served in several military positions before returning to India in early 1938.

World War II

When World War II began in 1939, Slim was a brigadier general. He commanded the Tenth Indian Infantry Brigade during the successful East African campaign in early 1941. He was then promoted to command the Tenth Indian Division, a key unit in the summer, 1941, struggle against Vichy French forces in Syria. This campaign removed a potential base for Nazi expansion into the vital Middle East.

In March, 1942, Slim was sent to Burma (now Myanmar) to command British and colonial troops, known as the Burcorps (short for "Burmese Corps"). They were being forced back by the Japanese invaders. Under Slim's leadership, Burcorps made the longest fighting retreat in British army history—over 900 miles (1,500 kilometers) from Rangoon, Burma, to the border of India. Slim was placed in command of the Fifteenth Indian Corps and then, in October, 1943, of the new Fourteenth Army.

In early 1944, Slim defeated a Japanese advance in the Arakan area. He then began preparing the Fourteenth Army for a major counteroffensive. The Japanese launched the Imphal offensive in March of 1944, intending to stop Slim by seizing and destroying his major supply base at Imphal in Burma. The Japanese achieved tac-tical surprise, but Slim responded by bringing in reinforcements by air.

Turning the Tide

The decisive point was the Battle of Kohima, key to the British position. Surrounded, the British held out through bravery and supplies from the Royal Air Force. By June, the Japanese were in retreat, which turned into a rout when Slim launched a series of well-planned and brilliantly executed attacks. Out of eighty-five thousand troops, the Japanese suffered at least fifty-three

William Joseph Slim *(Library of Congress)*

1403

U.S. and Chinese troops in the Burma campaign, 1944. *(Archive Photos)*

Extended Capital) liberated southern Burma, including the capital of Rangoon. For this victory, Slim was knighted and was named commander of the Allied South East Asia Command.

Following the war, Slim was promoted to field marshal and appointed chief of the Imperial General Staff. From 1953 until 1960 he was governor-general of Australia, and was raised to the peerage in 1960 as a viscount. He died in 1970. Field Marshal Sir William Slim was the epitome of the British Imperial colonial soldier, outstanding in both desert and jungle warfare. A veteran of the Indian army, he was fluent in the languages of the native troops he commanded, and inspired their confidence and respect through his coolness and poise.

thousand casualties and lost all their tanks and heavy weapons. Slim next launched an offensive (Operation Capital) that forced the Japanese from upper Burma. A second campaign (Operation

The Tenth Indian Division

Under William "Uncle Billy" Slim, the Tenth Indian Division played a major role in defending the vital Middle East against Nazi influence during the spring and summer of 1941. In May, the Tenth Indian Division moved into Iraq to counter a pro-German revolt and by early June had captured the capital of Baghdad, ensuring that vital oil supplies would be available to the British. Airfields in Syria, then under control of Vichy French forces, had been used to support the Iraqi revolt. When the Vichy French Syrian government refused to close the bases, British troops attacked from Palestine. They were joined by the Tenth Indian, which drove in from the east. The capture of the strategic strong point of Deir-es-Zor was a major step in forcing the surrender of the Vichy forces. The Tenth Indian Division then turned back to the east to invade Iran (then known as Persia), which was drawing closer to Germany. The British sought to expel German influence and open supply lines to the Soviet Union, invaded that June by the Germans. By September, Slim and the Tenth Division had reached the capital of Tehran and secured the country for the Allies.

Bibliography

Dear, I. C. B., ed. *The Oxford Companion to World War II*. London: Oxford University Press, 1995.

Dupuy, Trevor N., ed., with Curt Johnson and David L. Bongard. *The Harper Encyclopedia of Military Biography*. New York: HarperCollins, 1992.

Keegan, John, ed. *The Second World War*. New York: Viking, 1990.

———. *Who Was Who in World War II*. New York: T. Y. Crowell, 1978.

Lewin, Ronald. *Slim: The Standardbearer*. Hamden, Conn.: Archon Books, 1976.

Michael Witkoski

Joseph Roberts Smallwood

Born: December 24, 1900; Gambo, Bonavista Bay, Newfoundland (now part of Canada)
Died: December 17, 1991; St. John's, Newfoundland, Canada

First premier of province of Newfoundland (1949-1971)

Born in a lumber camp, Joseph Roberts Smallwood (Joh-sehf RO-bertz SMAHL-wood) was the son of Charles W. Smallwood (of English ancestry) and Minnie Devannah (of French and Irish ancestry). After dropping out of school in the ninth grade, Smallwood worked as a printer's apprentice and reporter in St. John's and Halifax before marrying Clara Oates, daughter of a fishing captain, in 1925. The couple had three children, Ramsay, William, and Clara.

Mixed Vocations

After struggling as a journalist in New York in the early 1920's, Smallwood, an admirer of social-ist William Coaker, returned to Canada and became a trade-union organizer in 1925. He started a weekly tabloid in Corner Brook in 1927 before becoming campaign manager for Sir Richard Squires's comeback election as prime minister of Newfoundland. Unable to win office in 1932, Smallwood returned to St. John's, where he edited and published *The Book of Newfoundland*, underwritten by businessman Chesley A. Crosbie, beginning in 1937. He became a successful newspaper columnist and radio host of *The Barrelman* before deciding to become a pig farmer in Gander. When Britain decided in late 1945 to grant Newfoundland self-rule, Smallwood's political interest was stirred again.

Confederation

Smallwood sold the piggery and promoted the idea of confederation—the uniting of Newfoundland with Canada—in newspaper letters. He won election in 1946 to Newfoundland's National Convention by an overwhelming majority. He and two other recruits (together they were nicknamed "the three Bolsheviks") made confederation their central topic. Smallwood was reviled for his statement regarding Newfoundland that "We are not a nation. We are a medium-sized municipality." It took two referendums to achieve a clear victory for confederation. Canadian prime minister William Lyon Mackenzie King signed the terms of union on December 11, 1948, assisting the new province with a transitional grant of $46.75 million over twelve years.

Provincial Premier

Smallwood, a Liberal, became the first premier of the province of Newfoundland. He won majority victories in 1949, 1951, and 1956. He insti-

Joseph Roberts Smallwood *(London Times/Archive Photos)*

The Province of Newfoundland

The easternmost Canadian province, Newfoundland consists of the island of Newfoundland, in the Atlantic Ocean near the Gulf of St. Lawrence, and Labrador, on the mainland. The island comprises 42,734 square miles, or 110,600 square kilometers. Newfoundland has many steep rock cliffs, inlets, marshes, and offshore islands. Discovered by John Cabot in 1497 and claimed by Sir Humphrey Gilbert in 1583, Newfoundland has abundant fur-bearing animals, waterfowl, fish (especially cod), hydroelectric power, copper, gypsum, iron, and zinc. Islanders rejected dominion status in 1869, but because of their poor economy they had to accept the administration of a British commission. In World War II, Newfoundland was an important air and radio base for Canada and the United States. Newfoundland did not become a part of Canada until 1949, when it officially became a province.

tuted loan banks for cooperatives and fisheries, a Public Utilities Commission, and a Hydro-Electric Commission. He also granted university status to Memorial College and introduced workers' compensation, slum clearance, and elemental medical coverage. He created new pulp and paper mills, mined natural resources, and attracted European investors for the Newfoundland and Labrador Corporation. However, increases in freight costs combined with failing fisheries led to massive unemployment. A 1959 loggers' strike resulted in the province's longest and most violent labor dispute.

There was continued progress on several fronts in the 1960's. Memorial University was sufficiently funded that it could offer free tuition and student salaries, making the province's per-capita spending on education the highest in the country. The first Canadian fisheries college was opened. Two large iron mines in Labrador and an asbestos mine on the Northeast Coast began operations. The Confederation Building was completed, and incomes rose while unemployment declined. In the 1966 election, Smallwood reduced the Conservatives to three seats out of forty-two. He fought off Quebec's claims to mineral-rich Labrador and to Churchill Falls. He developed a centralization plan whereby residents of outports (small fishing villages, many of them on islands) were given funds to relocate to mainland communities.

After the Premiership

Smallwood's projects strained the provincial budget, and he lost the 1971 election to Frank Moore's Progressive Conservatives. He tried unsuccessfully to get himself drafted as Liberal leader for the next election; he then launched the Liberal Reform Party to sabotage his old party. Smallwood won his seat but officially resigned from the House in June, 1977. He spent his last years promoting a role for Quebec within Canada, traveling to China and Cuba, and writing and editing books. Through more than twenty-two years of power, Smallwood was the chief force behind Newfoundland's progress. Confederation, Memorial University, and Churchill Falls were his lasting legacies.

Bibliography

Gwyn, Richard. *Smallwood: The Unlikely Revolutionary*. Toronto: McClelland and Stewart, 1968.

Horwood, Harold. *Joey: The Life and Political Times of Joey Smallwood*. Toronto: Stoddart, 1989.

Smallwood, Joseph R. *I Chose Canada: The Memoirs of the Honourable Joseph R. Smallwood*. Toronto: Macmillan, 1973.

Keith Garebian

1407

Alfred E. Smith

Born: December 30, 1873; New York, New York
Died: October 4, 1944; New York, New York

Governor of New York (1919-1921, 1923-1928) and U.S. presidential candidate (1928)

Alfred Emanuel Smith (AL-frehd e-MAN-ew-ehl SMIHTH) grew up on the Lower East Side of New York City in a district that was heavily Irish Catholic. His father, who operated a small trucking business, died when his son was twelve years old, leaving the family desperately poor. Smith dropped out of school at the age of fourteen without finishing the eighth grade and held various jobs, including a stint as a clerk at the Fulton Fish Market, in order to help support his mother and sister. In 1900 he married Catherine Dunn; they had five children.

Alfred E. Smith *(Library of Congress)*

Political Rise

Smith was fascinated by the colorful politics of New York City. He began to run errands for the local district leader, who was a major figure in Tammany Hall, the political machine that dominated Manhattan and exerted a powerful influence on the whole state. As a reward for his efforts, Smith was appointed process server (the person who delivers summons to appear in court) for the commissioner of jurors in 1895. In 1903 the district leader nominated Smith for the post of state assemblyman. Although bewildered during his first years in Albany, the state capital, Smith watched and learned, soon becoming one of the best-informed members of the Assembly. His vigorous defense of home rule during a debate over revising the New York City charter won him favorable attention from Democratic Party leaders who, when the party won a majority of the Assembly, chose him as majority leader in 1911 and as speaker in 1913.

Smith strenuously opposed measures that would adversely affect the operations of Tammany Hall, but he also developed an interest in practical humanitarian reforms that helped his constituents. The most important influence on Smith's growing interest in reform was what he learned from the investigating committee formed after the Triangle Shirtwaist Company fire in 1911 took the lives of 146 young women. Based on the committee's revelations, Smith sponsored wage and hour laws for women and children, workmen's compensation laws, and legislation regulating sanitation, health, and fire prevention in factories.

Governor of New York State

Popular with independent reformers as well as

machine politicians, Smith was the logical choice as the Democratic candidate for governor in 1918. Despite running in a predominantly Republican state, he won the governorship by a small margin. During the campaign Smith proposed reorganizing state agencies into a more efficient structure and establishing a state executive budget, but the Republican legislative majority ignored his carefully thought-out ideas. During the Red Scare of 1920, Smith vetoed several bills that threatened the civil liberties of radicals and refused to give his consent to the establishment of a state secret police.

Smith narrowly lost the 1920 election for governor, but he was elected with record pluralities in 1922, 1924, and 1926. At no time did Smith face a friendly legislature; Republicans controlled the Assembly in all eight years of his governorship and the state Senate in all but two years. Despite obstructive opposition, Smith achieved many of

New York governor Al Smith delivering a radio address. *(Archive Photos)*

Prohibition

The prohibition movement—the movement to make the sale and consumption of alcohol illegal—began as a temperance crusade in the early nineteenth century. Proponents, many of whom also supported antislavery crusades and other reform movements, tried to convince drinkers that consumption of alcohol was unhealthy and undermined the moral fabric of the republic. When persuasion failed, reformers demanded the complete prohibition of alcohol. Beginning with Maine in 1846, various states passed such laws during the nineteenth century; however, most were soon repealed.

Pressure for prohibition increased after 1900; by 1917 twenty-six states had enacted prohibition laws. That year Congress proposed an Eighteenth Amendment to the U.S. Constitution prohibiting the manufacture or sale of intoxicating liquor. Within thirteen months it had been ratified by the states, and Prohibition became the law of the land. Enforcement proved difficult, however. Illegal "speakeasies" replaced saloons, and gangsters organized the smuggling and sale of beer and liquor.

Many citizens were horrified by the police corruption and widespread disrespect for the law that accompanied Prohibition. When Al Smith in 1923 signed the repeal of a state law implementing the amendment, New York became the first of several states to admit that enforcement was unworkable. Prohibition was a major issue in the 1928 election, and Smith's defeat seemed to confirm its public support. However, opposition grew, especially after the onset of the Great Depression. In February, 1933, Congress proposed repealing the Eighteenth Amendment, and within a year the states ratified the Twenty-first Amendment, ending Prohibition.

The 1928 Presidential Campaign

The major issue on which the presidential candidates disagreed in 1928 was Prohibition. Herbert Hoover, the Republican candidate, favored full enforcement; Smith supported a local option plan that would let states decide what types of drink should be prohibited. Smith, a Roman Catholic, became the victim of a vicious smear campaign attacking his religion and his personal habits. He was accused of being a habitual drunkard and of planning to install the pope in the White House if he won the presidency. When Hoover triumphed with 21 million votes to Smith's 15 million and carried forty states, Smith blamed his loss on religious bigotry. He was certain that only anti-Catholicism explained Hoover's carrying five southern states that had regularly voted Democratic since the end of Reconstruction in 1877. However, with the country prosperous and at peace, it was unlikely that anyone could have beaten Hoover in 1928.

his goals. He was noted for his ability to explain complex matters, such as the value of an executive budget, in terms that the average citizen could understand. Smith marshaled public opinion in favor of his proposals, convincing the legislature to simplify the structure of state government and establish a state budget that produced sufficient economies to reduce taxes. Under Smith's leadership the state created an extensive park system, expanded the workmen's compensation system, and increased its enforcement of safety requirements.

Presidential Candidate

By 1924 Smith's reputation as a successful progressive governor made him a serious presidential contender, the first Catholic and the first descendant of recent immigrants to be so considered. However, any possibility of Smith's winning the two-thirds vote needed for nomination disappeared when the 1924 Democratic convention was torn apart by bitter debate as eastern urban delegates came within a few votes of inserting a condemnation of the Ku Klux Klan into the platform. William Gibbs McAdoo was the candidate of rural delegates from the South and West. (Most of these delegates strongly supported

Presidential candidate Al Smith (waving his hat) on a whistle-stop tour during his 1928 campaign. *(Library of Congress)*

Prohibition, under which the sale of liquor had been illegal in the United States since 1919.) Smith bitterly resented the bigotry that had been expressed during the fight over the Klan. The convention became deadlocked between the two candidates. Only after 103 ballots did the delegates settle on a compromise candidate, John W. Davis.

Smith gained the presidential nomination in 1928, winning on the first ballot, but the party divisions that had surfaced in 1924 continued to plague him. Anti-Catholic bigots, prohibitionists who disliked Smith's position on that issue, and even Democrats who could not accept the idea of a machine politician as president, deserted him. Although Smith lost the 1928 national election to Herbert Hoover, he received more votes than any previous Democratic candidate.

Contribution

Smith's reconstruction of New York's state government provided the structure upon which his successor, Governor Franklin D. Roosevelt, succeeded in building his reformist reputation during the first years of the Great Depression. Smith himself opposed the New Deal and supported Republicans during that time, but the new voters he had attracted to the Democratic Party, many of them children of immigrant families, provided the base for Democratic majorities during the next decades.

Bibliography

Handlin, Oscar. *Al Smith and His America*. Boston: Little, Brown, 1958.

Josephson, Matthew and Hannah. *Al Smith: Hero of the Cities*. Boston: Houghton Mifflin, 1969.

Moore, Edmund Arthur. *A Catholic Runs for President: The Campaign of 1928*. New York: Ronald Press, 1956.

Neal, Donn C. *The World Beyond the Hudson: Alfred E. Smith and National Politics, 1918-1928*. New York: Garland, 1983.

Sinclair, Andrew. *Prohibition: The Era of Excess*. Boston: Little, Brown, 1962.

Milton Berman

Ian Smith

Born: April 8, 1919; Selukwe, Rhodesia (now Shurugwi, Zimbabwe)

Prime minister of Southern Rhodesia (1964-1979)

Ian Douglas Smith (EE-uhn DUHG-luhs SMIHTH) was born on a ranch in Rhodesia (now Zimbabwe). After attending local schools, where he excelled at sports, Smith started college at Rhodes University in South Africa. With the outbreak of World War II in 1939, he volunteered for the Royal Air Force. He was shot down twice, yet served until war's end. Returning to South Africa, he earned his bachelor's degree and met Janet Watt. They married in 1948 and returned to Selukwe.

Ian Smith *(Library of Congress)*

Rise to the Top

In 1948 Smith ran for the Southern Rhodesian parliament as a member of the Liberal Party. He won, and he held his seat until 1953. That year saw the formation of the Central African Federation (also called the Federation of Rhodesia and Nyasaland), consisting of Southern Rhodesia, Northern Rhodesia (Zambia), and Nyasaland (Malawi). Smith switched to the United Federal Party and won election to the new federation parliament. By the end of the 1950's he had become the chief whip for Prime Minister Roy Welensky.

In the early 1960's, many African nations gained independence, and black Africans took control from white European colonizers. Nationalist movements developed in the Central African Federation, fostering desire for independence and equality among blacks. As it became clear that the federation would be disbanded, Southern Rhodesia became the focus of difficult debates. The other two states would gain independence and be ruled by black majorities. Southern Rhodesia, however, was ruled by whites, who made up less than 5 percent of the population. The government of Great Britain wanted to see reform of the Southern Rhodesian political system before independence. A revised constitution was proposed in 1961 that would slowly increase the political rights of blacks. Even that approach was unacceptable to some white Southern Rhodesians, including Ian Smith. He wanted independence from England but wanted white rule to remain intact.

In 1961, Smith helped form a party called the Rhodesian Front. In 1962, the party nominated Winston Field for Southern Rhodesian prime minister, and he triumphed. Smith was named the deputy prime minister. Field resisted British efforts to push reform, but conservatives were not satisfied with his efforts. In April, 1964, Field was forced to step down and Smith was chosen as his successor, becoming Southern Rhodesia's first native-born prime minister.

Declaration of Independence

In his first year in power, Smith cracked down on black nationalists. He imprisoned hundreds, including leaders Joshua Nkomo and Robert Mugabe. Smith made it clear that he was not afraid to defy England. Then, on November 11, 1965, he unilaterally declared the independence of Southern Rhodesia and initiated a rebellion. The British responded with economic sanctions, and the United Nations followed suit. The government of Southern Rhodesia held out in the face of the sanctions, receiving assistance from Portugal and South Africa. Considered a white supremacist outlaw by

Rhodesian prime minister Ian Smith with Nbabiningi Sithole of the Rhodesian government, talking to reporters after 1978 meetings in Washington, D.C. *(Archive Photos)*

some, Smith was viewed by others as a rebellious hero similar to the American patriots of 1776. At the start of the 1970's, Smith remained firmly in control.

The Rhodesian Front

Southern Rhodesia was a British colony controlled by whites, who constituted only about 5 percent of the population. While other African nations gained independence in the late 1950's, the British hesitated to grant independence to Southern Rhodesia until its black inhabitants received more rights. Leading politicians in Southern Rhodesia's United Federal Party began to initiate reforms in 1961 in the hope of gaining British approval.

These reforms sparked an exodus from the United Federal Party by conservative whites, such as Ian Smith, who formed a new right-wing party known as the Rhodesian Front. The Rho-

desian Front's 1962 candidate for prime minister, Winston Field, won the election. Smith became deputy prime minister, then replaced Field as prime minister in 1964. Smith and many of his advisers were farmers or ranchers, and his advisers became known as the "cowboy cabinet." They made no secret of their intention to maintain white rule or of their hostility toward the British. On November 11, 1965, Smith's government declared the independence of Southern Rhodesia. The Rhodesian Front remained the ruling party until 1979, when the combined effects of war and economic sanctions ended its reign.

The Pearce Commission

In 1965, Southern Rhodesian whites declared independence from Great Britain, determined to keep power from the country's blacks, who represented 95 percent of the population. In 1971, the prime minister of Southern Rhodesia, Ian Smith, and the British foreign secretary, Alec Douglas-Home, negotiated a new constitution that would gradually increase the political rights of blacks. The British required that the new constitution be approved by the black population. To gauge popular opinion, England sent a commission headed by Edward Pearce to Southern Rhodesia. After talking with blacks across the land, the Pearce Commission concluded in May, 1972, that the majority of blacks disapproved of the new constitution. The British abandoned it and suspended negotiations with Smith, who would finally be driven out of office in 1979.

The turning point came in 1974. Portugal had been fighting to maintain its control of Angola and Mozambique, and in 1974 the new Portuguese government stopped fighting and granted them independence. This move altered the situation in southern Africa, leaving only South Africa and Southern Rhodesia under white governments. South African leader John Vorster was attempting to improve his relations with black-led nations, and as part of this program he pressured Smith into easing up on black activists in Southern Rhodesia. Depending heavily on South African support, Smith could not deny the wishes of Vorster. He allowed Nkomo and Mugabe to be released from prison.

Mugabe went to Mozambique to help lead an army of refugees from Southern Rhodesia, Nkomo did the same in Zambia, and the war between the liberation armies and Smith's forces escalated in 1975. With the help of South Africa, Smith and his supporters fought ferociously. The war was brutal, with both sides committing atrocities, and it raged on into 1978. Combined with the ongoing economic sanctions, the fighting devastated Southern Rhodesia.

Founding of Zimbabwe

In 1978, Smith decided that he could not prolong the struggle indefinitely if he had to contend with both the economic sanctions and the war.

Rather than negotiate with the leaders of the liberation armies, Smith decided to seek a compromise settlement with other black leaders in the hope of gaining the approval of the British government. The most important black leader with whom he chose to compromise was Abel Muzorewa. The agreement that he and Smith reached in 1978 was known as the internal settlement, and it allowed for limited black participation in government and black suffrage. In the elections held in the spring of 1979, Muzorewa was elected the first black prime minister of Southern Rhodesia. Smith retained considerable power, however, particularly over the security forces.

Despite the election of Muzorewa, in the summer of 1979 Great Britain decided not to grant independence to Southern Rhodesia or to lift sanctions. Smith's last attempt to dictate the terms had failed. Instead, an all-parties conference was held in the fall of 1979 in London. Finally, in December, Mugabe and Nkomo agreed that their forces would stop fighting. A new constitution was drafted, and elections were scheduled for February, 1980. The people elected Mugabe as the first prime minister of the new independent nation of Zimbabwe, which officially came into being in April.

Despite his disappointment about Mugabe's election, Smith remained in Zimbabwean politics. As a member of parliament until 1987 and then as a private citizen, he criticized government policies. An uproar occurred in 1995 when he was not allowed to vote in Harare because he was registered in Selukwe. In 1997 Smith published his memoirs, blasting British and South African whites for betraying him. On the other hand, he praised Nelson Mandela and expressed optimism about the future of South Africa. Smith's historical reputation remains mixed: Smith will be remembered as part war hero and rebel, part white supremacist, and part shrewd politician.

Bibliography

Martin, David, and Phyllis Johnson. *The Struggle for Zimbabwe*. New York: Monthly Review Press, 1981.

Meredith, Martin. *The Past Is Another Country*. London: Pan, 1980.

Smith, Ian. *The Great Betrayal*. London: Blake, 1997.

Andy DeRoche

Margaret Chase Smith

Born: December 14, 1897; Skowhegan, Maine
Died: May 29, 1995; Skowhegan, Maine

U.S. congresswoman (1940-1949) and senator (1949-1973)

Margaret Madeline Chase Smith (MAHR-gah-reht MA-deh-lin CHAYS SMIHTH) was the daughter of Carrie Murray Chase and George Emery Chase, a barber in the mill and factory town of Skowhegan, Maine. After graduation from high school Margaret briefly taught school, then worked for the telephone company, the local newspaper, and as office manager for a local textile mill. She was active in women's business organizations and the Republican Party.

Margaret married experienced politician Clyde H. Smith in 1930, gaining valuable campaigning and public-service skills working in

Margaret Chase Smith *(Library of Congress)*

Washington, D.C., from 1936 to 1940 during his terms as a U.S. representative. After his death in 1940, Margaret won election to the second district congressional seat. During her thirty-two years of public service, Margaret Chase Smith, bearing her political trademark of the red rose, earned a reputation for independence, integrity, honesty, and courage.

Defender of Maine and National Security

Smith served in the House of Representatives from 1940 to 1949. As a member of the Naval Affairs Committee she developed a strong interest in military issues, using her influence to improve the status of women in the military. She showed independence from party politics and devotion to military preparedness by voting for both the Selective Service Act to draft soldiers for World War II and the Lend-Lease Act of 1941, which permitted President Franklin D. Roosevelt to send military supplies to nations whose security was linked to that of the United States. She had the foresight to support U.S. membership in the United Nations as well as participation in the European Recovery Plan as opportunities for the United States to exert leadership in world affairs. She cosponsored an Equal Rights Amendment to improve the status of women. Her activities to promote the seafaring interests, workers, and women of Maine gave her the support she needed to win an upset victory for a U.S. Senate seat in 1948.

Conscience of the Senate

Smith's service in the Senate from 1949 to 1973 earned for her a national reputation for courage and integrity. Smith delivered her famous "Declaration of Conscience" speech in 1950, defending basic American freedoms from the anticommunist scare tactics of Senator Joseph R. McCarthy. Her growing national reputation gained her appointment to the most powerful Senate committees, including the Appropriations, Armed Services, and Aeronautical and Space Sciences Committees. She took pride in setting a Senate record for casting the most consecutive roll-call votes. During a period of Cold War tensions in 1954, she visited the leaders of twenty-three nations to gauge support for U.S. policies. Her party loyalty bowed to personal principles when she voted against presidential nominees she considered unqualified to hold appointed office. She sparked controversy by openly criticizing the foreign policy of the John F. Kennedy administration. She played an important part in debates over the Anti-Ballistic Missile Treaty and other arms-control issues in the 1970's. She continued her practice of refusing to accept campaign contributions up to the time of her defeat for reelection by a Democratic candidate in 1972.

Margaret Chase Smith succeeded as an effective legislator in the predominantly male political domain. She was the first woman in American

U.S. senator Margaret Chase Smith at a 1963 press conference with Senator Ed Muskie (left) and President John F. Kennedy. *(Archive Photos)*

history to serve in both the House and Senate and the first woman from a major political party to have her name placed in nomination for the U.S. presidency. She received awards for distinguished national service, including the Presidential Medal of Freedom, the nation's highest civilian honor, and ninety-five honorary degrees from educational institutions. She was inducted into the National Women's Hall of Fame. The Margaret Chase Smith Library in Skowhegan, Maine, serves as a public resource for learning about public service and political events.

Speaking Out Against McCarthy

In the early years of the Cold War after World War II, Wisconsin senator Joseph R. McCarthy spearheaded investigations into alleged Communist Party infiltration into U.S. State Department positions. McCarthy's abusive investigative style and disregard for people's rights to dissent prompted Senator Margaret Chase Smith to deliver her famous "Declaration of Conscience" speech on June 1, 1950. She defended basic American rights to criticize, hold unpopular beliefs, and protest peaceably. She deplored McCarthy's use of senatorial power to spread hate, fear, and bigotry, and to ruin to the reputations of loyal Americans.

Senator Margaret Chase Smith was a staunch anti-communist; here she visits the U.S. naval base at Guantanamo Bay, Cuba, in 1962. *(Library of Congress)*

Bibliography

Fleming, Alice. *The Senator from Maine.* New York: Thomas Y. Crowell, 1969.

Gould, Alberta. *First Lady of the Senate: Life of Margaret Chase Smith.* Mt. Desert, Maine: Windswept House, 1990.

Morin, Isobel V. *Women of the U.S. Congress.* Minneapolis, Minn.: Oliver Press, 1994.

Willoughby G. Jarrell

Jan Christian Smuts

Born: May 24, 1870; Bovenplaats, near Riebeeck West, Cape Colony (now part of South Africa)
Died: September 11, 1950; Doornkloof, Irene, near Pretoria, South Africa

Prime minister of South Africa (1919-1924, 1939-1948)

Jan Christian Smuts (YAHN KRIHS-tyahn SMEWTZ) was the son of Abraham Smuts, a Boer farmer and a member of the colonial Parliament. His family wanted him to pursue a career as a pastor in the Dutch Reformed Church. He entered a local school at the age of twelve and then, in 1886, entered Victoria College (later known as the University of Stellenbosch). He met a brilliant woman student named Sibella Margaretha (nicknamed Isie) Krige, whom he later married in 1897. After an exemplary career studying arts and sciences at Victoria College, he obtained a scholarship to Cambridge University in England, where he studied law beginning in 1891. He proved to be a brilliant student of law and won many prizes and academic honors. He then studied at the Inns of Court in London and won first prize in his final examination. His work was so outstanding that most thought that he would undertake the practice of law in London. His heart was in South Africa, however, and in 1895 he returned there. He opened a law practice in Johannesburg a year later.

Smuts not only read law but also immersed himself in science, philosophy, and poetry. While studying in England, Smuts had read the poetry of the American Walt Whitman, which had a profoundly liberating effect on him. It freed him from the guilt associated with the strict Calvinism of the Dutch Reformed Church. Smuts even wrote a book on the work of Whitman, although he was unable to find a publisher for it.

Entry into Politics

The president of the South African Republic, Paul Kruger, became aware of Smuts's great ability and appointed him state attorney in 1898 at the remarkably young age of twenty-eight.

Smuts moved to Pretoria and from this point on was deeply involved in South African and world politics.

When the Boer War began in 1899, Smuts divided his time between government and military service. When Pretoria was occupied by British forces, he became a full-time Boer soldier, ultimately earning an independent command. He proved his brilliance during the guerrilla stage of the war (1900-1902) and led an attack that penetrated deep into the Cape Colony. He was in the field when the war ended but was summoned by

Jan Christian Smuts *(Library of Congress)*

1419

South African prime minister Jan Christian Smuts (center) in 1943 with British field marshal Harold R. Alexander and American general Dwight D. Eisenhower (right). *(National Archives)*

the British to take part in the peace conference at Vereeniging. He played a major role in the conference, concluding that Boer independence was an impossible dream and that the only hope for the people of the Transvaal and the Orange Free State was to accept their new status as British Crown Colonies. Along with Louis Botha, he founded the Het Volk (people's party) and gained election to the newly established Parliament. He

and Botha traveled to London in 1906 to persuade the British parliament to grant responsible government to the Transvaal. In 1910 he was instrumental in writing the constitution for the Union of South Africa. He became a member of a new party, the South African Party, which was formed by the merger of Het Volk and several other regional parties. Upon the establishment of union, Smuts became minister of defense, mines, and the interior.

World War I

The outbreak of World War I caused Smuts to return to military life, and he led successful campaigns in German South West Africa and East Africa. His abilities impressed the British government, and in 1917 he represented South Africa at the Imperial War Conference in London. British prime minister David Lloyd George asked him to join the war cabinet, where Smuts was largely responsible for the establishment of the Royal Air Force. Smuts was a natural conciliator and was a major proponent of a moderate peace treaty with Germany.

The Coalition Government of 1933

In 1923, J. B. M. Hertzog concluded an agreement with Frederick H. P. Cresswell, the leader of the Labor Party, to support the parliamentary candidates of the other party. The collaboration worked. Together they defeated Jan Christian Smuts's party and formed what was known as the Pact Government. It governed South Africa until 1933. The Great Depression, which began in 1929, led to a financial crisis in South Africa that in part was caused by the government's efforts to maintain a strict gold standard. In 1933, Hertzog accepted a proposal from Smuts to form a coalition government with himself as prime minister and Smuts as deputy prime minister and minister of justice. In 1934 the National Party and the South African Party joined to form the United Party. This period was known as the era of "fusion" government.

South West Africa

South West Africa, known since independence in 1990 as Namibia, is mostly desert but has immense deposits of precious gems. It was explored by the Portuguese, Dutch, and British prior to the nineteenth century, but the inhospitable nature of the land precluded the formation of a formal colony. In 1884 Germany established a protectorate and later annexed it. The first German settlers arrived in 1892. During World War I South Africa drove the Germans out and occupied the land. After the war, South Africa was given a mandate to administer it as a South African colony. In spite of requests from the United Nations to relinquish control, and a bloody rebellion conducted by the South West Africa People's Organization (SWAPO), South Africa continued its administration until 1988, when it agreed to grant the colony full independence.

Although these views did not prevail, be was one of the founding fathers of the League of Nations, the postwar organization that was to provide a forum for the peaceful resolution of disputes. He represented South Africa at the Peace Conference at Versailles in 1919 and was a principal author of the Covenant of the League of Nations. Smuts returned to South Africa to become prime minister following the death of Botha in 1919.

Postwar Activities

General James Barry Munnik (J. B. M.) Hertzog had resigned from the Botha cabinet in 1913 and founded the National Party. It drew support from Afrikaaners and others who favored severing ties with Great Britain. Although Smuts won the election of 1920, his party continued to lose support, and in 1924 Hertzog's coalition of the National and Labor Party defeated the South African Party.

Temporarily out of politics, Smuts turned his energies to scholarship. In 1926 he wrote a complex philosophical work, *Holism and Evolution*, which won scholarly acclaim. In 1930 he became a fellow of the Royal Society, and the following year he was appointed rector of St Andrew's University. He led the opposition until 1933 when financial crises led to the formation of a coalition government of national unity. Smuts was deputy prime minister until 1939. Upon the outbreak of World War II in 1939, the South African Parliament rejected Herzog's policy of neutrality and once again made the pro-British Smuts prime minister. He collaborated closely with Winston Churchill and other war leaders and represented South Africa at the 1945 San Francisco Conference; there he played a major role in drafting the charter of the United Nations. In 1948 the Nationalists once again won the general election, and Smuts was immediately offered the chancellorship of Cambridge University. He died two years later at Doornkloof, Irene, near Pretoria.

Bibliography

Muller, C. F. J. *Five Hundred Years: A History of South Africa*. Cape Town, South Africa: H & R Academia, 1981.

Pakenham, Thomas. *The Boer War*. London: Weidenfeld and Nicholson, 1979.

Smith, Iain. R. *The Origins of the South African War, 1899-1902*. Essex, England: Longman, 1996.

Warwick, Peter, and S. B. Speis, eds. *The South African War: The Anglo-Boer War, 1899-1902*. Essex, England: Longman, 1980.

C. James Haug

Anastasio Somoza García

Born: February 1, 1896; San Marcos, Nicaragua
Died: September 29, 1956; Ancón, Panama Canal Zone (now Panama)

Dictatorial leader of Nicaragua (1937-1956)

Anastasio ("Tacho") Somoza García (ah-nahs-TAH-see-oh "TAH-choh" soh-MOH-sah gahr-THEE-ah) was born in San Marcos in the coffee-growing region of Nicaragua. Like many sons of prosperous planters, Tacho went to the United States for his education. While attending the Pierce School of Business Administration in Philadelphia, he perfected the English language skills that would help him rise to power in Nicaragua.

Somoza used his language skills to provide translations when the United States intervened in Nicaragua to end an anti-American rebellion in

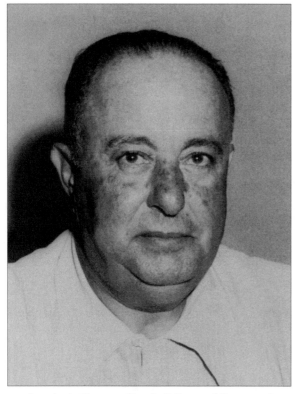

Anastasio Somoza García *(Library of Congress)*

1926. This work began Somoza's close relationship with U.S. representatives in Nicaragua. Somoza became so close to the Americans, in fact, that he was given the nickname El Yanqui ("the Yankee"). By providing special favors to U.S. Marine officers in the capital city of Managua, Somoza racked up a long list of favors due him. Somoza would later call in these favors to move to the leadership of the National Guard.

Somoza's Rise to Power

On March 31, 1931, a devastating earthquake destroyed most of Managua. In the midst of this crisis, Somoza proved skillful at recognizing opportunities. Since the quake severed all telephone, telegraph, and electrical services, ground transportation proved vital. Somoza secretly convinced taxi and truck drivers to go on strike so that he could use his influence to get the city moving again. Thus the tragedy helped Somoza portray himself as a hero of the people.

Somoza's family connections aided his rise to power. His wife, Salvadora, was the daughter of a leading Liberal (Dr. Luis N. Debayle) and granddaughter of a former president. Salvadora's Liberal connections convinced Somoza to join the Liberal rebellion to overthrow Conservative President Emiliano Chamorro in 1926. In 1932 Salvadora's uncle, Juan Bautista Sacasa, was elected president, virtually assuring Somoza a position of power in the new government. Because of his strong connections with Sacasa and with U.S. military officers, Somoza was chosen to lead the U.S.-supported paramilitary peacekeeping force called the National Guard.

It was from this position of power that Somoza orchestrated his own rise to the presidency. Somoza used the National Guard to eliminate his potential opponents. In 1933 he pretended to befriend rebel leader Augusto César Sandino after Sandino agreed to end his six-year guerrilla rebellion. When National Guard troops arrested Sandino and two Sandinista officers in Managua in February, 1934, Somoza refused Sandino's telephone calls for help. Within hours, Sandino and his officers were taken to an airfield and shot. Somoza later claimed responsibility for ordering the executions.

Throughout the 1930's, Somoza worked to solidify his power. He used the National Guard to force the Nicaraguan Congress to amend the constitution to assure his own election. To open his way to the presidency, he resigned as head of the National Guard, although he still ran it unofficially. With his power

A Sandinista honor guard marching in Managua in 1989 with a portrait of Augusto César Sandino, executed in 1934 by the National Guard when Somoza headed the force. At a rally following the march, President Daniel Ortega announced he would pardon National Guard members still in prison. *(Reuters/Lou Dematteis/ Archive Photos)*

over the military, and with the backing of the elites who cheered Sandino's death, Somoza forced President Sacasa to resign in June, 1936. His power and influence guaranteed his own

The Nicaraguan National Guard

In May, 1927, the United States established the Nicaraguan National Guard to defend peace, order, and the democratic process against attacks by Sandinista rebels. Equipped, trained, and commanded by U.S. Marine officers, the guard provided the Americans a method for controlling Nicaragua after the Marines withdrew in 1933. Immediately before the U.S. withdrawal, Anastasio Somoza García assumed leadership of the National Guard.

Under Somoza, the National Guard was well-armed and vicious. Used as a tool of repression by the Somoza dynasty, the guard was widely accused of rampant abuses of power, including beatings and murders of Sandinista rebels, Somoza's political opponents, and innocent bystanders—including at least two Red Cross volunteers. International outrage in response to the atrocities finally eroded U.S. support for the guard in the 1970's. The end of the National Guard came when, on July 18, 1979, guard officers fled into exile, leaving guard troops to surrender to the Sandinista troops marching into Managua.

The Sandinistas

When Nicaraguan rebel leader Augusto César Sandino initiated his war against the U.S. Marines in 1926, he personified the nationalist sentiments of many of his countrymen. In 1961 the popular memory of this patriot inspired the creation of the *Frente Sandinista de Liberación Nacional* (FSLN), or the Sandinistas. The FSLN was formed by the three leading rebel groups in opposition to the regime of Anastasio Somoza Debayle, whose father had masterminded the assassination of Sandino in 1934. Because of their nationalist and anti-imperial philosophy, the Sandinistas found most of their support among the rural peasants to whom Sandino himself had appealed.

Inspired by the successful 1959 Cuban Revolution of Fidel Castro, the FSLN embraced a leftist philosophy. In spite of U.S. Central Intelligence Agency (CIA) accusations that it was a communist organization, the FSLN remained separate from the Communist Party. The organization's leftist philosophy helps explain the lengths to which the United States went to eliminate it. U.S. efforts encompassed sending military advisers to Nicaragua in 1967 and, later, CIA establishment of the anti-Sandinista "Contras" in 1981 and the Ronald Reagan administration's illegal sending of arms to the Contras in the 1980's, a part of the Iran-Contra scandal.

election in November and his inauguration in January, 1937.

The Somoza Dynasty

As president, Somoza further modified the constitution to allow for his reelection to an eight-year term instead of the previous four-year term. He traveled to the United States in 1939, where he posed with Franklin D. Roosevelt, addressed Congress, and arranged for a $2 million loan from the Import-Export Bank. His sons, Luis and Anastasio, followed their father's lead by going to school in the United States. Both attended a military prep school in New York. Later, Luis entered Louisiana State University and Anastasio attended the U.S. military academy at West Point. They both later returned to Nicaragua to assume positions of leadership in the National Guard. Somoza secured the future of the dynasty by accumulating a huge fortune through corruption and extremely high taxes. It was estimated that after only ten years in office, his personal fortune topped $120 million and that he owned virtually all the land around Managua.

When his term in office expired in 1947, Somoza placed a series of hand-picked puppets in power and resumed command of the National Guard. Through it all, he maintained control as the virtual dictator of Nicaragua. Civil liberties were suppressed as political opponents were arrested and tortured. In 1950 Somoza returned himself to the presidency and arranged for his reelection in 1951.

In 1956 Somoza again revised Nicaragua's constitution to allow for yet another term as president. On the evening of September 21, 1956, at a party to celebrate his renomination, Somoza was shot four times by Rigoberto López Pérez, who was himself immediately shot and beaten to death. U.S. president Dwight D. Eisenhower ordered American military helicopters to carry Somoza to the Panama Canal Zone, where the best U.S. military surgeons struggled to save Somoza's life. In spite of these efforts, Somoza died on September 29, eight days after the shooting. That evening, Somoza's oldest son, Luis Somoza Debayle, president of the Congress, was elected acting president. His younger brother, Anastasio

Somoza Debayle, assumed control of the National Guard. The younger Somozas ruled as dictators in Nicaragua until 1979.

Bibliography

Crawley, Eduardo. *Dictators Never Die: A Portrait of Nicaragua and the Somoza Dynasty.* New York: St. Martin's Press, 1979.

Diederich, Bernard. *Somoza and the Legacy of U.S. Involvement in Central America.* New York: E. P. Dutton, 1981.

Walter, Knut. *The Regime of Anastasio Somoza, 1936-1956.* Chapel Hill: University of North Carolina Press, 1993.

Matthew A. Redinger

Paul-Henri Spaak

Born: January 25, 1899; Schaerbeek, near Brussels, Belgium
Died: July 31, 1972; Brussels, Belgium

Belgian politician and diplomat, advocate of European unity

Paul-Henri Charles Spaak (POHL o-REE CHAHRL SPOK) was born into a well-connected family. His father turned from practicing law to writing and eventually became director of the Brussels Opera. His mother, a socialist from a family active in both the arts and politics, was the first woman elected to Belgium's Senate. During World War I, Spaak was imprisoned in a German prison camp after trying to pass through the lines to join the Belgian army. He earned a law degree from the Free University of Brussels in 1921 and the next year married Marguerite Malevy, the daughter of an industrialist. A leftist firebrand, he became a Socialist Party deputy in the Belgian

Chamber of Representatives in 1932 and subsequently minister of transport and posts, then foreign minister. In the late 1930's, he became Socialist leader and then Belgium's youngest prime minister. After the war, during which he was a leading figure in the Belgian government in exile in London, he was again prime minister from 1947 to 1949 and foreign minister several times until 1957.

European Unification Efforts

Spaak is best remembered for his efforts to unify Europe, a commitment which led to his nickname, "Mr. Europe." This attachment to principles of integration had already developed during World War II, when Spaak was instrumental in establishing the Benelux Economic Union. Spaak was in the forefront of negotiations leading to far-reaching agreements on European union.

An international committee pressing for European unity organized a congress, which met at The Hague in May, 1948. The 750 delegates, among them some of Europe's leading statesmen, including Spaak, Winston Churchill, and Alcide de Gasperi, decided to establish the Council of Europe. Amid enthusiastic crowds, the council's Committee of Ministers' first session was opened in Strasbourg, France, by French foreign minister Robert Schuman on August 8, 1949. The Council of Europe decided to work in alphabetical order, and Belgium was first on the list, so Spaak became chairman of the first session of the Council of Europe's Consultative Assembly. A network of intergovernmental relations in fields as diverse as human rights, local government, education, research, culture, sports, and youth policy developed. However, the council was doomed to play an advisory role, debating

Paul-Henri Spaak *(Library of Congress)*

The Benelux Charter

Building on the 1932 Ouchy Convention, which was a step toward the economic integration of the Low Countries, the London-based governments-in-exile of Belgium, the Netherlands, and Luxembourg negotiated an agreement on economic union at the height of World War II. The Belgian-Luxembourg Economic Union (BLEU), formed in 1921, had already united the customs, trade, and monetary systems of Belgium and Luxembourg. The 1940 German occupation of the Netherlands led the Dutch to abandon their traditional neutrality and become more active in both European and world affairs. The result was the Customs Convention of September 5, 1944, a document later recognized as the founding charter of the Benelux Economic Union. A more lengthy treaty, signed on February 3, 1958, formalized the union and created a variety of shared institutions in virtually all aspects of national life. An inspiration for efforts to unify all of Europe, the Benelux union has been the most successful peaceable union of sovereign nations in history.

issues without having the authority to act. Spaak resigned in protest.

Spaak and the ECSC

Inspired by Schuman and Jean Monnet (the theoretician behind European integration), France, Germany, Italy and the Benelux nations established the European Coal and Steel Community (ECSC) on April 18, 1951. When the treaty went into force in 1952, institutions were established. Monnet presided over the High Authority, and Spaak was president of the ECSC's General Assembly during 1952 and 1953. Based on a report authored by Spaak, treaties establishing the European Economic Community (EEC) and European Atomic Energy Community (Euratom) were signed in Rome in March, 1957. They went into effect in January, 1958. Eventually these institutions, mainly headquartered in Brussels, were merged into the European Community, finally called the European Union.

Spaak was also a world figure. In 1949 he presided over the first General Assembly of the United Nations. In 1956 the North Atlantic Treaty Organization (NATO) chose him as secretary-general. He resigned in March, 1961, in order to resume his political career in Belgium, where he again became foreign minister. Spaak was also president of the Royal Belgian Academy of French Language and Literature.

Bibliography

Eyck, F. Gunther. *The Benelux Countries: An Historical Survey*. Princeton, N.J.: Van Nostrand, 1959.

Sampson, Anthony. *Anatomy of Europe*. New York: Harper & Row, 1968.

Spaak, Paul-Henri. *The Continuing Battle: Memoirs of a European, 1936-1966*. Boston: Little, Brown, 1971.

Randall Fegley

Joseph Stalin

Born: December 21, 1879; in Gori, Georgia, Russian Empire
Died: March 5, 1953; Kuntsevo, U.S.S.R.

Soviet totalitarian dictator (1928-1953)

Joseph Vissarionovich Dzhugashvili (ih-OH-sy-ihf vyih-suh-ryih-OH-nuh-vyihch jew-ga-SHVEE-lee)—the real name of Joseph Stalin (ih-OH-syihf STA-lyihn)—was the only son of a poor cobbler, Vissarion Dzhugashvili. His mother, Yekaterina, saved money from her meager income as a domestic servant in order to send Joseph to the seminary. The younger Dzhugashvili entered the Tiflis Orthodox Theological Seminary in 1893 and received high marks. By

1898, however, he had entered the growing revolutionary movement in the Russian Empire and was expelled from the seminary.

Siding with Vladimir Lenin's Bolshevik wing of the Russian Social Democratic Workers' Party, Dzhugashvili organized strikes, conducted political demonstrations and engaged in train robbery in the Caucasus region of the Russian Empire. For these acts he was imprisoned or exiled on numerous occasions between 1902 and 1917 by czarist authorities. During this period Dzhugashvili chose the name Stalin (Russian for "man of steel") as his pseudonym, rejecting his previous alias, "Koba." It was also during this period that Stalin's first wife, Yekaterina Svanidze, died. Having married Yekaterina in 1905, Stalin was extremely upset by his wife's early death in 1907. On the occasion of her funeral, Stalin reportedly confided in an old friend that she had "softened my stony heart" and with her death died his "last warm feelings for all human beings." His future actions certainly seemed to prove this statement correct.

Postrevolutionary Events

In early 1917, Stalin returned to St. Petersburg from exile and played a significant role in the planning of the Communist Revolution. From 1917 to 1922, Stalin was charged with directing nationalities policy for the newly installed Bolshevik government led by Lenin. In 1922 he was elected general secretary of the Russian Communist Party, at Lenin's suggestion. Though initially thought to be an innocuous position, the office of general secretary enabled Stalin to

Joseph Stalin *(Library of Congress)*

An idealized painting of Joseph Stalin (hand above map) leading a Central Committee meeting. In reality, a major part of the committee's plans involved bloody purges. *(Library of Congress)*

appoint loyal subordinates to positions of power and to intimidate his rivals. Before his death, Lenin wrote that Stalin (whom Lenin thought to be "crude" and "capricious") had amassed great power as general secretary, and he encouraged Stalin's removal. After Lenin's death, his words were not acted upon by Stalin's rivals; Stalin remained in his position and strengthened his hold on power.

To achieve these ends, Stalin moved against his rivals on the Politburo, the leading policy-making body of the Communist Party. Beginning with an ideological attack against the radical policies of Leon Trotsky, Grigoriy Zinoviev, and

The Stalin "Show Trials" of the 1930's

As Joseph Stalin's dictatorial powers grew in the 1930's, the totalitarian despot believed it necessary to hold staged trials of purported traitors. Such trials were held throughout the 1930's in order to exterminate Stalin's perceived rivals, to place responsibility for economic failures on the accused, and to serve as political education for the masses.

Branding the falsely accused people "agents of fascist Germany and Japan," "wreckers" of the Soviet economy and "conspirators" in plots to assassinate Stalin, the dictator's secret police organs obtained through torture "confessions" from top Soviet leaders that implicated them in the alleged crimes. Among the many tried and convicted by Stalin's rabid procurator general, Andrei Vyshinsky, were Nikolai Bukharin, Mikhail Tukhachevsky, and Leon Trotsky (tried in absentia). Upon finding the accused guilty of the crimes, the frenzied Vyshinsky would bark such orders as "Shoot the mad dogs, every one of them!" Stalin's secret police then carried out the condemned men's sentences, death by firing squad.

The Collectivization of Agriculture

A major plank of Joseph Stalin's plan for the rapid development of the Soviet economy in the late 1920's was the collectivization of agriculture. Collectivization sought forcefully to merge individual peasant farms into enormous collective (*kolkhoz*) or state (*sovkhoz*) farms. The collectivization campaign was undertaken in order to provide badly needed resources for the industrialization drive and to smash peasant resistance to Stalin's totalitarian state.

Within the space of seven years, the proportion of Soviet cropland collectivized by Communist Party officials and secret police troops rose from 3 percent to 94 percent. Resentful peasants responded by slaughtering livestock, burning crops, and secreting grain. Accordingly, Stalin instituted brutal measures, branding rebellious peasants "enemies of the people," deporting millions to labor camps in Siberia or the Soviet Union's far north, and inaugurating a premeditated famine that killed more than seven million peasants in Ukraine, the Soviet Union's primary grain-producing region. Stalin's collectivization policies were disastrous for Russian agriculture.

Crowds thronged Moscow's Red Square in 1953 for Joseph Stalin's funeral. *(National Archives)*

Lev Kamenev in the mid-1920's, Stalin had by 1928 rid the Politburo of these "left deviationists" and stolen their ideological program of heavy industrialization and collectivization of agriculture.

Soon thereafter, Stalin introduced a punishing drive toward full-scale industrialization and established five-year plans to serve both as all- important guides for the Soviet economy's rapid development and as measurements of success. In addition, the brutal policy of collectivizing the country's farmers onto enormous state or collective farms was begun. Meeting peasant resistance, Stalin reciprocated with savagery. His secret police, the NKVD, meted out summary judgment against those considered enemies of the people, carted off entire populations to Siberia, and imposed an artificial famine upon grain-producing areas of the Soviet Union. In the end, millions of peasants perished.

Purges and World War II

In early 1929, Stalin turned his ire against remaining Politburo members who were considered to be opponents of Stalin's harsh, maximalist policies. Within several years, Stalin totally discredited the members of the "right deviation," such as Nikolai Bukharin, Aleksei Rykov, and Mikhail Tomsky. Once again, Stalin's rivals were expelled from all positions of power. A thorough purging of party and government apparatuses soon followed their dismissals. Another victim of Stalin's brutality during this period was his second wife, Nadezhda Alliluyeva. Having learned of the many barbaric acts committed by her husband against both former friends and innocent Soviet citizens, she committed suicide under suspicious circumstances in November, 1932.

By the early 1930's, Stalin had vanquished his major rivals and obtained almost untrammeled power. Nevertheless, the paranoid leader still believed his position vulnerable to opposition. Therefore, after ordering the murder of the Leningrad party leader, Sergei Kirov, Stalin used Kirov's assassination as a pretext to annihilate those "enemies of the people" who were responsible. A massive purging of party, state, and military officials was undertaken. By the end of the 1930's, Stalin's NKVD had slaughtered more than one million party members and more than thirty-five thousand military officers. While cementing Stalin's control, these acts negatively affected the performance of the Soviet government and military in the opening months of World War II.

After recovering from the initial shock of Adolf Hitler's invasion in June, 1941, General Secretary Stalin—who by now was also premier of the Soviet government—added three more titles to his name: supreme commander in chief of Soviet armed forces, chairman of the state defense committee, and generalissimo. As such, Stalin led the stoic Soviet people through four years of war. The Soviet Union suffered more than twenty million casualties in World War II. In the aftermath of victory, many Soviet citizens believed that the excesses of the Stalinist regime would abate.

Their hopes were not fulfilled, however, as Stalin pressed for continued sacrifice, further industrialization, and greater loyalty from his nation and subordinates. Opposition, either real or perceived, was still extinguished with brutal ferocity. In addition, a personality cult arose around Stalin, as sycophantic yes-men lauded the increasingly senile dictator with numerous honors and renamed entire cities and squares after him. Such deeds could not ameliorate the suspicions of the paranoid leader. Indeed, by 1952 Stalin was preparing a new purge of party and government leaders. His plans never came to fruition, however, as Stalin died in March, 1953, of a cerebral hemorrhage.

Bibliography

Brzezinski, Zbigniew K. *The Permanent Purge: Politics in Soviet Totalitarianism.* Cambridge, Mass.: Harvard University Press, 1956.

Conquest, Robert. *Stalin: Breaker of Nations.* New York: Viking, 1991.

Duranty, Walter. *Stalin & Co.: The Politburo, the Men Who Run Russia.* New York: William Sloane Associates, 1949.

McCauley, Martin. *Stalin and Stalinism.* 2d ed. London: Longman Group, 1995.

Shearer, David R. *Industry, State, and Society in Stalin's Russia, 1926-1934.* Ithaca, N.Y.: Cornell University Press, 1996.

Thomas E. Rotnem

Adlai E. Stevenson

Born: February 5, 1900; Los Angeles, California
Died: July 14, 1965; London, England

U.S. politician and diplomat, United Nations ambassador (1961-1965)

Adlai Ewing Stevenson II (AD-lay EW-ihng STEE-vehn-suhn thuh SEH-kuhnd) was the son of Lewis and Helen Stevenson; his father was a newspaper executive and Democratic Party official. His grandfather, also named Adlai, had been vice president under Grover Cleveland and had been nominated again for the office during the 1900 campaign of William Jennings Bryan. After his youth in Bloomington, Illinois, Stevenson graduated from Princeton University. After briefly attending Harvard Law School, he returned to work on the family newspaper, the

Adlai E. Stevenson *(Library of Congress)*

Pantagraph. While still working at the *Pantagraph*, Stevenson gained his law degree from Northwestern Law School.

Marriage and Government Service

On December 1, 1926, Stevenson married Ellen Borden. The couple moved to Chicago, where Stevenson practiced law. The Stevensons eventually had three sons, but they divorced in 1949. During the 1930's, Stevenson became active in Chicago politics, and in 1933 he accepted a position in the Agricultural Adjustment Administration, a part of President Franklin D. Roosevelt's New Deal program. Stevenson then returned to Chicago, becoming well known as president of the Council on Foreign Relations. In 1941 he joined the staff of Frank Knox, secretary of the Navy, and was active as a congressional liaison and on missions overseas. In 1945 Stevenson received his most important assignment: assisting with the creation of the United Nations.

Stevenson was drafted to run for governor of Illinois in 1948. His freshness, intelligence, and commitment led to a smashing victory, and he became only the third Democrat elected Illinois governor since the Civil War. Talk began of Stevenson as the Democratic nominee for president in 1952. His outstanding record as a hardworking, highly effective governor increased his popularity, and he went to the Democratic convention as the favorite of President Harry S Truman.

Twice a Candidate

In Chicago the Democrats nominated Stevenson, and in his eloquent acceptance speech he promised to "talk sense to the American people." Stevenson waged an intelligent, even intellectual campaign against the enormously popular Republican nominee, Dwight D. Eisenhower. Eisenhower had commanded Allied troops against Nazi Germany during World War II. Despite the enthusiasm Stevenson aroused, he could not surmount Eisenhower's lead, and he was defeated in November. However, his defeat did not diminish his reputation or his standing in the Democratic Party. He made an around-the-world tour to great acclaim. At home, he fearlessly spoke out against the reckless attacks of demagogic Republican senator Joseph R. McCarthy while many remained silent.

In 1956 Stevenson was again nominated by the Democrats. In a break with tradition, he left the nomination of the vice presidential candidate to the convention. After a hard-fought contest, which saw freshman senator John F. Kennedy of Massachusetts nearly the nominee, Senator Ernest Kefauver of Tennessee was the choice. Pitted against the ever-popular Eisenhower, Stevenson lost again in November, although the Democrats won a majority in Congress.

A Public Servant Until the End

Stevenson's appearance at the 1960 Democratic convention touched off an enormous spontaneous demonstration, but the presidential

Illinois governor Adlai Stevenson addressing the New York State Liberal Party in 1952 during his run for the presidency. *(Archive Photos)*

nomination went to John F. Kennedy, who won a narrow victory that fall. Stevenson, who had hoped to be named secretary of state, was appointed ambassador to the United Nations. In

---

The Presidential Campaign of 1952

Faced with the apparently deadlocked Korean War, President Harry S Truman chose not to run for reelection in 1952. The Republicans nominated Dwight D. Eisenhower, who had been commander of Allied forces in Europe during World War II. (The war had ended some seven years earlier.) The Democrats nominated Adlai Stevenson, the intelligent, witty governor of Illinois.

Against Eisenhower's great popularity, Stevenson attempted to appeal to the American voter's intelligence. A collection of his speeches, with a foreword by author John Steinbeck, became a best-seller. Then Eisenhower promised that, if elected, he would "go to Korea." Although such a visit meant little, it had great symbolic value. The statement is regarded by many as the single event which led to Stevenson's defeat that November. After the election, Stevenson wryly recalled an Abraham Lincoln story about a boy who stubbed his toe: "He was too old to cry, but it hurt too much to laugh."

that post, he charmed delegates with his wit, sophistication, and intelligence. During the Cuban Missile Crisis of October, 1962, he showed great determination. After presenting photographic evidence of the growing Soviet military presence in Cuba, he demanded a response and promised, "I am prepared to wait for my response until hell freezes over." In the end, the Soviets withdrew their missiles from the island. Stevenson continued to grow in reputation and stature. His health, however, had begun to decline. On the evening of Wednesday, July 14, as he was walking through London, he collapsed and died of a heart attack. Stevenson has been called "the best president the United States never had."

Bibliography

Baker, Jean H. *The Stevensons: Portrait of an American Family*. New York: W. W. Norton, 1996.

Boller, Paul F. *Presidential Campaigns*. New York: Oxford University Press, 1984.

Broadwater, Jeff. *Adlai Stevenson and American Politics*. New York: Twayne, 1994.

Davis, Kenneth. *The Politics of Honor: A Biography of Adlai Stevenson*. New York: G. P. Putnam, 1967.

Martin, John Bartlow. *Adlai Stevenson of Illinois*. New York: Doubleday, 1977.

McKeever, Porter. *Adlai Stevenson: His Life and Legacy*. New York: William Morrow, 1989.

Michael Witkoski

Henry L. Stimson

Born: September 21, 1867; New York, New York
Died: October 20, 1950; Huntington, New York

U.S. secretary of state (1929-1933) and secretary of war (1940-1945)

Henry Lewis Stimson (HEHN-ree LEW-ihs STIHM-suhn), a statesman and champion of the sanctity of international agreements, established a reputation as one of the most respected and admired figures of the early twentieth century. During the course of his distinguished career in public service, Stimson served in the cabinets of four presidential administrations. He also chaired the committee that made the final recommendation to use the atomic bomb during World War II.

Early Career

Henry Stimson was born in New York City, the son of Lewis Atterbury Stimson and the former Candace Wheeler. Following his mother's death in 1875, Stimson and his sister were sent to live with their grandparents. He studied Greek and Latin at the Sanver School of Languages prior to being sent away to boarding school at Phillips Academy in Andover, Massachusetts. Stimson went on to receive his undergraduate degree from Yale University in 1888, eventually completing his legal studies at Harvard Law School in 1890. He joined a well-respected Wall Street law firm after completing law school.

President Theodore Roosevelt appointed Stimson the U.S. attorney for the Southern District of New York in 1906, the first of many such presidential appointments. He resigned his position as U.S. attorney in 1909 to run for the office of governor of New York. Stimson won the Republican nomination for governor in 1910 but failed in his bid during the general election. President William Howard Taft appointed Stimson his secretary of war in 1911, a position he held until 1913, when the Democrats regained the White House and he was forced to resign. During World War I

Stimson served in the U.S. Army as a colonel in the artillery. After the conflict ended in 1918, he again returned to New York City to practice law.

Stimson again entered public service in 1927, when he was called upon by President Calvin Coolidge to work with the U.S. military force occupying Nicaragua. His directive from Coolidge was to arbitrate elections and reestablish a constitutional government in that country. Nicaragua, like many Central American and Caribbean countries at that time, was occupied by American forces in an effort to protect U.S. investments and establish U.S. supremacy in the region. Stimson's shrewd handling of the

Henry L. Stimson *(Library of Congress)*

1435

A blindfolded secretary of war Henry L. Stimson reaches for the first Selective Service lottery number in 1940. *(Library of Congress)*

Nicaraguan situation so impressed Coolidge that he appointed Stimson governor-general of the Philippines in 1928. One year later, newly elected president Herbert Hoover selected Stimson as his secretary of state.

Secretary of State

As secretary of state, Stimson led the American delegations to the London Naval Conference in 1930 and the Geneva Disarmament Conference in 1932. Agreements to adhere to restrictions on the development and deployment of military weapons were negotiated at both conferences. The 1931 Japanese invasion of Manchuria led to his announcement the following year of what is referred to as the Stimson Doctrine, under which the United States would not recognize the validity of political change brought about by violation of international obligations or treaty rights. Stimson wanted the United States to respond in some manner to the Japanese atrocities being carried out in

The Stimson Doctrine

The groundwork of the Stimson Doctrine was actually securely established in the late 1890's by Secretary of State John Hay, who established the "doctrine of the open door" regarding China. At that time the leadership in China was weak, divided, and vulnerable to outside forces, especially the Japanese. Hay asserted that all nations should have the freedom to trade in China and that Chinese territorial integrity would be secured. In 1931 Japan invaded China and occupied Manchuria. U.S. secretary of state Henry Stimson viewed the Japanese invasion as a violation of agreements signed by Japan. In January, 1932, Secretary Stimson reasserted Hay's open-door policy. Establishing a policy now known as the Stimson Doctrine, Stimson declared that the United States would not recognize the legitimacy of political change brought about by violation of international obligations or treaty rights.

Dollar Diplomacy

Henry Stimson was an enthusiastic advocate of "dollar diplomacy," the active use of the power of the United States against other countries to promote and protect private U.S. investment abroad. Dollar diplomacy is most often associated with U.S. foreign policy toward Latin America during the early twentieth century, the time encompassing most of Stimson's tenure of public service. The policy was based on the belief that U.S. investment abroad, especially in Latin America, would benefit not only the economy of the developing nation but also the U.S. investor. U.S. military intervention, if required, was considered an acceptable means of ensuring stability and preventing the emergence of leftist governments that might threaten investments. Stimson, a conservative Republican who served under four presidents during the height of dollar diplomacy, often stated his belief that the role of government was to preserve law and order—and thus to protect property and investments.

China, but the United States had no desire to engage in a conflict with Japan at that time. Following Franklin D. Roosevelt's defeat of Hoover, Stimson again returned to the practice of law in 1933.

Concerned about the course of U.S. foreign policy, Stimson met with President-elect Roosevelt just prior to his inauguration to brief him on issues of national security. The meeting with Roosevelt, for which Stimson received much criticism from other members of the Hoover administration, was a very friendly encounter and left an indelible impression on Roosevelt. As a private citizen, Stimson continued to speak out publicly regarding the potential threat to American security posed by the Japanese. He also spoke of the threat from the fascist and communist leaders of Europe and Asia. He advocated increased military spending, warning that the United States was unprepared for a major conflict.

World War II

President Roosevelt appointed Stimson his secretary of war in 1940. The appointment of such a high-profile Republican has been interpreted as an effort by Roosevelt to unify the nation as the threat of war loomed on the horizon. Stimson was criticized by fellow Republicans for accepting the appointment, but he stated that the welfare of the nation was more important than politics. Roosevelt, who had been very impressed by Stimson's tenure as secretary of state under Hoover, saw him as the obvious choice.

With Stimson's guidance, Roosevelt began the break from U.S. isolationist policies of the past. Military spending reinvigorated the American economy after the lengthy depression of the 1930's. Although the United States was unprepared for the war with Japan that began with the Japanese bombing of the Pearl Harbor navy base in December of 1941, the U.S. military quickly recovered under Stimson's leadership. As Roosevelt's chief adviser on atomic policy, Stimson was among the first to suggest the use of atomic bombs in the war against Japan. After Roosevelt's death in April, 1945, President Harry S Truman made the final decision to act on Stimson's recommendation, hoping that the use of the new weapon would bring about a swift conclusion to the war. The United States dropped an atomic bomb on Hiroshima on August 6, 1945, and on Nagasaki on August 9.

In response to critics, Stimson later stated that the use of the bomb was necessary to avoid the loss of American military personnel in a bloody invasion of Japan. He argued that an invasion might have resulted in more than one million casualties. Shortly after the Japanese surrender in 1945, President Truman awarded Stimson the Distinguished Service Medal.

Bibliography

Current, Richard N. *Secretary Stimson: A Study in Statecraft*. New Brunswick, N.J.: Rutgers University Press, 1954.

Hodgson, Godfrey. *The Colonel: The Life and Wars of Henry Stimson, 1867-1950*. New York: Alfred A. Knopf, 1990.

Morison, Elting E. *Turmoil and Tradition: Henry L. Stimson*. Boston: Houghton Mifflin, 1960.

Rappaport, Armin. *Henry L. Stimson and Japan: 1931-1933*. Chicago: University of Chicago Press, 1963.

Rhodes, Richard J. *The Making of the Atomic Bomb*. New York: Simon & Schuster, 1987.

Donald C. Simmons, Jr.

Louis St. Laurent

Born: February 1, 1882; Compton, Quebec, Canada
Died: July 25, 1973; Quebec City, Quebec, Canada

Prime minister of Canada (1948-1957)

Louis Stephen St. Laurent (lew-EE stay-FEH sa loh-RO) was brought up by a French-speaking father and an English-speaking mother. As a result, he was fluently bilingual. His elementary education occurred at home, after which he began studies for the Roman Catholic priesthood. His interests lay elsewhere, however, and he studied law at Laval University in Quebec City. This study led to a distinguished legal career in which he was appointed professor of law at Laval in 1914. In 1929 St. Laurent became head of the Quebec Bar Association and from 1930 to 1932 served as president of the Canadian Bar Association. From 1937 to 1940 he was counsel to the Rowell-Sirois Royal Commission on Dominion-Provincial Relations. All this was accomplished while St. Laurent was building a reputation as one of Quebec City's most successful lawyers.

The Political World

Before his entry into politics, St. Laurent was not active in any party. However, in 1940, Ernest Lapointe, the lieutenant to Liberal prime minister William Lyon Mackenzie King, died. St. Laurent was suggested as his successor. At first King's overtures were refused, but when Cardinal Villeneuve and Quebec premier Adelard Godbout intervened he agreed despite the considerable financial sacrifice the move would entail.

The first task was to seek election in a by-election in Quebec East. Quebec had a deserved reputation for political dirty tricks that included heavy-handed, even abusive, heckling. At first St. Laurent did not fare well in this atmosphere (as a lawyer, he was much more at home in the boardroom than the courtroom). However, at one particularly raucous meeting, St. Laurent tried to calm the unruly crowd by talking to them in a fatherly fashion. Much to his surprise, the approach worked. This style ultimately earned him the nickname "Uncle Louis" and served him well in his political career. In Ottawa, St. Laurent was immediately given the Justice portfolio, which he held until 1946. During the World War II years, however, his most important function was to represent Quebec's interests in the King cabinet. Because he had the prime minister's ear, he is often given credit for persuading King to wait as long as he did to impose conscription, thus avoiding the national unity crisis which had divided Canada in World War I.

Louis St. Laurent *(National Archives)*

In 1945 St. Laurent, who had intended to serve only one term, was persuaded to run again. Easily reelected, he was given the prestigious post of external affairs minister. Moreover, after this election Prime Minister King told St. Laurent that he wanted him as his successor. Despite his denial of interest in the position, St. Laurent was persuaded to contest the leadership when King retired in 1948. In 1949 and again in 1953 he led the Liberal Party to substantial majorities.

The Prime Ministerial Years

The first term of the new government included a number of accomplishments. Newfoundland entered confederation as the tenth province. The Trans-Canada Act was passed, providing for construction of a coast-to-coast roadway. An agreement was also signed with the United States for construction of the long-advocated St. Lawrence Seaway, although construction did not begin until 1954.

St. Laurent also appointed the Royal Commission on Arts, Letters, and Sciences, headed by Vincent Massey. In 1952 Massey became the first Canadian-born governor-general. This position (as the queen's representative and head of state in her absence) has been held by Canadians ever since. Internationally the most important event of the time was the involvement in the Korean War from 1950 to 1953.

In the Liberal government's second term, the St. Lawrence Seaway was begun. St. Laurent also instituted a policy which has become the backbone of Canadian confederation: equalization payments. Under this program, financially well-off provinces such as Ontario contribute funds which are given to poorer provinces to equalize wealth and to allow all provinces to offer social programs at the same level. In 1957 the Canada Council was established to foster Canadian culture. The other great accomplishment of the second term was the Trans-Canada Pipeline—although, ironically, it led to the downfall of the St. Laurent government.

The Election of 1956

As the Liberals neared the end of their second term, they were optimistic about their reelection. Not only did the government enjoy a substantial budgetary surplus, but also the polls showed that the Liberals had a considerable lead over the Conservatives and their newly elected leader, John Diefenbaker. Tactical errors, however, led to an alteration of these circumstances by election time in 1957.

The Trans-Canada Pipeline had been portrayed as a project as important to Canada in the twentieth century as the Canadian Pacific Railway was in the nineteenth. However, when the Conservatives learned that the government's

---

Newfoundland Joins Canada

Negotiations for Newfoundland to join Canada were ongoing from the mid-nineteenth century. In the meantime, the colony of Newfoundland was ruled by an appointed commission. At the end of World War II the newly elected Labor Party government in Great Britain decided that the residents of Newfoundland should vote on whether to unite with Canada. A 1946 convention was held, at which Newfoundlanders decided to abide by the results of a referendum. In the 1949 vote, which bitterly divided political parties and even families, the pro-confederates won by the narrowest of margins. In March, 1949, the British America Act was amended. On April 1, 1949, Joseph Roberts Smallwood was appointed the first premier of the new province of Newfoundland.

Canada and NATO

The North Atlantic Treaty Organization (NATO) was the brainchild of Canadian diplomat Escott Reid, who in 1947 was concerned about the postwar weakness of Great Britain and France and increasing isolation on the part of the United States. He proposed the alliance to Louis St. Laurent, who dispatched senior diplomat Hume Wrong to London and Washington, D.C. NATO, which was Canada's first peacetime alliance, was formed in 1949. It was with the escalation of tensions connected with the Cold War in the 1950's and 1960's that NATO assumed major importance.

choice of contractor was an American company, they decided to delay passage of the pipeline bill by filibustering. The Liberals' response was to introduce "closure," a limitation to the debate time devoted to the legislation. Despite opposition protests that closure violated parliamentary practice, the legislation was upheld by the speaker. Near fistfights broke out in the House amid the draping of the speaker's chair with the Union Jack and the singing of "God Save the Queen." In the ensuing campaign this incident was cited by the Conservatives as one of many examples of Liberal arrogance.

Another incident involved old-age pensions. The Conservatives argued that the government's surplus justified a substantial increase in the monthly pension payment. When the finance minister, Walter Harris, reluctantly agreed to a six dollar increase, his opponents began to portray "six-buck Harris," as they dubbed him, as unsympathetic to those in need.

Finally there was St. Laurent's own performance. By 1956 he seemed to have lost interest in politics. During the pipeline debate he was more often on the golf course than in the House of Commons. The result was that in 1957 the Conservatives, led by the western populist Diefenbaker, won a minority government. Though St. Laurent indicated that he would stay on as leader, he was persuaded to resign. He was succeeded by his former assistant at External Affairs, Lester Bowles Pearson.

Bibliography

Pickersgill, J. W. *Louis St. Laurent*. Don Mills, Ontario: Fitzhenry and Whiteside, 1981.

_____. *My Years with Louis St. Laurent: A Political Memoir*. Toronto: University of Toronto Press, 1975.

Thomson, Dale C. *Louis St. Laurent: Canadian*. Toronto: Macmillan, 1967.

Gerald J. Stortz

Gustav Stresemann

Born: May 10, 1878; Berlin, Germany
Died: October 3, 1929; Berlin, Germany

German politician and diplomat, winner of 1926 Nobel Peace Prize

Gustav Stresemann (GOOS-tahf SHTRAY-zeh-mahn) was the son of Ernst Stresemann, a Berlin brewer and beer distributor. Educated at the Andreas Realgymnasium and the University of Leipzig, Stresemann read voraciously in history and economics while earning a Ph.D. In 1902, at age twenty-four, Stresemann founded the Union of Saxon Industrialists and became its managing director. A year later he joined the National Liberal Party, and in 1907 he was elected to the Reichstag (legislature) for the first time. In 1903 he married the daughter of industrialist Adolf Kleefeld.

Gustav Stresemann *(National Archives)*

Nationalist

Stresemann combined a concern for social welfare with an abiding confidence in the superiority of the German Empire. An admirer of Otto von Bismarck and Alfred von Tirpitz, he strongly supported Germany's military expansion in the early twentieth century. After World War I began, he complained only that Germany was not prosecuting the war forcefully enough. He had expected a quick victory. In July, 1917, Stresemann led the National Liberal Party's attack on those politicians who argued for peace. He opposed the November 11, 1918, armistice and later said that Germany should refuse to sign the 1919 Versailles Treaty.

A republican government known as the Weimar Republic was created in Germany after Emperor William II (Kaiser Wilhelm) abdicated in November, 1918. Although he was elected to its constituent assembly in 1919, Stresemann did not favor this government. He saw a republican regime as inherently weak and believed that it would be unable to resist the overly harsh treatment he believed Germany had received from the Allies. When an attempt to overthrow the Weimar Republic (named for the city of its headquarters) was made in 1920, Stresemann was willing to accept the results of the illegal action. The attempt, called the Kapp putsch, failed, however, and gradually Stresemann began to adjust to republican politics. It is an irony of Stresemann's life that his reputation as a statesman rests on his determination to defend the republic and make it a success. He turned against extreme nationalists after the murders of Matthias Erzberger in 1921 and Walther Rathenau in 1922. Both Erzberger and Rathenau, who was foreign minister at the time of his assassination, had firmly embraced the republic.

Foreign Minister

For a brief time beginning in August, 1923, Stresemann served as chancellor of the Weimar government. His administration collapsed after fifteen weeks, but he was made minister of foreign affairs in the new ministry organized by Wilhelm Marx. While he occasionally served as chancellor during the next six years, Stresemann retained the foreign office until his death.

Stresemann's primary objectives as foreign minister included moderate revisions of the Versailles Treaty and reestablishing Germany's position in the European community. It was a difficult undertaking: Many in Europe were not prepared to forgive Germany for instigating World War I. Within Germany, Stresemann confronted the strident opposition of various nationalist organizations that continued to reject the republic and all moderation in foreign policy.

While serving as foreign minister, Stresemann achieved the reorganization of the war reparations that Germany was required to pay to the victorious Allies after World War I. He worked with American financier Charles Dawes to establish the Dawes Plan (1924), which reduced the amount of Germany's annual reparations payments. In 1929 he cooperated with American lawyer Owen D. Young on the Young Plan, a further revision of the payment schedules. Stresemann had hoped that these alterations would provide breathing room for Germany's economy. The Dawes Plan did assist Germany's remarkable recovery from 1924 to 1929, but the Great Depression of 1929 meant the end of economic progress.

Primary Achievements

Stresemann's outstanding achievements came in 1925 and 1926. In 1925 he participated in discussions with Austen Chamberlain, British foreign minister, and Aristide Briand, French foreign minister, in Locarno, Switzerland. The Locarno meeting resulted in the signing of the Locarno Treaty, which created an unusual optimism about the possibility of friendly relations among the European powers.

Stresemann's apparent willingness to cooperate with other European countries, as well as his moderate approach to the revision of the Versailles Treaty, led to the acceptance of the Weimar Republic into the League of Nations in 1926. Stresemann and Briand had strongly promoted this

Weimar Culture, 1919-1933

The creation of the Weimar Republic in 1919 brought forth a cultural energy in Germany that is often described as the "Weimar renaissance." Disillusionment resulting from Germany's defeat in World War I instigated a significant challenge to prewar cultural realism. Expressionism dominated the 1920's as German artists, writers, architects, and academicians became more introspective. The focus was on portraying the truth in the human soul rather than objective reality.

Politically, the Weimar cultural elite generally rejected the extreme nationalism of pre-World War I Germany and the bourgeois capitalism associated with it. Instead, cultural leaders embraced democracy, internationalism, and socialism. Their opposition to the notion of German superiority in Europe, and particularly their satirization of that notion, led to bitter opposition from German conservatives. In the last days of the Weimar Republic, just before and after Adolf Hitler assumed the chancellorship, many of the republic's cultural giants emigrated to the United States to continue their work.

The Locarno Treaty

The Locarno Treaty was an attempt to seek cooperation and harmony among Western European states after World War I. Negotiated at Locarno, Switzerland, and officially signed in London on December 1, 1925, the treaty created a sense of good will known as the "spirit of Locarno." The principal contributors were Gustav Stresemann, Aristide Briand, and Austen Chamberlain.

Locarno provided that Germany, Belgium, and France would never attack each other except in self-defense or to fulfill League of Nations obligations. England promised to defend Belgium and France if either were attacked. Strese-

mann affirmed that Germany accepted the boundaries established by the Versailles Treaty as inviolable. In return, it was agreed that Allied forces would leave the occupied Rhineland zone in 1930, five years ahead of schedule. Locarno appeared to confirm that the Weimar Republic renounced military action as a method for revising the Versailles Treaty. This situation paved the way for Germany's entrance into the League of Nations. The "spirit of Locarno," however, failed to survive the Great Depression, which began in 1929, and the advent of Adolf Hitler as German chancellor in 1933.

international recognition for the "new" Germany. For their efforts to advance the cause of peace, Stresemann and Briand were jointly awarded the 1926 Nobel Peace Prize. In 1928 Stresemann gave his endorsement to the Kellogg-Briand Pact outlawing war, and in 1929 he supported Briand's suggestion for a United States of Europe. Stresemann's unexpected death on October 3, 1929, was a major blow to the future stability of the Weimar Republic and to European international cooperation.

Stresemann's strength lay in his ability to adjust to the reality of Germany's World War I defeat. His reputation as one of the twentieth century's most successful statesmen rests on his willingness to suppress his inclination toward nationalism and work to revive European confidence through creating a reasonable German foreign policy.

Bibliography

Bretton, Henry L. *Stresemann and the Revision of Versailles: A Fight for Reason.* Stanford, Calif.: Stanford University Press, 1953.

Gatzke, Hans. *Stresemann and the Rearmament of Germany.* Baltimore: Johns Hopkins University Press, 1954.

Grathwol, Robert P. *Stresemann and the DMUP: Reconciliation or Revenge in German Foreign Policy, 1924-1928.* Lawrence: University of Kansas Press, 1980.

Turner, Henry. *Stresemann and the Politics of the Weimar Republic.* Princeton, N.J.: Princeton University Press, 1963.

Warren, Donald R. *The Red Kingdom of Saxony: Lobbying Grounds for Gustav Stresemann, 1901-1909.* The Hague: M. Nijhoff, 1964.

Ronald K. Huch

Alfredo Stroessner

Born: November 3, 1912; Encarnación, Paraguay

Dictatorial president of Paraguay (1954-1989)

As president of Paraguay from 1954-1989, General Alfredo Stroessner (ahl-FRAY-thoh STREHS-nur) presided over one of the longest military dictatorships in Latin American history. The son of a German immigrant to Paraguay, Stroessner grew up in the southern part of the country.

Military Career

In 1929 Stroessner entered the Military Academy in Asunción. He distinguished himself for bravery during the Chaco War, a conflict between Paraguay and Bolivia that lasted from 1932 to 1935. By the end of the war, Stroessner had risen to first lieutenant. By 1940 he was a major, and that year he was sent for special military training in Brazil. He then came to command Paraguay's main artillery unit and was afterward assigned to the staff headquarters of the army.

Civil war broke out in Paraguay in 1947. Stroessner remained loyal to the government, crucially defending the capital, Asunción. Paraguay had two major political parties, and it was the Colorado Party that was victorious at the end of the war. However, rivalries for office split the party into factions. Although for a brief period Stroessner had to go into exile because he backed a losing faction, he later used his artillery unit to support victorious coups, thereby receiving appointment as commander of the army in 1951.

President of Paraguay

Three years later Stroessner seized the presidency for himself, occupying the position for a quarter of a century. He held power based on the dominance of the military and the Colorado Party. As a military hero, he had the loyalty of many troops. He built upon that base by purging disloyal officers in 1955 and again in 1959. He strengthened his hold over the party by allowing its many bickering factions to fight among themselves and progressively to eliminate each other so that he remained the sole, dominant power. The dominance of the Colorado Party gave him a massive organization for control of civilian and political life.

The Stroessner regime was conservative. It did not seek to destroy the existing political or socio-economic power structure. Rather, it sought to reinforce it under the control of one man. The fervid anticommunism of the regime at a time when Marxists such as Cheddi Jagan in British Guiana and Fidel Castro in Cuba were emerg-

Alfredo Stroessner *(National Archives)*

Paraguay's Colorado Party

The Colorado Party is strongly incorporated into the national life of Paraguay. Founded in the middle of the nineteenth century, its purpose was to control presidential succession, political appointments, and the distribution of spoils. The hold of the Colorado Party on Paraguay was broken by its rival, the Liberal Party, during the first half of the twentieth century. However, following the return of the Colorado Party to power in 1947, it became even more dominant. This dominance was furthered by the organization and vigilance with which Alfredo Stroessner molded it so that it would serve as a vehicle for his regime. The party was organized in every part and at every level of Paraguayan society. It served as an efficient machine for distributing patronage and maintaining a hierarchy of clients and patrons. Although the party was no longer commanded by Stroessner, it continued to win elections with impressive majorities.

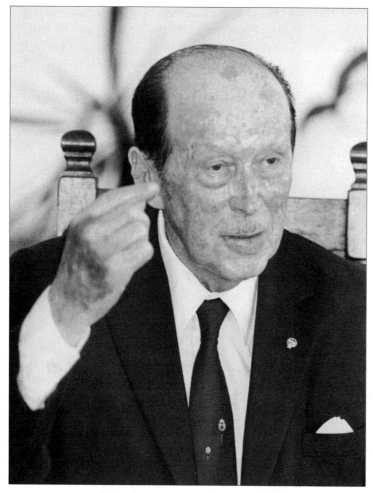

Alfredo Stroessner (*National Archives*)

ing in the region earned Stroessner the support of the United States. Stroessner tolerated widespread illegal activities by military and political leaders, opposed land reform, and encouraged foreign investment. Until the early 1980's his regime was generally accepted by Paraguayans. The high point of his rule occurred in 1982 with the inauguration of the Itaipú Dam. Built in conjunction with Brazil on a river boundary between the two countries, the mammoth dam was able to supply electricity and the means for modernization to all of Paraguay.

However, several economic problems developed, and they exacerbated political and military tensions. Inflation began to increase, and capital for investment declined, resulting in reduced economic activity and unemployment. The repressive character of the Stroessner regime became more apparent as more critics appeared and were tortured, jailed, and killed. Increasing segments of the Colorado Party wanted to free themselves from the hold of

Stroessner. Moreover, seeing the challenges to his regime, the army produced its own challengers to his government, resolved to maintain the authority of military with or without Stroessner. In February of 1989 the commander of the army ousted Stroessner, who then went into exile in Brazil.

Bibliography

Hanratty, Dennis M., and Sandra W. Meditz, eds. *Paraguay: A Country Study*. 2d ed. Washington, D.C.: U.S. Government Printing Office, 1990.

Lewis, Paul. *Paraguay Under Stroessner*. Chapel Hill: University of North Carolina Press, 1980.

Miranda, Carlos. *The Stroessner Era*. Boulder, Colo.: Westview Press, 1990.

Edward A. Riedinger

Suharto

Born: June 8, 1921; Kemusu, Argamulja, Java, Dutch East Indies (now Indonesia)

President of Indonesia (1968-1998)

Suharto (sew HAHR-toh), or Soeharto, in the Dutch-influenced spelling, was born the son of poor Javanese parents, his father being a minor official in the sultanate of Jogjakarta. He was educated in a Dutch-language high school and through military training. In 1947 he married Siti Hartinah; they had four daughters and two sons.

Military Career

From childhood Suharto was interested in a military career, and he was one of a small group of Indonesians who received military training

Suharto *(Library of Congress)*

from the Dutch colonial army (1940-1943); he achieved the rank of sergeant. When the Japanese invaded during World War II, he joined the Japanese-trained Indonesian army and advanced to company commander (1943-1945). After Indonesian independence was proclaimed in 1945, Suharto distinguished himself in the struggle against the Dutch in Central Java (1945-1949), especially in Jogjakarta in 1948. Suharto helped suppress an insurrection in the South Moluccas in 1950, rose rapidly through the ranks to colonel, and was made a division commander in the late 1950's. He was promoted to brigadier general in 1960. He directed efforts to expel the Dutch from western New Guinea in 1961, for which he was promoted to major general in 1962.

Defeat of President Sukarno

On September 30, 1965, a group of communist Chinese-inspired military conspirators kidnapped and murdered six top army generals and proclaimed a new revolutionary government. General Suharto, then commander of the army strategic reserve in Jakarta, displayed great composure and tactical ability as he discovered the identities of the conspirators and crushed the coup.

Subtle complicity between the popular and charismatic President Sukarno and the coup conspirators was discovered. Student demonstrations against President Sukarno were encouraged by the military, which was predominantly anticommunist. During a year of chaotic struggle for power between General Suharto and President Sukarno, 300,000 or more communists and innocent bystanders were killed by the military and rioting mobs. On March 11, 1966, President Sukarno was forced to grant broad powers to General Suharto. Suharto was named acting president in March, 1967, then president in March, 1968. He was reelected president in 1973, 1978, 1983, 1988, 1992, and 1997.

The New Order

As president, Suharto immediately set about rebuilding Indonesia, based on the twin pillars of political stability and economic development. Indonesia renewed its membership in the United Nations, from which Sukarno had withdrawn in 1965, and sought improved relations with the United States. The Marxist Parti Komunis Indonesia (PKI) was banned, and a new cabinet was formed to focus efforts on national development. There was relatively free expression of (non-communist) ideas, and ten political parties flourished until they were reorganized into three officially recognized parties in 1972-1973.

Suharto at the celebration of Indonesia's fiftieth anniversary in 1995. *(Reuters/E. Nuraheni/Archive Photos)*

By 1971, Suharto's efforts had reduced inflation to less than 10 percent per year—down from 650 percent per year in 1965. In the 1970's and 1980's, Suharto's policies attracted substantial foreign investment to Indonesia, and revenues from its substantial oil reserves were invested largely in essential public infrastructure such as schools, hospitals, highways, and factories. Be-

---

Resisting the Dutch

Although he received his earliest military training in the Dutch colonial army, Suharto's role was significant in retaining independence from the Dutch after it was proclaimed in August, 1945. The Dutch insisted that they retained sovereignty over all of Indonesia and attempted to retake it by force of arms. They instituted a reign of terror, breaking into Indonesian homes, burning them down, and shooting civilians. By December, 1945, they had killed more than eight thousand persons in Jakarta.

Suharto served ably in Tentara Negara Indonesia, the Indonesian army that fought against attempts by the Dutch to regain control of the islands after the Japanese departed at the end of World War II. He was a distinguished battalion commander in the struggle against the Dutch in Central Java (1945-1949). Suharto led the attack against the Dutch army that was occupying Jogjakarta in 1948, temporarily recapturing the provisional capital from forces having superior numbers and armament. Suharto later directed efforts to expel the Dutch from western New Guinea in 1961, extending Indonesian control over that territory in 1963.

The 1975 Invasion of East Timor

The area covered by Indonesia is as tall (north to south) and wider (east to west) than the United States. Indonesia includes some 13,500 Pacific islands. In 1974, the only portion of this archipelago not under Indonesian control was part of the island of Timor. When the former Portuguese colony in East Timor collapsed, civil war erupted between factions there. Some sought independence, and others wished to be part of Indonesia.

At that time, communist victories in Southeast Asia were creating fears of instability, and Suharto was fighting against a Marxist insurgency in North Sumatra. Suharto sent troops into East Timor and annexed it in 1975, ostensibly in response to requests for support from the pro-Indonesia faction. Recognition of Indonesian sovereignty over East Timor was withheld by Portugal, the United Nations, and most major governments. A small group of Fretilin guerrillas continued to agitate for independence.

In November, 1991, Indonesian troops believed that they were fired upon by East Timorese mourners attending a funeral in the city of Dili. The troops shot and killed about 170 unarmed persons. Subsequently, two top generals were fired and ten soldiers were sentenced to a year in prison for human rights violations.

tween 1966 and the late 1990's, the Indonesian economy expanded by more than 450 percent, despite brief contractions in the early 1980's and late 1990's.

Embattled Indonesian president Suharto announcing his resignation in May, 1998. *(Reuters/Enny Nuraheni/Archive Photos)*

Suharto received international awards recognizing Indonesia's success in food production and family planning. Indonesia achieved self-sufficiency in rice production in 1985. Both the mortality rate and the birthrate declined precipitously as health care improved. Indonesia's progress in alleviating poverty was praised by the World Bank in 1990; both the percentage of the population and the number of persons living in poverty were halved in 1990 compared to 1976. At the close of the twentieth century, illiteracy had almost disappeared among persons under twenty years of age, even in poorer rural areas. As part of his nation-building efforts—and because of the fear of a Marxist takeover in the former Portuguese colony of East Timor—Suharto completed the extension of Indonesian control over territory in the central archipelago by annexing East Timor in 1975.

Family Business

As the economy of Indonesia grew, so did the wealth and business interests of Suharto's family, which was given preferential treatment by the government. In 1998, each of Suharto's six children controlled assets in excess of $100 million (one controlled assets of more than $2 billion), including a government-legislated monopoly on the buying and selling of cloves, the only road from Jakarta to its international airport (a toll road), a "national car" manufacturer subsidized by the government, and a failed national bank that had been bailed out by the government. The business connections of the Suharto family increased in visibility after the death of Suharto's wife in 1996.

When the Indonesian economy abruptly crashed in late 1997, public sentiment turned strongly against the wealthy, and the Suharto family was at the top of the list. Suharto's Golkar Party had won substantial majorities in parliamentary elections held the previous May, but his formal reelection to the presidency in March of 1998 was marred by criticism of Indonesia's economic performance, his advancing age (he was seventy-seven), and his family's extreme wealth. During violent demonstrations in May, 1998, rioters destroyed some business offices of the Suharto family, while students seized the Parliament building, demonstrated against nepotism and government corruption, and called for Suharto to resign.

After four students were shot to death by snipers during demonstrations at Trisakti University, Suharto hastily returned from a conference in Egypt to try to quell the disturbances. He found that his support had evaporated, but he insisted on a constitutional transition of power to his vice president, B. J. Habibie. Suharto resigned the presidency on May 20, 1998, after serving thirty-two years, the longest tenure of any Asian leader in modern history.

Bibliography

Dahm, Bernhard. *History of Indonesia in the Twentieth Century*. New York: Praeger, 1971.

Hill, Hal, ed. *Indonesia's New Order: The Dynamics of Socio-economic Transition*. Honolulu: University of Hawaii Press, 1994.

Neill, Wilfred T. *Twentieth Century Indonesia*. New York: Columbia University Press, 1973.

Michael S. Hamilton

Sukarno

Born: June 6, 1901; Surabaya, Dutch East Indies (now Indonesia)
Died: June 21, 1970; Jakarta, Indonesia

First president of independent Indonesia (1949-1967)

Sukarno (sew KAHR-noh), or Soekarno, in the Dutch-influenced spelling, was the son of a Muslim Javanese schoolteacher and a Hindu Balinese temple dancer. He was a sickly child named Kusno at birth. When he was thirteen his father hoped that his prospects would improve with a luckier name and changed it to Sukarno ("best hero"), derived from Karna, a hero in the Hindu epic *Mahabharata*. After graduating from a Dutch-language high school in Surabaya and from engineering school at Bandung Institute of Technology in 1926, he opened an engineering firm in Bandung and founded the Partai Nasionalis Indonesia (PNI, the Indonesian National Party), urging immediate independence from the Dutch.

Sukarno *(National Archives)*

Nationalist Revolutionary

Sukarno was fiercely nationalistic, creative, and eclectic in his political views. Born in what was then the Dutch East Indies, Sukarno chafed under the heel of Dutch colonial occupation. While still in high school, he began writing inflammatory articles advocating the overthrow of the Dutch government.

Jailed in 1929 when the PNI was banned, Sukarno was released in 1932 and became chairman of the new Partai Indonesia (Indonesia Party). He was arrested again in 1933 and detained until 1942, when he was released by Japanese invaders during World War II. The Japanese liberated Indonesia from the Dutch, and sought out Sukarno to assist in administering affairs for them. They promised eventual independence.

The Five Principles (Panjat Sila)

On June 1, 1945, with the Japanese watching him closely, Sukarno made a famous speech proposing the Panjat Sila (five principles) of a political philosophy upon which an independent Indonesian state would be founded. The Panjat Sila were national unity, respect for a just and civilized global humanity, popular sovereignty based on consensus and mutual assistance, social justice based on political and cultural equality of all persons, and faith in one God in a context of religious tolerance. Sukarno claimed that these principles were a combination of nationalism, Marxism, and Islam. Eventually the Panjat Sila became accepted as Indonesian state ideology.

Indonesian Independence

After the bombing of Hiroshima by the United States in August, 1945, Sukarno was told by the Japanese that he was free to form an Indonesian government. Then, two days later, he was told that independence was out of the question because Japan had surrendered Indonesia without a change of government. That day, August 17, 1945, Sukarno wrote and proclaimed a brief declaration of Indonesian independence in Jakarta. August 17 continues to be celebrated each year as Indonesian Independence Day.

First President of Indonesia

Sukarno assumed the role of president and called for the people to claim their independence rather than return to colonial domination. They seized weapons abandoned by the Japanese and from 1945 to 1949 resisted efforts by the Dutch to regain control. On December 27, 1949, sovereignty was transferred from the Dutch to the Republic of Indonesia through offices of the United Nations.

Indonesian president Sukarno (left) with Ghana's president Kwame Nkrumah at New York's Waldorf Hotel in 1960. *(Archive Photos)*

Sukarno proved to be a more effective revolutionary than head of government. He produced no coherent programs for national development, and the economy faltered while he pur-

The Afro-Asian Bandung Conference of 1955

Sukarno sought a foreign policy of neutrality toward both the United States and the Soviet Union, seeking to avoid involvement in the Cold War between them. Sukarno organized a conference of Afro-Asian states in Bandung, Indonesia, in 1955, to discuss alternatives to alignment with either country. This meeting was one of several attempts to form a nonaligned movement.

The leaders of about thirty independent states met to discuss the possibility of closer cooperation in order to form a third pole of world power separate from the United States and the Soviet Union. Of note were attendance by India's Jawaharlal Nehru and communist China's Zhou Enlai. Also notable was the inability of participants to agree on much. At Sukarno's urging, they did agree to condemn "colonialism in all its manifestations," and they vowed to settle disputes between themselves by negotiation rather than by force. However, the Philippine, Pakistani, and Turkish leaders interpreted "colonialism in all its manifestations" to include actions by China, and the second statement was nullified by armed border conflicts between China and India in 1959.

Indonesia's Withdrawal from the United Nations

In May, 1961, the prime minister of Malaya announced a plan to create a Federation of Malaysia, composed of Singapore, Malaya, Brunei, and the British colonies of Sabah and Sarawak on northern Borneo. Fearing an attempt by the British to isolate Indonesia from its friends in China, Sukarno opposed the plan and secretly supported an uprising in Brunei during 1962.

In the summer of 1963, Sukarno agreed to accept creation of Malaysia if a U.N. referendum demonstrated popular support in Sabah and Sarawak. The referendum was not completed in September, 1963, when Britain announced formation of Malaysia. In summer of 1964, Sukarno sent armed volunteers into northern Borneo, but they were quickly defeated by the Malayan army. This confrontation was condemned by the United Nations, which admitted Malaysia to membership in November, 1964. China urged Sukarno to withdraw in protest over the Malaysia issue. Indonesia withdrew from the United Nations on January 20, 1965, returning in 1966 after Suharto assumed power.

---

sued an extravagant personal lifestyle. The nation did make significant gains in education, health, cultural self-awareness, and formation of a national identity—from hundreds of island cultures with different languages—but at tremendous cost.

In the 1950's, Sukarno dismantled the parliamentary democracy created by the 1945 constitution, establishing an appointed council to direct "guided democracy"—an approach that undermined capitalism in favor of socialist policies. He secured substantial amounts of foreign aid from the United States and the Soviet Union in the early 1960's but made poor spending decisions. In international relations, Sukarno encouraged resistance to policies of other nations that appeared to have imperialistic intentions as he sought greater prestige for Indonesia in world affairs. Several assassination attempts were made on Sukarno, the first in 1957 by a fundamentalist group that sought creation of an Islamic state in West Java. Insurrections erupted in Sumatra and Sulawesi in 1958. Sukarno liberated the western half of New Guinea from the Dutch between 1961 and 1963.

Sukarno organized a conference of Afro-Asian states in 1955 to discuss alternatives to alignment with either the United States or the Soviet Union. In 1963 he opposed formation of the Federation of Malaysia. After the United States and the Soviet Union failed to support Sukarno, he turned increasingly toward communist China. This conflict led to withdrawal of Indonesia from the United Nations in 1965.

A Marxist Parti Komunis Indonesia (PKI), with links to the Soviet Union, had formed in 1920. It staged an unsuccessful coup attempt against Sukarno in 1948. However, as Sukarno's support in the PNI wavered, the PKI increasingly supported his policies. Sukarno courted its support beginning about 1959 and rewarded PKI leaders with positions of ministerial rank in 1962.

Sukarno's Downfall

On September 30, 1965, a group of communist and military conspirators kidnapped and murdered six top army generals and proclaimed a new revolutionary government. The coup attempt was crushed by General Suharto, commander of the army's strategic reserve in Jakarta. Complicity between Sukarno and the conspirators was later discovered. Suharto and Sukarno engaged in a chaotic power struggle in 1965 and

1966 in which an estimated 300,000 people were killed by the military and by rioting mobs. Suharto finally forced Sukarno to give him broad powers in March, 1966. Suharto was named acting president in March, 1967, and president in March, 1968. Sukarno retained the hollow title of "lifetime president" in deference to his role in founding the country.

Sukarno's greatest contribution was his leadership of the Indonesian nationalist movement between 1945 and 1949, when he galvanized resistance against a return to colonial domination. He married seven times and had seven children, including a daughter, Megawati Sukarnoputri, a leader of the "pro-democracy movement" of the late 1990's. Sukarno died at the age of sixty-nine from a chronic kidney ailment.

Bibliography

Bharadwaj, Ram Dev. *Sukarno and Indonesian Nationalism*. Delhi, India: Rahul, 1997.

Dahm, Bernhard. *History of Indonesia in the Twentieth Century*. New York: Praeger Publishers, 1971.

Neill, Wilfred T. *Twentieth Century Indonesia*. New York: Columbia University Press, 1973.

Penders, C. L. M. *The Life and Times of Sukarno*. Teaneck, N.J.: Fairleigh Dickinson University Press, 1974.

Michael S. Hamilton

Sun Yat-sen

Born: November 12, 1866; Cuiheng Village, Xiangshan County, Guangdong Province, China
Died: March 12, 1925; Beijing, China

Chinese revolutionary and political figure, leader of Chinese Nationalist Party (the Kuomintang, founded 1912)

Sun Yat-sen (SOON YAHT-SEHN), whose original name was Sun Wen (SOON WUHN), attended village schools until age thirteen, then was taken to Hawaii. (The name Sun Yat-sen may also be rendered into English as Sun Yixian and as Sun I-hsien.) In Hawaii he studied at missionary schools and became fluent in English. At age twenty-one he moved to Hong Kong and studied medicine, graduating in 1892. In 1894 he prepared a memorandum sketching proposed reforms for China's imperial government, but he was rebuffed in his efforts to present it to a leading official. From that point he became devoted to the overthrow of the Chinese monarchy.

Revolutionary Agitator

Later in 1894, Sun returned to Honolulu and organized many Chinese residents into the Society to Revive China, devoted to creating a republican form of government. In October, 1895, he organized an armed uprising in Canton, but it failed. Fleeing prosecution as a traitor, Sun spent the period 1895-1911 outside China. He traveled widely and made many contacts with Chinese people overseas, raising money and enlisting supporters for a possible revolution. In 1896 Sun went to England, where he made the mistake of entering the Chinese embassy in London. Chinese officials seized him and indicated that he would be sent back to China to be executed. However, the newspapers raised such a furor that Sun was released. The experience convinced him that his revolutionary mission was divinely favored.

Sun spent another year in England, much of it studying Western writers on social and political topics. Then he moved to Japan, where large numbers of young Chinese had come to study. In 1900 he helped organize another revolutionary uprising in Waichow, but it also failed. In August, 1905, Sun founded the United League (T'ung-meng-hui), merging his earlier society with other revolutionary groups and enlisting many student supporters. In his speeches and prolific writings, Sun elaborated his Three People's Principles (San Min Chu I). The Chinese army and other government departments became increasingly infiltrated with young men who wished to see a government more favorable to modern-

Sun Yat-sen *(Library of Congress)*

Sun Yat-sen (seated, center) spearheaded the movement to overthrow the Qing government. *(Library of Congress)*

ization and liberalization. After more failed uprisings, rebels teamed with army units in October, 1911, in Wuchang, to initiate a revolution which ultimately forced the imperial regency to abdicate.

Sun in Government

Sun Yat-sen was traveling in the United States when the revolution broke out, but he quickly returned to China. On December 29, 1911, he was formally elected provisional president of the new

---

The Three People's Principles

Sun Yat-sen's most important intellectual creation originated in his efforts to form revolutionary groups among overseas Chinese. He had articulated the essential elements as early as 1905, but the conclusive version of the Three People's Principles did not emerge until his 1924 lectures, which were transcribed and published. The first principle was nationalism. Sun was distressed at the weakness of the Chinese nation and the ease with which it was abused and dominated by foreign powers. Before 1911, this principle also involved denunciation of the Ching (Manchu) dynasty, viewed as alien invaders.

The second principle was democracy. Sun aspired to see China become a republic with a government loosely modeled on that of the United States. He favored participatory democracy but gave less stress to personal liberty and more stress to a powerful and effective national government. The third principle was the people's livelihood. Sun favored a mixed economy, hoping to blend the dynamic qualities of private capitalism with social justice involving the regulation of private capital and equalization of land rights.

The Kuomintang

Sun Yat-sen's most enduring creation was the Kuomintang (KMT), the Nationalist Party. The party was formed in August, 1912, with a commitment to help create a democratic constitution. It competed effectively for votes but fell into disarray in the following years. In 1920, Sun reorganized the KMT, incorporating a commitment to the Three People's Principles, formalizing his own position as party head, and committing the party to the temporary "tutelage" of the public pending their readiness for full political participation. The reorganization, therefore, included hints of one-man control of the party and one-party control of the government.

In 1922, Sun agreed that members of the Chinese Communist Party (CCP), formed in 1921, could join the KMT. He formed a connection with the Soviet government, which furnished him with money and military assistance. The Whampoa Military Academy was established to train officers for a KMT military force, under the direction of Chiang Kai-shek. After Sun's death in 1925, Chiang established himself as leader of the KMT and led successful military campaigns to gain control of the Chinese government. Chiang failed to defeat the Communists, however. Weakened by the war against Japan (1937-1945), Chiang and the KMT were driven out by the Communists in 1949. Chiang moved the Nationalist Party to the island of Formosa (Taiwan), where the KMT became an instrument for impressive economic development.

republic by a council of national leaders meeting in Nanjing. However, the real power in China remained with the military and its leader, Yuan Shikai. A national assembly meeting in Beijing elected Yuan as premier. Hoping to enlist Yuan's power to support democratic principles, Sun agreed to turn the presidency over to Yuan if the latter would support a republican form of government. In February, 1912, Sun's brief term as president ended.

Yuan appointed Sun to be director-general of the railway system. Sun traveled all over the country and drew up a grandiose but not very realistic plan for a vast increase in railway mileage. In 1912 he transformed the United League into a political party called the Kuomintang (KMT) to present candidates for elections under the working leadership of Song Jiaoren. The KMT did very well in the elections, but Yuan was moving toward creation of a military dictatorship. Song was assassinated, and the KMT parliamentary representatives were dispersed by force. Sun fled to Japan in August, 1913. He was able to return when Yuan died unexpectedly in June, 1916. Military force was still the deciding factor in Chinese politics, and the country became divided among regional warlords. In October, 1915, Sun married Song Qingling, whose father was one of Sun's closest friends and largest financial supporters. The Song family evolved into one of the most powerful in China before 1949.

Political Struggles

During 1917-1918, Sun struggled unsuccessfully to try to form a constitutional government for the Guangdong region in south China. In November, 1917, he appointed Chiang Kai-shek as his personal military adviser. From June, 1918, to November, 1920, he lived in Shanghai. There he wrote *The International Development of China* (1920), urging the Western Allies who had just been victorious in World War I to invest heavily in a socialist plan for China's economic development. The Allies were not interested, so Sun turned for help to the new communist government of the Soviet Union.

During 1920-1923, Sun intermittently held power in Guangdong and devoted his attention to building the KMT, aided by Chiang Kai-shek. In November, 1924, Sun traveled to Beijing to try to persuade northern warlords to join him in unifying the country. He fell ill, however, and died from cancer in March, 1925. His protégé, Chiang Kai-shek, traded heavily on his closeness to Sun and became the effective head of the Chinese national government between 1928 and 1949.

Assessment

Sun Yat-sen was an energetic and personable man who inspired many devoted followers. Most scholarly evaluations, however, paint him as glib but naïve. He had no talent for administration. Though he was never a communist, his ideas helped to turn the KMT into an instrument of one-party rule and to support centralized bureaucratic control of the economy.

Bibliography

Chang, Sidney H., and Leonard H. D. Gordon. *All Under Heaven: Sun Yat-sen and His Revolutionary Thought*. Stanford, Calif.: Hoover Institution, 1991.

Seagrave, Sterling. *The Soong Dynasty*. New York: Harper and Row, 1985.

Sharman, Lyon. *Sun Yat-sen: His Life and Its Meaning*. Hamden, Conn.: Archon Books, 1965.

Wilbur, C. Martin. *Sun Yat-sen, Frustrated Patriot*. New York: Columbia University Press, 1976.

Paul B. Trescott

Robert A. Taft

Born: September 8, 1889; Cincinnati, Ohio
Died: July 31, 1953; New York, New York

U.S. senator (1939-1953) and three-time presidential candidate

Robert Alphonso Taft (RO-burt al-FON-zoh TAFT) was a U.S. senator, a leader of the Republican Party, and an unsuccessful contender for the presidential nomination in 1940, 1948, and 1952. He was the son of former U.S. president William Howard Taft. After graduating from Yale University and Harvard Law School, Taft practiced law in Cincinnati. In 1914, he married Martha Wheaton Bowers. They had four sons. He was a member of the Ohio House of Representatives from 1921 to 1926 and the Ohio Senate in 1931 and 1932. During World War I, he served as assistant consul for the U.S. Food Administration. He then helped manage American relief efforts in Europe.

Robert A. Taft *(Library of Congress)*

His experiences in war-torn Europe and his upbringing in a prominent and wealthy midwestern family helped shape his conservatism and nationalism. He was opposed to government interference in the economy and to diplomatic alliances and foreign entanglements. Taft fought for a reduction in the power of the presidency. He opposed concentrated power, economic folly, and the weakening of the constitutional power of the Senate.

U.S. Senator

When Taft arrived in the U.S. Senate in 1939, President Franklin D. Roosevelt and his New Deal dominated the nation's economic, political, and social agenda. Democrats outnumbered Republicans by a wide margin in Congress. Soon after he became a senator, Taft became a member of the committees on appropriations, banking and currency, and education and labor. Taft, a critic of Roosevelt's New Deal, quickly took advantage of the political opportunity created by the emergence of the conservative coalition—an alliance of opposition Republicans and Southern Democrats disenchanted with the New Deal.

Almost by default, he became the leader of Republican opposition to Roosevelt. His reputation was that of a sober-sided, hard-working, and brilliant legislative strategist. By the time the Republicans won control of the Senate in the 1946 elections, he was the Republican Party's majority leader. His success stemmed from his legislative know-how. Taft spearheaded the 1947 passage of the Taft-Hartley Act, which Republicans designed to restore equity in collective bargaining between labor and management. When President Harry S Truman vetoed the proposed legislation, Taft guided the successful effort to override the veto. Taft's major influence was on domestic policy. From 1946 to 1952, he was head of the powerful Republican Policy Committee, and he became majority leader in 1953.

"Mr. Republican"

The Taft influence was apparent in many of President Dwight D. Eisenhower's decisions in the 1950's, especially those relating to military strategy, defense spending, and the need for a balanced budget. Taft helped push President Eisenhower's programs through Congress. He strengthened the conservative tradition in American politics and revived the Republican Party. In addition, Taft helped Congress regain some measure of influence over diplomatic and military affairs. He was a nationalist. As he was probably the most powerful legislator and opposition party leader of his day in Congress, Taft earned his nickname, "Mr. Republican." In 1955, he was

U.S. senator Robert A. Taft, second from left, with other government figures responsible for war production and economic planning during World War II, in 1943. *(Library of Congress)*

included in the Senate's circle of its greatest members—Henry Clay, Daniel Webster, John C. Calhoun, and Robert M. LaFollette.

Bibliography

Baker, Richard A., and Roger H. Davidson, ed. *First Among Equals: Outstanding Senate Leaders*

The Taft-Hartley Labor Relations Act

U.S. senator Robert A. Taft of Ohio and Representative Fred Hartley, Jr., of New Jersey, both Republicans, shepherded the Taft-Hartley Act through Congress and then successfully overrode President Harry S Truman's veto of the measure. Truman branded Taft an enemy of labor and the act a "slave labor law." The act regulates labor and management behavior in disputes. Taft and Hartley believed that unions had become too powerful and should be restrained. The act curtailed the Wagner Labor Act of 1935, which organized labor. It allowed a president to block strikes that imperiled national welfare by obtaining a federal court injunction for an eighty-day "cooling-off" period. The Taft-Hartley Act was the only major change in New Deal legislation to pass Congress in the 1940's. It is the only one to bear Taft's name and was one of his major accomplishments.

of the Twentieth Century. Washington, D.C.: Congressional Quarterly, 1991.

Hernon, Joseph Martin. *Profiles in Character: Hubris and Heroism in the U.S. Senate*. Armonk, N.Y.: M. E. Sharpe, 1997.

Lee, R. Alton. *Truman and Taft-Hartley: A Question of Mandate*. Westport, Conn.: Greenwood Press, 1966.

Patterson, James T. *Mr. Republican: A Biography of Robert A. Taft*. Boston: Houghton Mifflin, 1972.

Robbins, Phyllis. *Robert A. Taft: Boy and Man*. Cambridge, Mass.: Dresser, Chapman & Grimes, 1963.

Fred Buchstein

William Howard Taft

Born: September 15, 1857; Cincinnati, Ohio
Died: March 8, 1930; Washington, D.C.

President of the United States (1909-1913)

William Howard Taft (WIHL-yuhm HOW-urd TAFT) was the son of Alphonso Taft, a member of President Ulysses S. Grant's cabinet. William graduated second in his class from Yale College and earned a law degree from Cincinnati Law School. The young Taft worked as a lawyer, a prosecuting attorney, a judge, a tax collector, and a law school professor and dean. Under President Benjamin Harrison, he served as the solicitor general of the United States. He married Helen Herron in 1886. One of their three children was Robert A. Taft, who became an important Republican senator from Ohio.

Foreign Achievements

In 1900 Taft headed a commission to establish a civil government for the Philippine Islands, newly acquired by the United States. Later, as governor of the Philippines, he tackled problems of civil unrest, education, health, roads, railroads, and economic development. He worked to lower U.S. tariffs on Philippine goods. He also extended most of the protections of the Bill of Rights to the Philippine people and encouraged their progress toward a popular assembly. Taft won a political struggle with U.S. Army general Arthur MacArthur (father of General Douglas MacArthur) and settled a land dispute with the Roman Catholic Church. His governorship was a success.

Taft reluctantly returned to Washington in 1904 to become President Theodore Roosevelt's secretary of war. A major project of the time was construction of the Panama Canal, and Taft figured in the decision to fit the canal with locks so that it could be built more quickly and cheaply. Roosevelt dispatched him to many foreign capitals as a mediator. He worked to end the Russo-Japanese War (1904-1905) and to lessen tensions between Japan and the United States. In Cuba he brought an end to a rebellion by taking control briefly as provisional governor.

A Troubled Presidency

In 1908, with Roosevelt's backing, Taft was nominated for president by the Republican Party. He defeated Democrat William Jennings Bryan to become, in 1909, the twenty-seventh president of the United States. His administration can be credited with many lasting accomplishments. Taft favored passing constitutional amendments to allow income taxes and the direct election of

William Howard Taft *(Library of Congress)*

Former president William Howard Taft (seated, center) serving on the U.S. Supreme Court. *(Library of Congress)*

The Presidential Election of 1912

The events leading up to the presidential election of 1912 were among the most sensational in American history. In 1908 President Theodore Roosevelt helped his adviser and friend William Howard Taft win the Republican nomination for president and then helped him win the election. He hoped that Taft would further his progressive reforms.

Taft, however, proved weak and somewhat conservative. The restless Roosevelt sided with the liberal progressives against Taft. When many people, including the progressives, rallied behind him, Roosevelt became a candidate to replace Taft as the Republican nominee for president in 1912. Taft warned that Roosevelt intended to become a dictator. Roosevelt

charged that Taft had sold out to big money. In states with primary elections, Roosevelt won national delegates, but in states where the old convention system prevailed, Taft won. After party regulars gave Taft a number of disputed delegates, he won the nomination on the first ballot. Roosevelt left the Republican Party and formed the Progressive (or Bull Moose) Party to nominate him.

Meanwhile, the Democratic Party nominated Woodrow Wilson, the reform-minded governor of New Jersey and former president of Princeton University. Taft knew that he would lose the three-sided race, but he fought on to make sure that Roosevelt was defeated. He was happy when Wilson won.

senators. He presided over changes in the postal system and the creation of pure food laws, and he began steps that led to creating a national budget. His administration initiated a number of lawsuits designed to break up large industrial monopolies such as the U.S. Steel Corporation. His wife also left a highly visible legacy: She had Washington, D.C.'s now-famous cherry trees planted.

Yet Taft's presidency was a troubled one. Unlike the vigorous Roosevelt, he could not hold together his party's factions. The "progressives" of the western states resented the profits reaped by eastern industrial interests. In Congress, conservative easterners wanted high tariffs, while the westerners wanted to lower the cost of living by lowering tariffs. Taft had promised some lower tariffs, but he was not a strong leader. The Payne-Aldrich bill, the tariff bill that Congress eventually passed, was perceived not to lower tariffs but actually to raise them. Taft was blamed, and progressives in Congress became his enemies. When he got Congress to approve reciprocal tariffs with Canada, the Canadians rejected the idea.

Taft's conservation policies also brought him grief. President Roosevelt wanted Taft to reappoint his aggressive secretary of the interior, James R. Garfield. Taft appointed Richard Ballinger instead. Ballinger was then accused by the crusading conservationist Gifford Pinchot of im-

William Howard Taft had a difficult term as U.S. president. A genial man but not a strong leader, he could not unite the different factions of his party. *(Archive Photos/ Museum of the City of New York)*

The Judiciary Act of 1925

Long before he became chief justice of the United States in 1921, William Howard Taft knew the court system needed reform. Because lawyers could bring any case before the Supreme Court, the Court spent too much time deciding inconsequential matters. By 1921 new cases so clogged the Supreme Court's docket that many could not be heard for over a year. Taft favored allowing the Court to decline hearing certain appeals, and he organized support from lawyers nationwide. The Judiciary Act of 1925 (also known as the Judge's Bill) gave Supreme Court judges the power to refuse to hear some cases appealed to them. The only automatic appeals would be from state supreme courts about the constitutionality of a state statute. Since 1925 the Court has thereby been able to act more quickly on the cases it does agree to hear.

properly turning over Alaskan coal land for exploitation. Although a congressional committee cleared Ballinger, he resigned because of the resulting furor in the press. Taft fired Pinchot from his job as head of the Forest Service, further enraging progressives.

Taft was a large, even fat, man, and many disaffected citizens made cruel jokes about his size. To make matters worse, Taft's energetic wife suffered a stroke. The Senate changed the arbitration treaties that he had negotiated with Britain and France so drastically that he declined to sign them. Even so, Taft wanted to run for a second term. He was nominated by the Republican Party in 1912, but he was defeated by Democrat Woodrow Wilson in a three-way race.

The Chief Justice

After his defeat, Taft taught law at Yale and was elected president of the American Bar Association. In vain, he urged the United States to join the League of Nations. In 1921 President Warren G. Harding appointed him chief justice of the United States. In addition to his legal abilities, Taft brought to his job presiding over the Supreme Court his growing conservatism and considerable dignity. His greatest achievement was procuring passage of the Judiciary Act of 1925. Other landmarks were decisions upholding workers' right to strike and the president's power to fire public officials.

Accomplishments and Defeats

Taft had the misfortune to follow the charismatic Theodore Roosevelt as president, and his natural complacency and affability led to many discouraging defeats. Yet his achievements before and after his presidency were great, and historians agree that he was a thoroughly honest man who, though he often resisted change, brought about important reforms.

Bibliography

Anderson, Judith Icke. *William Howard Taft*. New York: W. W. Norton, 1981.

Burton, David H. *The Learned Presidency: Theodore Roosevelt, William Howard Taft, Woodrow Wilson*. Rutherford, N.J.: Fairleigh Dickinson University Press, 1988.

_____. *Taft, Holmes, and the 1920's Court*. Madison, N.J.: Fairleigh Dickinson University Press, 1998.

Mason, Alpheus Thomas. *William Howard Taft: Chief Justice*. New York: Simon & Schuster, 1965.

Pringle, Henry F. *The Life and Times of William Howard Taft: A Biography*. New York: Farrar & Rinehart, 1939.

Ross, Ishbel. *An American Family: The Tafts, 1678-1964*. Cleveland, Ohio: World Publishing, 1964.

George Soule

Mother Teresa

Born: August 26, 1910; Shkup, Albania, Ottoman Empire (now Skopje, Macedonia)
Died: September 5, 1997; Calcutta, India

Roman Catholic nun and charity worker, winner of 1979 Nobel Peace Prize

Mother Teresa (MUH-thur teh-RAY-sah) was born Agnes Gonxha Bojaxhiu (AHG-nehs gohn-CHAH boh-yahch-YEW). Gonxha means "flower bud" in Albanian. Her father was a financially successful Albanian citizen and patriot who died when Agnes was about eight years old. Her mother, a woman of extraordinary character, raised young Agnes as a Catholic and took her on many acts of charity in their neighborhood. They provided food and clothing for the needy, bathed sick people, and bandaged wounds. In 1922, at the tender age of twelve, Agnes decided, as she put it, "to go out and give the life of Christ to the people." She became a Catholic nun at eighteen and joined the Irish order of the sisters of Loreto, famous for their missionary work in India. She took the name Sister Mary Teresa after Saint Theresa of Lisieux, patroness of missionaries. Sister Teresa traveled to Darjeeling, India, in January, 1929, to do her novitiate and took her lifetime vows in May, 1937. For twenty years she served as either a geography teacher or principal at St. Mary's High School in Calcutta.

Spiritual Turning Point

Mother Teresa claimed that the turning point in her life came on September 10, 1946, while she was traveling on a train to Darjeeling. She described her spiritual experience as "the call within the call": God wanted her to leave her present duties and devote her life to the poor. Throughout her life Mother Teresa combined deep compassion for the poor with shrewd organizational skills. Despite initial opposition from the Catholic Church, she proceeded within the next few years to form a new Calcutta order, which eventually became known as the Congregation (or Order) of the Missionaries of Charity.

Within ten years she had become famous throughout India, and the order became established in more than twenty cities. International notice came in the 1960's, when Mother Teresa left India for the first time in more than thirty years to work in Venezuela (1965), Tanzania (1968), and Australia (1969). By the time of her death, almost six hundred clinics, orphanages, soup kitchens, maternity houses, refugee centers, and homes for the poor, sick, and dying were set up in 105 countries and were staffed by approximately forty-five hundred nuns, five hundred brothers, and thou-

Mother Teresa after receiving the 1979 Nobel Peace Prize. *(Reuters/Scan Foto/Archive Photos)*

Mother Teresa in Calcutta in 1971, distributing rice and blankets to the needy. *(Archive Photos/Popperfoto)*

sands of volunteers. They were feeding 500,000 families a year, teaching twenty thousand slum children, and treating ninety thousand lepers.

Worldwide Acceptance

Mother Teresa became a universal beacon of light and hope radiating pure, selfless goodness. She was a familiar figure on the world stage, appearing at well-publicized scenes of national disasters. The world's most powerful politicians and celebrities courted her favors and friendship. Even the political leaders of Cuba, the former Soviet Union, and China opened their doors to her missionary work. Throughout her life

Leprosy

Mother Teresa's humanitarian concern for the abandoned and the dying was well illustrated by her love for lepers, the classic rejects of society. Leprosy is known medically as Hansen's disease. In India during the 1950's, more than thirty thousand lepers lived in the Calcutta area. Most Bengali citizens viewed them with fear and loathing. In 1956, Mother Teresa organized a mobile clinic—a blue van filled with medicines, disinfectants, and food—to help lepers who could not travel to a dispensary. Within a year, eight leprosy stations had been set up for the mobile unit. Two years later, Mother Teresa established a permanent place for lepers at Titagarh, already known for its leper colony, located about an hour from Calcutta. Today the self-supporting center treats approximately three hundred patients needing full hospital care and encourages rehabilitated lepers living by the hospital to work at various crafts.

The Congregation of the Missionaries of Charity

Mother Teresa created the nucleus of what was to become the Congregation of the Missionaries of Charity in 1949. She wanted to establish an order dedicated to helping the poor and dying in Calcutta. She quickly rallied supporters for her new mission in life from her former students. At the same time she applied for, and received, Indian citizenship, drafted a new constitution which strictly regimented the new disciples, and applied for permission to the archbishop of Calcutta, Ferdinand Perier, to recognize the congregation. The archbishop was particularly impressed that Mother Teresa added a fourth vow to the expected three of poverty, chastity, and obedience. It was that all members live by the vow of giving "wholehearted and free service to the poorest of the poor." The Congregation of the Missionaries of Charity was launched on October 7, 1950, limited at first to the Calcutta diocese.

Mother Teresa was showered with honors: the Nehru Award for International Understanding (1972); the first Albert Schweitzer International Prize (1975); the Nobel Peace Prize (1979); and the honorary Order of Merit, presented by Queen Elizabeth (1983). Three months before her death she was honored by the United States with the Congressional Gold Medal (1997).

Controversy

Serious controversy continually dogged Mother Teresa's religious mission and philosophy. Criticism came immediately upon the establishment of her first house dedicated to the dying poor. Volunteer Calcutta doctors protested that she was interested only in the patients' spiritual salvation, not in their physical health. One of the first and fiercest critics was Australian writer and feminist Germaine Greer, who characterized Mother Teresa as a religious imperialist for her uncompromising stand on abortion even in cases of rape, severe medical complications, and extreme malnutrition. Many critics also attacked her evangelizing, conservative religious intolerance of homosexuality and her support for denying women the priesthood. She was further criticized for turning her back on the Albanian people, suffering under many years of communist rule.

Severe criticism arose in the 1990's in the form of the 1994 television documentary *Hell's Angels*, followed a year later by the book *Missionary Position*, both by British journalist Christopher Hitchins. He savagely excoriated Mother Teresa, stating that she tried to portray Calcutta as a black hole of despair in desperate need of her ministry rather than as the cultural mecca it really is. Hitchins claimed that Mother Teresa raised millions of dollars for the Catholic Church and the convents but that very little of the money actually went to hospitals. She obsequiously fraternized with some of the world's most despised political leaders, he said, thereby sacrificing her moral stature for financial support. Hitchins also alleged that Mother Teresa never made an attempt to assert her authority on world leaders to support political and social reforms.

Throughout her remarkable career Mother Teresa ignored her critics. She traveled all over the globe, repeating her simple message by helping the unwanted and forgotten. Dressed in her traditional white cotton sari, decorated with three blue stripes, she remained continually in the public consciousness for several decades. Mother Teresa, a frail-looking woman troubled by illness all her life, battled daily against ignorance, disease, poverty, and injustice. No other humanitarian figure in the twentieth century, with the possible exception of Albert Schweitzer, was so universally beloved, admired, and honored.

Bibliography

Egan, Eileen. *Such a Vision of the Street: Mother Teresa, the Spirit and the Work*. New York: Doubleday, 1985.

Mother Teresa. *A Simple Path*. New York: Ballantine Books, 1995.

Muggeridge, Malcolm. *Something Beautiful for God: Mother Teresa of Calcutta*. New York: Harper & Row, 1971.

Sebba, Ann. *Mother Teresa: Beyond the Image*. New York: Doubleday, 1997.

Spink, Kathryn. *Mother Teresa: A Complete Authorized Biography*. San Francisco: HarperCollins, 1997.

Terry Theodore

U Thant

Born: January 22, 1909; Pantanaw, Burma (now Myanmar)
Died: November 25, 1974; New York, New York

Burmese diplomat, secretary-general of the United Nations (1961-1971)

The names of Burmese babies born on a Friday traditionally begin with T, Ht, or Th. Thant means "clean" or "pure." The preceding U ("uncle") is a term of respect, employed once a person has distinguished himself, reached sufficient age, or both. The result is roughly "Mr. Clean," an apt moniker for the life U Thant (EW TAHNT) would lead.

Emerging Talents in an Emerging Nation

Thant was educated at National High School, Pantanaw, and at University College, Rangoon. In Rangoon he met Thakin Nu (later U Nu, the first premier of independent Burma). Thant returned to National High School as senior master teaching history and English, later headmaster and superintendent. At twenty, he won the All Burma Translation Competition. Two years later he placed first in the nation on the Anglo-Vernacular Secondary Teachership Examination. Thant also was an author and aspiring journalist. He published several books, beginning with *Cities and Their Stories* in 1929. In addition, he was known for expressing his opinions on current issues through frequent letters to the press.

In 1945, Nu persuaded Thant to become press officer for the Anti-Fascist People's Freedom League (AFPF), the leading nationalist coalition. Thant was the first director of broadcasting and then secretary of the Ministry of Information after Burma's independence in 1948. In fact, Thant held multiple titles; Nu relied upon him heavily.

Serving at the United Nations

Thant was named Burma's permanent representative to the United Nations (U.N.) in 1957. He served as vice president of the U.N. General Assembly's fourteenth session in 1959, and he was named acting secretary-general in the wake of Dag Hammarskjöld's death in 1961. Controversy over U.N. activity in the Congo had led Soviet premier Nikita Khrushchev to propose that the office of secretary-general be replaced by a troika from the East, the West, and the nonaligned nations. Thant's appointment was unanimous, ending the stalemate over restructuring. The vote was to be unanimous twice more: Having completed Hammarskjöld's term, Thant was appointed to another three years in 1962 and to a

U Thant *(Archive France/Archive Photos)*

U.N. secretary-general U Thant (left) with U.S. senator J. William Fulbright in 1967. *(Library of Congress)*

five-year term in 1966. If his appointment was determined by East-West tensions, it was the gap between north and south—that is, between rich and poor nations, and development of the latter—about which the third U.N. secretary-general cared most.

Perhaps U Thant's greatest achievement came as peacemaker in the Cuban Missile Crisis of 1962. Thant issued an appeal for a two- to three-week cooling-off period: He asked the Soviets for a moratorium on arms shipments and asked the United States to suspend its blockade of Cuba. Thant also traveled to Havana to meet with Cuba's Fidel Castro, who was quite unhappy about being caught in the middle of the showdown between the superpowers. While it cannot be said that the secretary-general was directly responsible for averting nuclear catastrophe, he certainly spoke up for the rest of the world in the confrontation.

The low point of his tenure followed his withdrawal of the United Nations Emergency Force (UNEF) from the United Arab Republic, at Egypt's request, in 1967. An Arab-Israeli war, the Six-Day War, followed. Thant believed that he had no legal right to refuse Egypt's request, but the pullout was heavily criticized.

Assessment

Thant has been described as no less effective as U.N. secretary-general than his predecessors, Trygve Lie and Dag Hammarskjöld, were. The same could be said of Thant relative to his suc-

The British in Burma

Burma (now Myanmar) was annexed to British India in pieces, across three successive wars between 1824 and 1885. The British took part of Lower Burma in the first Anglo-Burmese War (1824-1826). They captured the rest of Lower Burma and part of Upper Burma in the second (1852), and all of Burma became a province of colonial India after a third war, lasting only four-teen days (1885). In 1935 Burma became separate from India and was allowed limited self-government. Japan occupied Burma during World War II, but British authority was restored in 1945. Full Burmese independence came in 1948. Like Ireland and the United States, Burma is a former possession that did not become a part of the British Commonwealth.

U.N. secretary-general U Thant, center, presenting U.S. president Richard Nixon (left) with commemorative stamps and medals in celebration of the United Nations' twenty-fifth anniversary in 1970. *(Archive Photos)*

cessors. The nature of the United Nations and the secretary-generalship makes it difficult to be any less ambiguous. By one measure at least, the third U.N. secretary-general might be considered its most effective: Never has there been more at stake than at the height of the Cold War.

Bibliography

Bingham, June. *U Thant: The Search for Peace*. New York: Knopf, 1966.

Nassif, Ramses. *U Thant in New York, 1961-1971*. London: C. Hurst, 1988.

Thant, U. *View from the UN*. Garden City, N.Y.: Doubleday, 1977.

J. P. Piskulich

Margaret Thatcher

Born: October 13, 1925; Grantham, Lincolnshire, England

First woman prime minister of Great Britain (1979-1990)

Margaret Hilda Roberts Thatcher (MAHR-gah-reht HIHL-dah RO-burtz THAT-chur) was born into a lower-middle-class British family. Strongly influenced by her father, who was a grocer, lay preacher, and alderman, Margaret sought to be the best at school. She attended Oxford University, majoring in chemistry. Her family and her Methodist upbringing imbued her with strict moral principles and shaped her political views. In 1951 she married Denis Thatcher, a wealthy businessman whose assets permitted her to study law and pursue a political career while raising a family. The Thatchers had twins, Mark and Carol, born August 15, 1953. Denis Thatcher was always a resolute supporter of his wife's political endeavors and, after his retirement, became the "first gentleman" of British politics when Margaret became prime minister.

Thatcher's Early Political Career

While at Oxford, Margaret Thatcher became active in politics and in the Conservative Party. She ran twice for Parliament before her marriage and was defeated. In 1959 she ran successfully for Parliament. Her ambition, hard work, and the fact that there were few Conservative women in Parliament helped her to advance in the party. She held several positions in the "shadow cabinet" in the late 1960's when the Conservatives, led by Edward Heath, were in opposition. During the government of Edward Heath, she was secretary of state for education and science (1970-1974). After Heath's defeat, she was elected head of the Conservative Party in 1975, with the support of the party's conservative wing. After 1975 she began to espouse her own views.

Thatcher as Prime Minister

Thatcher became prime minister in 1979. She did not come to power with a fully developed philosophy. She was, however, determined to break the cycle of what she perceived to be dependency on government, to reduce the size of the government by privatizing government holdings and cutting back the number of civil servants, and to reduce the power of the unions. These policies became the core of Thatcherism. She achieved her goals, but in so doing she sacrificed the long-held principle of full employment. Her policies also increased the gap between the rich and poor in the United Kingdom.

Margaret Thatcher *(National Archives)*

Unlike other Conservative prime ministers, Thatcher did not come from the upper classes. She shared their "Oxbridge" (education at Oxford or Cambridge University) link but not their class origin or background. She saw herself as middle class, and more than any other prime minister before her, she spoke for the middle class in a country historically divided between the upper class and working class. Through her marriage and education, she moved from the lower middle class to the upper middle class and from the nonconformist Methodist Church toward the Church of England, although she never officially became an Anglican.

Conviction, not Compromise

Thatcher disdained the politics of compromise which had driven the great consensus in post-World War II British politics. A person of resolute beliefs and convictions, she did what she thought was right, regardless of whether others agreed. Her strongly expressed convictions and policies contributed to her nickname, the

British prime minister Margaret Thatcher in Paris in 1990 after signing a European defense treaty. *(Reuters/Gary Hershorn/ Archive Photos)*

The Falkland Islands War

The Falkland Islands (also known as the Malvinas) lie off the coast of Argentina. They were part of Britain's colonial empire. There has been a long-standing dispute between Britain and Argentina over ownership of these islands. The fewer than two thousand inhabitants of the islands generally identify with the United Kingdom and have resisted being united with Argentina. In 1982, however, the military junta then governing Argentina invaded the Falklands. War between Britain and Argentina ensued. The war was brief but costly—both in the short and long run—since Britain, as well as Argentina,

lost many troops and ships. Furthermore, Britain took on a greater obligation to protect the islands in the future. The war strengthened the image of Thatcher as a tough leader, but it was perhaps not typical of her overall policy toward colonial possessions. The return of Hong Kong to China in the agreement of 1985, which provided for the transfer of Hong Kong to China over a twelve-year period, is perhaps more indicative of Britain's colonial policy. The British response to the Falklands crisis was an emotional one. Hong Kong was approached more dispassionately, even though it was indubitably a greater asset.

The British Election of 1987

Margaret Thatcher won three elections, in 1979, 1983, and 1987. She was the only British prime minister in the twentieth century to be reelected twice, although her party never received 50 percent of the vote. The unprecedented third election created an illusion of invincibility, which did not reflect the fact that her popularity was actually declining both in the party and in the country. After 1987 she became even more resolute in her policies, further confirming the image of the Iron Lady.

Thatcher's electoral success in 1987 can be attributed to several factors. The economy was healthy, despite growing unemployment. Thatcher's foreign policy, especially her resolute positions vis-à-vis the European Community (EC) and the Soviet Union, reestablished the firm British voice in international relations. Finally, her opposition was divided because of a split several years earlier in the Labour Party. In 1987 the Labour votes and the breakaway Social Democrat (SDP)-Liberal Alliance votes, if added together, constituted a majority, but the Conservatives profited from their split.

Margaret Thatcher after being knighted at Windsor Castle in 1995. At left is her husband, Denis. *(Martin Keene, "PA" Photo Library/Archive Photos)*

Iron Lady. Thatcher reduced the power of cabinet ministers and enhanced the power of the prime minister. In foreign policy, she was best known for her opposition to increased political integration of Europe. She strongly supported the single European market, but she refused to surrender British sovereignty to Europe. Her growing bias against identification with a new Europe turned some of her staunch cabinet allies against her in 1990 and contributed to her downfall.

In domestic politics her resolute stance was exemplified by the poll tax, a per-capita tax on residents that replaced the traditional tax on housing. Thus a couple living in a mansion and a couple living in a small row house would pay essentially the same poll tax, even though the former had far greater assets. This extremely unpopular tax alienated her from the common people, many of whom had previously supported her, and it was probably the domestic issue that most contributed to her forced resignation on November 22, 1990. In her last years as prime minister, she became increasingly resolute and unbending, until other Conservative Party leaders rebelled and requested her resignation. Her successor, John Major, was, to some degree, her choice, but he was also someone the party knew could be managed.

The Legacy of Thatcherism

Margaret Thatcher was the longest-serving British prime minister in the twentieth century. She reversed the tide of government ownership, trimmed the welfare state, and helped to turn Britain away from its class-based establishment toward meritocracy. The question has frequently been raised whether Thatcher helped advance the cause of women. Not a feminist herself, she nevertheless demonstrated through her life that a woman could be a highly effective politician and prime minister. There was also a Thatcher style, characterized by faultless grooming, taste-ful suits, perfect hairdos, and subdued jewelry. She therefore confirmed a personal style for women political leaders, which others tended to emulate.

Bibliography

Genovese, Michael, ed. *Women as National Leaders*. Newbury Park, Calif.: Sage Publications, 1993.

Jenkins, Peter. *Mrs. Thatcher's Revolution: The Ending of the Socialist Era*. Cambridge, Mass.: Harvard University Press, 1988.

Thompson, Juliet S., and Wayne C. Thompson. *Margaret Thatcher: Prime Minister Indomitable*. Boulder, Colo.: Westview Press, 1994.

Young, Hugh. *The Iron Lady*. New York: Farrar Strauss, 1989.

Norma C. Noonan

Clarence Thomas

Born: June 23, 1948; Pin Point, Georgia

U.S. jurist and Supreme Court justice (named 1991)

Born in the tiny community of Pin Point, Georgia, south of Savannah, Clarence Thomas (KLA-rehntz TO-muhs) was only two years old when his father abandoned the family. Thomas's mother worked as a maid to support her three children, but after their home burned, Clarence and his brother were sent to live with their maternal grandfather in Savannah.

Thomas's grandfather was a devout Roman Catholic and a hard taskmaster. Following his wishes, Thomas attended Catholic educational institutions and did well in school. He first attended Immaculate Conception Seminary in Missouri, but he left after his first year, citing the

Clarence Thomas *(Reuters/Mike Theiler/Archive Photos)*

racism he encountered there. In 1971, he received his B.A. from Holy Cross College. In 1974, he received a degree from Yale Law School, to which he had been admitted under the school's affirmative action program.

Legal Career

After leaving law school, Thomas was unable to secure an offer from a major law firm, a situation he blamed on racial prejudice. Eventually, he accepted a position on the staff of Missouri attorney general John Danforth. In Danforth's offices, Thomas—fearful of being stereotyped—carefully avoided work on assignments addressing specifically African American concerns. He also clearly signaled his political conservatism, joining both the Republican Party and the African American conservative movement.

Thomas worked briefly in the private sector, but in 1979 he returned to work for Danforth, who was by that time a U.S. senator. As one of only a handful of prominent conservative African Americans in the Washington political arena, Thomas came to the attention of President Ronald Reagan's administration, which employed Thomas first, from 1981 to 1982, as assistant secretary for civil rights, then, from 1982 to 1990, as director of the Equal Employment Opportunity Commission (EEOC). In 1990, President George Bush appointed Thomas to the prestigious District of Columbia Circuit Court of Appeals.

In 1991, Justice Thurgood Marshall, an African American, retired from the Supreme Court. Despite illness and old age, Marshall had stayed on the Supreme Court in the hope that a Democratic president would be elected—who would, presumably, appoint a successor who shared Marshall's liberal orientation and concern for civil rights. In the end, Marshall had to leave the Court while a Republican president was still in office. His retirement left vacant what some observers regarded as the "African American" seat because they assumed that another African American would be appointed to fill it.

Supreme Court Nomination

Indeed, George Bush nominated Thomas for the seat. During his Senate confirmation hearings, Thomas did not encounter hostility about his conservative orientation, but rather questions concerning his judicial qualifications and his unwillingness to be forthcoming about his attitudes toward controversial matters such as abortion. Then, shortly before the Senate was to vote on his nomination, a former female employee named Anita Hill came forward with allegations that Thomas had harassed her sexually. Thomas weathered the intense scrutiny that followed and was finally confirmed by a vote of 52-48, the slimmest margin given any Supreme Court nominee in a century. On November 1, 1991, he became

Clarence Thomas being sworn in to testify in his Senate Judiciary Committee confirmation hearing in 1991. *(Arnold Sachs/CNP/Archive Photos)*

The Thomas Confirmation Hearings

On Saturday, October 5, 1991, three days before the Senate was scheduled to vote on the nomination of Clarence Thomas as the next justice of the U.S. Supreme Court, one of his former employees, Anita Hill, went public with her accusations that he had sexually harassed her. Hill had worked for Thomas in the Civil Rights Division of the Department of Education and later at the Equal Employment Opportunity Commission (EEOC). To some observers, the fact that Hill had followed Thomas to the EEOC tended to undermine the testimony she gave before the Senate Judiciary Committee in hearings that were called to investigate her allegations.

The hearings, which went on for three days and were broadcast on national television, included testimony from both Thomas and Hill, as well as from character witnesses for both sides. Surprisingly, since both Thomas and Hill were African American, Thomas—proclaiming the hearings "a high-tech lynching"—characterized the events as an exercise in racism. In the end, although Thomas's nomination was confirmed, Hill managed to put the issue of sexual harassment on the national agenda.

only the second African American to sit on the nation's highest tribunal.

Once on the Court, Thomas kept a low profile and remained aloof from his fellow justices. He continued to demonstrate a marked conservatism, voting most often with Justice Antonin Scalia, the most outspoken conservative on the Court headed by Chief Justice William Rehnquist.

Bibliography

Mayer, Jane, and Jill Abramson. *Strange Justice: The Selling of Clarence Thomas.* Boston: Houghton Mifflin, 1994.

Phelps, Timothy M. *Capitol Games: Clarence Thomas, Anita Hill, and the Story of a Supreme Court Nomination.* New York: Hyperion, 1992.

Smith, Christopher E. *Critical Judicial Nominations and Political Change: The Impact of Clarence Thomas.* Westport, Conn.: Praeger, 1993.

Lisa Paddock

Bal Gangadhar Tilak

Born: July 23, 1856; Ratnāgiri, Maharashtra, India
Died: August 1, 1920; Bombay, India

Indian nationalist leader

Bal Gangadhar Tilak (BAHL GAHN-gah-thur TEE-lahk) was born to a high-caste family of moderate means. He studied mathematics and then law. By the age of twenty-four he had decided to dedicate himself to the cause of Indian freedom. In 1880 he started the New English School at Poona in order to promote nationalism through educational institutions. The school was so successful that in 1884 he established the Deccan Educational Society in order to administer the Poona school and to establish more schools and colleges, such as Fergusson College, Poona, and Willingdon College at Sangli. The importance of the society was that it recognized that education in the vernacular was the means to effect social, political, and cultural change. Two newspapers, *Kesari*, in the Marathi language, and *Mahratta*, in English, were started in 1881. In 1890 Tilak resigned from the society, as he believed it was moving away from its original goals.

Political Activities

After his break with the society, Tilak acquired sole possession of *Kesari* and *Mahratta* and became deeply involved in politics. He was a vehement and consistent critic of the British. He believed that the Indian National Congress (founded in 1885) would never make an impact on the British if it confined its activities to the elite classes and did not involve the masses. He revived the Ganapati festival in 1894 and started the Shivaji festival in 1896 in order to increase national pride and unity among the Hindus. During the weeklong festivities Tilak attacked the activities of the Christian missionaries and the social reform legislation that the British were passing.

He became increasingly critical of moderate reformers and loyalists. He railed against British rule and argued that British economic policies were the cause of India's poverty and the recurrence of famine and epidemics. He criticized British activities so vehemently during the plague of 1896-1897 that he was blamed for the murder of three British officials, charged with sedition, and sentenced to eighteen months of hard labor.

He emerged from prison with a large following of people who wanted a more vigorous response to British rule. He supported boycott and independence movements in Bengal and encouraged

Bal Gangadhar Tilak *(Kim Kurnizky)*

1481

Indian Home Rule Leagues

Two Home Rule Leagues were established in 1916, one by Indian nationalist Bal Gangadhar Tilak, the other by Annie Besant (1847-1933), a British theosophist, feminist, and labor organizer. The term "home rule" was taken from the movement for independence in Ireland and was first used by an Indian in 1905. The leagues were organizations that fought for freedom for India, and they represented a more aggressive stance than had previously been taken toward British rule. Indians were disappointed at how little power was given to Indians by the Government of India Act of 1909, and there was resentment at the loss of freedom due to laws passed during World War I. Tilak and Besant wished to bring the Indians of the Indian National Congress, who had divided into "moderates" and "extremists," together in opposition to the British. By 1918 Tilak's league had some thirty-two thousand members, while Besant's league had fewer numbers. The aim of both leagues was Indian independence within the British Empire. They both produced pamphlets, gave talks, and engaged in social and educational work to involve the masses in political action. By 1919 Tilak's league was largely a moribund organization because of lack of organization, the increase of communal tension between Hindus and Muslims, and the British announcement in 1917 that further constitutional reforms would occur.

Englishwoman Annie Besant, founder of an Indian home rule league. Like Bal Gangadhar Tilak, she wanted to bring Indian moderates and extremists together. *(Archive Photos)*

However, the Home Rule Leagues brought political action to the masses and mobilized more Indians in the movement for freedom than had been active before 1916.

---

similar movements in Maharashtra. He became known as an "extremist." His alliance with politicians in Bengal and the Punjab alarmed both the British and the Congress, and this situation led to Congress splitting in 1907 between "moderates" and "extremists," with Tilak the leader of the extremists.

In 1908 the British linked the increase in the amount of terrorism with the radical press. For his articles in *Kesari* he was sentenced to six years' deportation. He served his term in Mandalay prison in Burma. After his release in 1914 he tried to bring all Indians together in the Congress Party.

The Home Rule League

In 1916 Tilak formed the Home Rule League to fight for freedom for India. By 1918 Tilak's league had some thirty-two thousand members. He produced pamphlets, gave numerous talks, and engaged in social and educational work to involve the masses in the nationalist movement. By 1919, however, the league had lost most of its support because of its lack of organizational structure and communal tension between Hindus and Muslims. Moreover, the British announced in 1917 that further constitutional reforms would occur. However, Tilak, who has been called the "father of the Indian freedom struggle," brought political action to the masses and mobilized Indians in the fight for freedom. It was fitting that he died the same day that Mahatma Gandhi began his non-cooperation movement in 1920, as Gandhi adopted many of the aims that Tilak had espoused.

Bibliography

Cashman, Richard I. *The Myth of the Lokamanya: Tilak and Mass Politics in Maharashtra*. Berkeley: University of California Press, 1975.

Pradhan, G. P. *Lokamanya Tilak*. New Delhi: National Book Trust, 1994.

Wolpert, Stanley. *Tilak and Gokhale: Revolution and Reform in the Making of Modern India*. Berkeley: University of California Press, 1962.

Roger D. Long

Alfred von Tirpitz

Born: March 19, 1849; Brandenburg, Prussia (now Kostrzyn, Poland)
Died: March 6, 1930; Ebenhausen, near Munich, Germany

German naval commander, creator of Germany's High Seas Fleet

Alfred Peter Friedrich Tirpitz (AHL-freht PAY-tayr FREED-rihk TIHR-pihtz) was born to a one-time noble Prussian family with a long record of bureaucratic service. A poor student, Alfred entered the Prussian navy as a cadet in 1865. He rose to become chief of staff to the commander of the Baltic Naval Station (1890) and chief of staff to the Supreme Command of the German Imperial Navy (1892-1896). In 1896 he commanded the Far Eastern Squadron, being recalled in 1897 to become chief of the Naval High Command, a position he held for twenty years. In 1900 Kaiser

Alfred von Tirpitz *(Library of Congress)*

William (Wilhelm) II ennobled Tirpitz, who added *von* to his surname.

Building the Imperial Navy

Tirpitz firmly believed that Germany needed a strong fleet of powerful surface ships to compete for overseas colonies and to maintain a balance of power locally with Great Britain. He persuaded the kaiser, the public, and many in the Reichstag (the German parliament) that large sums of money should be devoted to developing the High Seas Fleet. Nationalist organizations supported him, and events such as the Spanish-American War, the Boxer Rebellion, and the Russo-Japanese War reinforced the drive. Tirpitz-designed naval bills (or supplements) passed the Reichstag in 1898, 1900, 1906, 1908, and 1912. Naval expenditures accounted for 24 percent of Germany's budget by 1908; naval personnel increased from twenty-seven thousand in 1897 to eighty thousand in 1914. Growth led to open rivalry with Britain, especially after introduction of Great Britain's huge *Dreadnought* battleship in 1906.

When World War I came in 1914, Tirpitz's construction program was far from complete. Though second only to Britain's Royal Navy, the fleet was unprepared to confront it directly. Naval strategists shifted emphasis to submarines in the autumn of 1914; Tirpitz called for their unrestricted use in January, 1915. Political and moral considerations kept Germany's leaders from conducting unrestricted submarine warfare, however, and Tirpitz resigned; his resignation was finally accepted in March of 1916.

Tirpitz and the Political Right Wing

Frustration with military policy led Tirpitz to participate in conservative nationalist politics during and after the war. Reactionaries considered overthrowing both the kaiser and the chancellor (Theobald Bethmann-Hollweg), and Tirpitz was mentioned as a candidate for chancellor. His staunch conservatism, broad popularity, and energetic defense of a strong Germany attracted many supporters, especially in the German Fatherland Party. In the summer of 1918 he wrote his memoirs, in which he defended his past policies of naval construction and his opposition to the wartime leadership. He subscribed to the idea that Germany had been "stabbed in the back" by naïve liberal politicians. Military defeat in November, 1918, naval mutinies, and Bolshevik revolutionary turmoil fueled reactionary politics.

A German warship in World War I. Between 1898 and 1912, Alfred von Tirpitz had convinced the German government to spend significant amounts of money to build its High Seas Fleet. *(Archive Photos)*

The victorious Allies imposed a new government on defeated Germany, the Weimar Republic. This indignity convinced many Germans, including Tirpitz, to advocate right-wing revolt and dictatorship. In the early 1920's he struggled to create a united conservative political front among veterans, industrialists, nationalists, and paramilitary groups such as the National Socialists (the Nazis). Though he thought Adolf Hitler a useful popular leader, he disdained him as "a

The German High Seas Fleet

Founded in 1907, imperial Germany's *Hochseeflotte*, or High Seas Fleet, was initially commanded by the kaiser's brother, Admiral Prince Heinrich. By August, 1914, the fleet consisted of 13 dreadnoughts (battleships), 4 battle cruisers, 8 light cruisers, and 152 smaller craft. Much inferior in numbers, gun size, and tradition to Britain's Home Fleet, it engaged the Royal Navy only once during World War I, at Jutland on May 31, 1916.

Despite somewhat heavier British losses, Germany never seriously risked its fleet again. On October 29, 1918, the famous Kiel Mutiny occurred, in which German sailors refused to serve upon hearing of a "suicide sortie." After the armistice on November 21, the German navy handed over to Great Britain all major ships for temporary anchorage in Scapa Flow. On June 21, 1919, the German commander of the imprisoned fleet ordered the ships scuttled, rendering them worthless to the victorious Allies' navies.

fanatic inclined to craziness whom pampering has made unrestrained." He also did not share Hitler's anti-Semitism. When the politics of *putsch* (overthrow) failed, Tirpitz ran successfully for the Reichstag from Bavaria in 1924. Suggestions that he become chancellor were quashed by both center and left-wing parties, who resented his position on submarine warfare and his advocacy of military dictatorship. Field Marshal Paul von Hindenburg's election as president ended Tirpitz's hope of political power. Retiring from the Reichstag in 1928, he continued to agitate for right-wing political unity and better treatment of Germany by the international community until dying from a heart attack in 1930.

Tirpitz's expensive and controversial fleet helped lead to, but displayed little activity during, World War I. His political activism after the war helped pave the way for fascist success in Germany in the 1930's.

Bibliography

Scheck, Raffael. *Alfred von Tirpitz and German Right-Wing Politics, 1914-1930*. Atlantic Highlands, N.J.: Humanities Press International, 1998.

Steinberg, Jonathan. *Yesterday's Deterrent: Tirpitz and the Birth of the German Battle Fleet*. New York: Macmillan, 1966.

Tirpitz, Alfred von. *My Memoirs*. New York: Dodd, Mead, 1919.

Weir, Gary E. *Building the Kaiser's Navy: The Imperial Naval Office and German Industry in the von Tirpitz Era, 1900-1919*. Annapolis, Md.: Naval Institute Press, 1992.

Joseph P. Byrne

Josip Broz Tito

Born: May 7, 1892; Kumrovec, Austro-Hungarian Empire (now Croatia)
Died: May 4, 1980; Ljubljana, Slovenia, Yugoslavia (now Slovenia)

President of Republic of Yugoslavia (1953-1980)

Josip Broz Tito (YOH-seep BROHZ TEE-toh) was born Josip Broz to a Croatian-Slovenian peasant family in the Austro-Hungarian Empire. His early career was as an itinerant manual laborer, and later a recruit into the Austro-Hungarian army. At the outbreak of World War I in 1914, he was sent to the eastern front, wounded, and sent as a prisoner to Russia. There he encountered the communist movement, which he joined after the Russian Revolution in 1917. He returned in 1920 to Croatia with his Russian wife as a communist agent and union organizer in the new Kingdom of Serbs, Croats, and Slovenes (Yugoslavia after 1929).

Early Political Career

Tito began his political work in Zagreb, Croatia, but was arrested and sentenced to five years in prison in 1928. In 1935, assuming the pseudonym Tito, he returned to Russia, where he met Joseph Stalin, successor to Vladimir Lenin as Soviet dictator, and worked for the Comintern (the Communist International). Adolf Hitler was expanding Germany's boundaries and threatening Europe. War was beginning to be seen as inevitable. Tito returned to Yugoslavia in 1939 to reorganize the Communist Party, and he became its secretary-general. His attempts to convince Yugoslavians of the correctness of Stalin's view of class war were hampered by the nonaggression pact that Stalin signed with Hitler in 1939. World War II began in September of that year.

Serbia's refusal to sign a nonaggression pact with Germany in March, 1941, after a military coup seized power and established young King Peter Karadjorjevic as ruler, led to swift retribution from Germany. On April 6, 1941, Germany bombed Belgrade and quickly occupied the country, sending king and government into exile.

Partisan Commander

The rapid fall and dismemberment of Yugoslavia by the Nazis, after establishing a puppet regime in Croatia, was made even worse by the vicious civil war that erupted between Serbs and Croats. Anti-Nazi groups, such as Draža Mihailović's Serb Četniks, spent more energy fighting rival Croat Ustaše than fighting the Germans. Here Tito's military genius became apparent, as he established the Partisans, composed of all ethnic factions, to conduct guerrilla warfare against

Josip Broz Tito *(National Archives)*

Josip Broz Tito (center) dancing with residents of Kola, Yugoslavia, while on the campaign trail in 1950. *(Library of Congress)*

Postwar Yugoslavia

After World War II, there was little doubt that Tito's communists would inherit the leadership of Yugoslavia. Tito's reputation as war hero and political leader was, if not untarnished, at least intact, and his commitment to the unification of Yugoslavia under communist rule was believed by many to be the best route to achieving a viable government after the dislocations of the war. Tito's slogan of "brotherhood and unity" stressed the hope of burying the fratricidal atrocities of the war under the mantle of a new beginning.

Tito's photograph graced every public building and many storefronts in the country, and he commanded popular support. His 1948 standoff with Stalin and his subsequent introduction of limited economic incentive for Western-style entrepreneurial activity encouraged the Western powers

the Germans after their invasion of the Soviet Union in June, 1941. Although there was infighting with the Četniks, Tito's forces were able to command loyalty to the Yugoslav, and communist, cause.

The Partisans

Tito's leadership of the Partisans was based on his assessment that the royalist, Serb-led Četniks and the Croat-led Ustaše were leading the country into chaos at a time when unity was badly needed. He formed the Partisans, composed of members of all ethnic groups, and focused on fighting the Nazis and their collaborators on Yugoslav territory. This communist-dominated force, particularly after their 1943 successes at the battles of the Neretva and the Sutjeska, drew Allied attention as the Yugoslavian faction most deserving of military and material support. (In reality, the Partisans were fighting the Četniks as well as the Nazis.) Their success in getting Allied support ensured their success. The Partisans, aided by the Soviet army, were instrumental in liberating Serbia in 1944. They gained political control by the end of the war. Tito then legitimated his government at the expense of the monarchy through dubious elections. He purged noncommunists and "collaborators" from the government and had established the Federal People's Republic of Yugoslavia by the end of 1945. During the 1991 civil war between the Serbs and the Croats, the terms "Četnik" and "Ustaša" resurfaced as epithets of abuse, but the term "Partisan" did not.

Tito and Stalin

Tito began his career in Russia as a communist under Joseph Stalin's tutelage. He was suitably rewarded for his efforts on behalf of the Cominform (a European organization of mainly ruling Communist Parties) by being named secretary-general of the Communist Party of Yugoslavia at a time when fellow party members were being purged. However, differences of opinion between himself and Stalin on issues of Balkan foreign policy emerged after World War II, and these differences led Tito to defy his former mentor. Stalin's attempt to purge Tito from his position of leadership in 1948 was unsuccessful because of Tito's military strength. This attempt was followed by the expulsion of the Communist Party of Yugoslavia from the Cominform. The unforeseen consequence of this move was that Tito began to seek his own road to socialism.

to view him as a renegade from the Stalinist camp. The promise of military support from the West, along with the issuing of huge loans to make economic rebuilding possible, increased his standing.

Tito made a name for himself as a diplomatic leader of nonaligned nations in the mid-1950's. Many countries wished not to get involved in the confrontational Cold War politics that seemed a threat to world peace. Internally, his strategy of worker self-management was seen by many as a move away from a command economy, as he sought to broaden the concept of socialist worker participation. This movement caused political conflict, however, and was not particularly successful.

Tito's Last Years

Tito was, in his later years, notable as the leader who returned Yugoslavia to stability in world politics. He was a flamboyant dresser, an admirer of beautiful women, and a collector of palaces, hunting lodges, and fine automobiles. Although not regarded as a strict dictator, Tito carried out purges within the Communist Party, imprisoned and exiled political opponents, and made sure that none of his reforms was carried further than he intended.

Antagonisms between ethnic groups became increasingly apparent during his final years, as

At his peak, photographs of Josip Broz Tito seemed to be everywhere in Yugoslavia. Here members of the Yugoslav Youth Labor Brigade march to a construction site armed with banners, hand tools, and a portrait of Tito. *(National Archives)*

did economic difficulties due to inability to repay earlier loans. There was also resentment in the wealthier republics, as their wealth was redistributed to the poorer regions of Macedonia, Kosovo, and Montenegro.

Ethnic problems worsened in the late 1970's. Tito's unwillingness or inability to deal with them made his death in 1980 seem like a portent of impending doom. During his final years he established a new constitution (in 1974). It gave greater autonomy to individual republics and autonomous regions and provided for a rotating presidency, with himself as leader, to ease the transition after his death. However, ethnic divisions among Serbs, Croats, Slovenes, and Kosovo Albanians caused the breakup of Yugoslavia under his successors during the early 1990's. Tito was reevaluated as a national leader after Yugoslavia's disintegration. He was variously accused of betraying the Serbs by altering the internal borders of the republics and of failing other ethnic groups by perpetuating the Serb domination of the government and army.

Bibliography

Auty, Phyllis. *Tito: A Biography*. Rev. ed. Harmondsworth, England: Penguin, 1974.

Pavlowitch, Stevan K. *The Improbable Survivor: Yugoslavia and Its Problems, 1918-1988*. Columbus: Ohio State University Press, 1988.

_____. *Tito: Yugoslavia's Great Dictator, a Reassessment*. Columbus: Ohio State University Press, 1992.

Ulam, Adam B. *Titoism and the Cominform*. Reprint. Westport, Conn.: Greenwood Press, 1971.

Gloria Fulton

Hideki Tojo

Born: December 30, 1884; Tokyo, Japan
Died: December 23, 1948; Tokyo, Japan

Prime minister of Japan (1941-1944)

Hideki Tojo (hee-deh-kee toh-joh) was the son of an army general in a family with a long military tradition. After graduating from military academy in 1905, he held a series of regimental staff assignments. He then graduated from the Military Staff College with honors in 1915. He married the vivacious Katsu Ito in 1909, and the couple had seven children between 1911 and 1932.

Military Promotions

Following World War I, Tojo was resident officer in Germany, a country he always admired. He advanced to the chief of the organization section of the Army General Staff in 1931, the year that Japanese troops took control of Manchuria. In 1935, he was transferred to the Kwangtung Army of Manchuria, where he served as head of the powerful military police, the Kempeitai.

Within the army, Tojo associated himself with the "Control Faction," which emphasized discipline, and opposed the ultranationalist "Imperial Way Faction." When extremists attempted a *coup d'état* in 1936, he gained prominence by suppressing their supporters in Manchuria. With his clique of effective officers, Tojo became known as the "razor" because of his shrewdness and attention to details. In 1937, he was promoted to chief of staff of the Kwangtung Army, and he played a key role in the early stages of Japan's war against China.

Early Political Career

In May, 1938, Tojo returned to Tokyo as vice minister of war, and he used this position to promote an expansionist policy of "freeing Asia from the Western yoke," a concept that later developed into the Greater East Asia Co-prosperity Sphere. He was an efficient administrator and persuasive speaker, and he was popular with most factions of the military. For these reasons he was appointed minister of war in the second cabinet of Premier Fumimaro Konoye in July, 1940.

As war minister, Tojo was able to exercise considerable influence within the cabinet. Never sympathetic to representative democracy, he fully supported the establishment of the Imperial Rule Assistance Association, which replaced Ja-

Hideki Tojo *(National Archives)*

U.S. Marines firing a captured Japanese gun during the 1944 battle for Saipan. *(National Archives)*

withdraw troops from both China and Indochina, Premier Konoye attempted to pursue negotiations. Tojo, representing the military perspective, was determined not to allow any withdrawals. He participated in an imperial conference that gave the government until October 15 to attain minimum objectives. Meanwhile, Tojo and other military leaders made secret preparations for war, and Konoye resigned after he failed to meet the deadline.

Prime Minister

When Tojo was appointed prime minister on October 17, 1941, the change in government was popular with the Japanese public. The *jushin*, or senior statesmen, hoped that Tojo's appointment would restrain the army, but they were soon disappointed. Although continuing to negotiate with the United States, Tojo was convinced that agreement was impossible. He gave advance approval for the surprise attacks that occurred at Pearl Harbor and other Western bases on December 7.

pan's political parties, and he played a leading role in negotiating the Tripartite Pact with Italy and Germany. After deciding that Japan's future lay in the south rather than the north, he was one of the principal architects of the invasion of southern Indochina in July, 1941.

When the United States demanded that Japan

The Kwangtung Army

The Chinese province of Kwangtung (or Guandong) was a Japanese leasehold in southern Manchuria from 1905 until 1945. Japan created the Kwangtung Army in 1906 to defend the territory, especially the zone around the Southern Manchurian Railway. Officials of the army were accountable to the emperor rather than under civilian control. During the 1920's they favored strong measures to suppress a rising tide of Chinese nationalism. A staged explosion

on the tracks near Mukden in 1931 gave the Kwangtung Army an excuse to occupy all of Manchuria and to establish the puppet state of Manchukuo. In 1939, the Kwangtung Army lost 18,000 soldiers in border clashes with the Soviet Red Army at Nomonhan. The Soviet Red Army attacked Manchuria on August 9, 1945, and 80,000 of the 787,000 soldiers in the Kwangtung Army were killed within two weeks.

The Fall of Saipan, 1944

Saipan, 14 miles (23 kilometers) long, is one of the Mariana Islands in the Central Pacific. Mandated to Japan in 1920, it served as a supply area with strategic airbases during World War II. After the Allies won victories in New Guinea and the Marshall Islands, one of their major goals was to take control of the Marianas. The Marianas were close enough to Japan to serve as launching sites for B-29 air attacks. The Mariana campaign began with Saipan.

On June 15, 1944, a landing force of seventy-seven thousand U.S. Marines went ashore on the southern coast. Although the thirty thousand Japanese defenders fought ferociously, the Americans had the advantages of air support and naval fire. The capture of the island, planned to take three days, required three weeks. By July 1, most of the soldiers in the Japanese garrison were dead. As the fighting officially ended on July 9, an estimated 22,000 civilians, fearing atrocities by the invaders, committed mass suicide by jumping from Marpi Point. U.S. casualties on Saipan totaled thirty-five hundred deaths and more than ten thousand wounded. Japan's loss of the island was the immediate cause for Premier Hideki Tojo's resignation.

Military leaders, however, were responsible for deciding on the exact locations and details of the operations.

With the early Japanese successes in World War II, Tojo became the strongest prime minister in modern Japanese history, and he personally assumed control of most important ministries. He generally allowed military commanders to formulate and regulate policies within the occupied territories. Therefore, he was not directly responsible for atrocities such as the Bataan "death march," although he never made any attempt to ameliorate such behavior. In domestic affairs, he supported the emergency law of 1942, providing officials with special powers to control the press and arrest political opponents. Tojo's prestige and influence naturally declined after Japan began to suffer defeats, and the fall of Saipan forced him to resign on July 19, 1944.

Postwar Fate

Tojo was disgraced and without influence at the time of Japan's surrender in 1945. When the Americans came to arrest him, he shot himself in the chest, but he recovered in an American hospital. In prison, he spent most of his time in Buddhist meditations. When prosecuted as a Class A war criminal, he accepted responsibility for initiating and conducting the war, and he did what he could to exonerate the emperor from any blame. While continuing to defend Japanese goals, he insisted that mistreatment of prisoners and other abuses had been contrary to his orders. Found guilty of war crimes, he was hanged with six other wartime leaders in 1948.

Although Tojo ruled as a virtual dictator from 1941 to 1944, he never exercised the totalitarian control found in Adolf Hitler's Germany or Joseph Stalin's Russia. His narrow ideology was founded on traditional notions of military virtue and Japanese nationalism, with an emphasis on strict authority and firm discipline. Because he was unable to appreciate other viewpoints, he could not understand why all Asians did not welcome Japanese domination. Although quite intelligent, he was a stubborn and emotional man who took great risks based on limited knowledge and unrealistic expectations.

Bibliography

Browne, Courtney. *Tojo: The Last Banzai*. New York: Holt, Rinehart and Winston, 1967.

Butow, Robert. *Tojo and the Coming of the War.* Princeton, N.J.: Princeton University Press, 1961.

Hoyt, Edwin. *Warlord: Tojo Against the World.* Lanham, Md.: Scarborough House, 1993.

Shillony, Ben-Ami. *Politics and Culture in Wartime Japan.* New York: Oxford University Press, 1981.

Toland, John. *The Rising Sun: The Decline and Fall of the Japanese Empire, 1936-1945.* New York: Random House, 1970.

Thomas T. Lewis

Leon Trotsky

Born: November 7, 1879; Yankova, Ukraine, Russian Empire
Died: August 20, 1940; Coyoacán, Mexico, near Mexico City

Russian revolutionary leader, oversaw creation of the Red Army (1918-1921)

Born to a Jewish family, Lev Davidovich Bronstein (LYEHF duh-VIH-duh-vyihch bruhn-SHTIN)—later Leon Trotsky (LYEE-on TROHT-skoo-ih)—was sent to Odessa at the age of ten. Eight years later he moved to Nikolayev for further education. In 1897 he committed himself to a life of revolution. The South Russian Workers' Union that he joined was soon rounded up by the authorities. Trotsky married fellow revolutionary Alexandra Sokolovskaya in prison in Moscow. After a year and a half in prisons they were sentenced to four years of exile in Siberia. With his wife's approval, Trotsky escaped in 1902 and made his way to London under his new name, Trotsky. There he promptly became an associate of Vladimir Ilich Lenin.

European Travels and the First Soviet

From 1902 to 1905 Trotsky took part in the struggles of the intellectuals living in France, England, and Switzerland to define "the revolution." On a speaking trip to Paris he met Natalie Sedova, with whom he was to live in common law for the rest of his life. At first close to Lenin, Trotsky split with him in July, 1903, at the congress that created the Russian Social Democratic Party. He sided with the minority, or Mensheviks (although he never officially joined their party). They opposed the majority, or Bolsheviks, mainly over Lenin's vision of the dictatorship of the proletariat: Lenin argued that an executive party led by Lenin himself should rule the state on behalf of the people.

Although Trotsky later made efforts to reconcile the two parties, he was awkward and inconsistent, repeatedly failing back and attacking Lenin. As a result he was a revolutionary without a faction. The situation was rescued in 1905. Trotsky rushed from Geneva to St. Petersburg when he heard that a czarist attack on nonviolent demonstrators on "Bloody Sunday"—January 22, 1905—had triggered unrest. The unrest became the unsuccessful revolution of 1905. The St. Petersburg Soviet (communist council) of Workers' Deputies was formed. In October of 1905, unions paralyzed the city. Trotsky fled briefly to the safety of Finland but returned and became deputy leader of the Soviet. For the last eleven days of the Soviet, Trotsky was actually its leader. By December the revolution had run its course, and the czar's forces were again in control. Trotsky agreed to the Soviet's peaceful surrender. He was exiled for life to Siberia.

Leon Trotsky *(National Archives)*

1495

Leon Trotsky and other Russian revolutionary leaders reviewing the Red Army in Moscow. *(Library of Congress)*

Exile Again

Trotsky escaped before he arrived in Siberia. He made his way safely to Finland and later to Vienna, where his sons were born in 1906 and 1908. He lived in the suspended state of an exiled revolutionary except for work as a war correspondent in the Balkans. When World War I broke out, he left Vienna quickly for Switzerland

---

Trotsky's Siberian Exile

Arrested in 1898 and jailed variously in Nikolayev, Odessa, and Moscow (where he married Alexandra Sokolovskaya), Leon Trotsky was sentenced to four years' exile in Siberia in 1899. He was moved to Ust-Kut, a tiny peasant village on the Lena River, in the summer of 1900. There he read *Das Kapital* for the first time as well as Lenin's manifesto, *What Is to Be Done?* After the birth of their first daughter, the Trotskys moved to Verkholensk, where Trotsky studied with other Marxist exiles. He also wrote for a liberal newspaper in Irkutsk. Shortly after the birth of a second daughter in 1902, and with his wife's full support, he escaped alone to the south and east to join the central movement that was beginning to organize Marxism in Russia. The movement's voice was Lenin's journal, *Iskra*.

The Red Army, 1918-1921

Leon Trosky's leadership of the Red Army was more a triumph of his personal fervor than of military skill. In the early campaigns of Russia's civil war he exhorted the troops, traveling by armored train to the battlefronts. He soon won an argument with the Bolshevik leadership that allowed him to recruit skilled former czarist officers. The first engagements, which evicted the Czechoslovak Legion from the Upper Volga region, began September 10, 1918. In the spring of 1919 a White Army under Admiral Kolchak was forced from the Upper Volga region. When Kamenev was made commander in chief, he and Trotsky clashed. Shortly thereafter, both Moscow and Petrograd were under threat. In Octo-

ber, 1919, Trotsky personally oversaw the defense of Petrograd, and on October 21, with the support of armed factory workers and military students, Yudenich's army was driven from the city.

When war with Poland erupted in 1920 in Ukraine, Trotsky assisted by managing transport, but Warsaw was not taken. A truce with Poland in October, 1920, allowed Trotsky to move troops into the final campaign of the civil war against Baron Peter Wrangel in the Crimea. His last action was filled with bitter irony: The Kronstadt naval base near Petrograd revolted against severe economic strictures, and Trotsky had to quell internal Soviet rebellion.

and proceeded to Paris as a correspondent. From there he helped organize the Zimmerwald Conference and Manifesto. However, Trotsky's French newspaper, *Nashe Slovo*, so upset the French government that he was expelled, spending two months in Spain. Spain tried to expel him to Cuba, but he went to New York instead, arriving with his family in January, 1917. There he wrote and spoke, met with nascent socialist organizations, and was well received. He soon sought to return to Russia, where the 1917 revolution was beginning, but he was detained for several months by British authorities when his ship docked in Halifax.

Russia in 1917 and After

Lenin arrived in Petrograd (formerly St. Petersburg) before Trotsky did. Trotsky, although not fully aligned with the Bolshevik vision, supported Lenin's drive to take over the new provisional government by any means. Lenin had to flee temporarily to Finland, so it was Trotsky who oversaw the reorganization of the Soviet which put the organization in Bolshevik hands in Sep-

tember, 1917. On November 7 the provisional government fell.

Trotsky refused to head the new government, instead becoming commissar for foreign affairs. He found himself handling crises in transport, food, and publications as well. He oversaw a costly but necessary peace with Germany. He soon resigned but was immediately named chairman of the Supreme War Council to contend with White Russian resistance. From 1918 to 1921 he oversaw the creation of the Red Army and its victory in the civil war.

From Lenin to Stalin

Trotsky was less suited to bureaucracy than to revolution. He turned down Lenin's offer of deputy chairman in 1922, and soon the political situation changed with Lenin's illness; Lenin died in 1924. Trotsky had not prepared to use the army as a power base and was outside the "Old Bolshevik" group now led by Joseph Stalin. Stalin had maneuvered Trotsky out of power by 1928. Trotsky did not actively oppose him until it was too late, and he was sentenced to reasonably liberal internal exile near the Chinese border in 1928.

Exile and Assassination

Since even internal exile did not completely sever his connections with his anti-Stalin elements, Trotsky and his family were sent to Constantinople (Istanbul) in 1929. They obtained residence in France in 1933, in Norway in 1935, and finally asylum in Mexico in 1937 at the home of painter Diego Rivera. By this time Stalin's show trials had repeatedly condemned Trotsky, and a number of his followers had been hunted down outside Russia. Trotsky moved into a fortified house, but despite bodyguards and police he was assassinated in 1940 by an agent wielding an ice pick.

Leon Trotsky was a passionate, untiring revolutionary, an intellectual in action for the highest moral reasons. His failures at political intrigue cost his life and the lives of thousands of his Russian supporters. Nevertheless, he was one of the key men who launched Russia into the modern age.

Bibliography

Cliff, Tony. *Trotsky: Towards October*. Chicago: Bookmarks, 1989.

_____. *Trotsky: The Sword of the Revolution, 1917-1923*. Chicago: Bookmarks, 1990.

_____. *Trotsky: Fighting the Rising Stalinist Bureaucracy, 1923-1927*. Chicago: Bookmarks, 1991.

Dugrand, Alain. *Trotsky in Mexico*. Manchester, England: Carcanet, 1992.

Howe, Irving. *Leon Trotsky*. New York: Viking, 1978.

Payne, Robert. *The Life and Death of Trotsky*. New York: McGraw-Hill, 1977.

Warth, Robert D. *Leon Trotsky*. New York: Twayne, 1977.

Peter Brigg

Pierre Elliott Trudeau

Born: October 18, 1919; Montreal, Canada

Two-time prime minister of Canada (1968-1979, 1980-1984)

Pierre Elliott Trudeau (pee-AYR eh-lee-UHT trew-DOH) was born in Montreal to a wealthy French-Canadian businessman and an English-Canadian mother. After being educated by Jesuits, he attended the University of Montreal before continuing his education at Harvard University and the London School of Economics. Trudeau did not marry until 1971, when Margaret Sinclair became his wife. They had three children before divorcing in 1984.

Entering Politics in Quebec

After a year abroad, Trudeau returned to Quebec in 1949 and actively opposed the provincial government of Maurice Duplessis, well known for its corruption and authoritarianism. He and several others began publishing a journal called *Cité Libre*, which became a forum for critics of both the government and Quebec society in general. Trudeau was especially controversial because of his strong attacks on French-Canadian nationalism, which he argued reinforced Quebec's backwardness and promoted intolerance.

By the 1960's Quebec was rapidly modernizing, and French-Canadian nationalism grew just as quickly. Trudeau, now a law professor at the University of Montreal, continued to argue that remaining a part of Canada rather than seeking independence was the best option for Quebecers. This message made Trudeau popular with the federal government of Prime Minister Lester B. Pearson, which was seeking to rejuvenate itself in Quebec.

Moving to Ottawa

In 1965 Pearson appointed Trudeau and two other prominent Québécois to his government. Two years later, Trudeau became the minister of justice and gained national attention for his liberalization of laws governing abortion, divorce, and homosexuality. The national profile paid off for Trudeau in 1968. Pearson resigned and Trudeau, now age forty-eight, became the new Liberal leader and Canada's fifteenth prime minister. Shortly afterward, Trudeau called an election. During the campaign the Canadian electorate experienced "Trudeaumania" as the attractive and single Trudeau proved an exciting option to voters. The Liberals under Trudeau decisively won the election.

Pierre Elliott Trudeau *(Library of Congress)*

Canadian prime minister Pierre Trudeau addressing the nation. *(Archive Photos)*

The Years in Power

The reality of governing proved difficult for the intellectual Trudeau. He almost immediately had to deal with growing discontent in Quebec.

In 1969, official bilingualism was introduced in an effort to protect the place of French Canadians in Canada. The policy, however, proved unpopular with many English-speaking Canadians. It also did little to reduce nationalist sentiment in Quebec. During the 1960's, some Québécois used violence in an effort to gain independence. In October, 1970, events reached a crisis stage after the British high commissioner to Canada and a Quebec provincial cabinet minister were kidnapped by members of the Front de Libération du Québec, a terrorist organization. In response Trudeau invoked the War Measures Act, legislation which suspended Canadian civil liberties. The British hostage was eventually freed, but the Quebec cabinet minister was mur-

The Liberal Party

The Liberal Party, a Canadian political party, has been nicknamed "Canada's government party." The nickname is an accurate reflection of reality. During the twentieth century, members of the Liberal Party have held power in Canada for sixty-nine years.

The party itself originated in the nineteenth century. Its key to electoral success has been the ability to win support in both English and French Canada, specifically the province of Quebec. Quebec voters have tended to vote in a block, usually for the Liberals, whereas English Canada tends to split its vote, with the Liberals still winning a substantial portion. In order to ensure the continuance of this linguistic coali-

tion, the party has, since the nineteenth century, alternated between French and English Canadian leaders.

Only during World War I and in the 1980's did the Liberal coalition founder. During the former, the party was relegated almost exclusively to Quebec because of its opposition to the conscription of Canadian men for military service overseas. During the 1980's, the party lost power after its dominant leader of the second part of the twentieth century, Pierre Trudeau, retired. By 1993, however, it was rejuvenated, winning the election through a return of strong support in Quebec and parts of English Canada.

Trudeau and the "Pentagon Pip-squeaks"

Pierre Trudeau's last term in office (1980-1984) coincided with a dramatic escalation in tensions between the United States and the Soviet Union. Determined to reduce tensions, Trudeau embarked on an international peace mission in 1983 and 1984. Traveling to several countries, Canada's prime minister called for a reduction in the number of nuclear weapons. He and his mission were widely criticized, especially in the United States. In return, the Canadian prime minister referred to his American critics as "Pentagon pip-squeaks." Nevertheless, nothing tangible was achieved in his mission. In fact, it was during this period that the Canadian government gave permission to the United States to test its newly developed cruise missile over Canadian soil. Critics pointed out the contradiction between Trudeau's defense and foreign policies.

dered. Canadians generally approved of Trudeau's handling of the crisis, but he was also widely criticized, especially in Quebec, for his use of such draconian measures.

By the early 1970's, a combination of economic problems and the rapid pace of change introduced by his government had upset many Canadians. In the 1972 federal election Trudeau and the Liberals were reduced to a minority government. Two years later Trudeau called a new election, this time winning a majority government.

The economy and problems with Quebec continued to bedevil Trudeau in the latter half of the 1970's. Runaway inflation proved difficult to control, and in 1976 a party seeking the peaceful separation of Quebec from Canada was elected in that province. By paying so much attention to Quebec, Trudeau alienated western Canadians. By 1979 discontent with the Trudeau government was widespread. In the election of that year the Trudeau government was narrowly defeated by the Progressive Conservatives under the leadership of Joe Clark. Trudeau announced his retirement, and his political career appeared over.

Pierre Trudeau arriving in Havana in 1976; Cuban premier Fidel Castro is at left. It would be twenty-two years before another Canadian prime minister, Jean Chrétien, would visit Cuba. *(AP/ Wide World Photos)*

The Return and the End

Before the Liberals could select a leader to replace Trudeau, however, Joe Clark was forced to call an election. Trudeau won a majority government and returned to office in 1980. His final term would see his government involved in several controversial measures. In 1980 the separatist government in Quebec held a referendum asking Quebecers to provide it with a mandate to negotiate for a sovereign Quebec. The referendum was defeated by Trudeau and the federalist side, in part because of a promise by the prime minister that constitutional change would occur. That change came two years later when Trudeau managed to repatriate and amend the Canadian constitution. The Charter of Rights and Freedoms was added to the constitution, enshrining Canadian civil rights in law for the first time. However, Trudeau's heavy-handed handling of the constitutional issue only further isolated and alienated Quebec; its government symbolically refused to sign the new constitution. An attempt to nationalize the Canadian energy sector also angered western Canadians. Finally, high inflation and high unemployment gripped Canada throughout Trudeau's final years. Because of these problems and fiscal mismanagement, the federal government began to experience increasingly large budgetary deficits, contributing to a burgeoning national debt and future financial difficulties.

In 1984 Trudeau announced his retirement. He was succeeded as party leader and prime minister by John Turner. Trudeau returned to private life as a lawyer in Montreal. In the 1980's and 1990's he continued to speak out on issues related to the constitution and the place of Quebec in the Canadian confederation. His most lasting legacy was the 1982 constitutional change, especially the Charter of Rights and Freedoms, which has had a dramatic impact on the nature of Canadian society. Other problems related to regional alienation, French-Canadian nationalism, and economic turmoil were exacerbated during his time in office.

Bibliography

Clarkson, Stephen, and Christina McCall-Newman. *Trudeau and Our Times*. Toronto: McClelland & Stewart, 1990.

Gwyn, Richard J. *The Northern Magus: Pierre Trudeau and Canadians*. Toronto: McClelland & Stewart, 1980.

Trudeau, Pierre Elliott. *Federalism and the French Canadians*. New York: St. Martin's Press, 1968.

_____. *Memoirs*. Toronto: McClelland & Stewart, 1993.

Steve Hewitt

Rafael Trujillo

Born: October 24, 1891; San Cristóbal, Dominican Republic
Died: May 30, 1961; Ciudad Trujillo (now Santo Domingo), Dominican Republic

Dictatorial head of the Dominican Republic (1930-1961)

Rafael Leónidas Trujillo Molina (rah-fah-EHL lay-oh-NEE-thahs trew-HEE-yoh moh-LEE-nah) was the third of eleven children born to José and Altagracia Trujillo Valdéz. José Trujillo operated as a businessman and independent contractor, dealing in lumber, tobacco, coffee, and cattle. Rafael Trujillo received only a modest education and before entering public life held only minor clerical positions in the local telegraph office and at a sugar mill.

Early Career

In 1915 the U.S. government began a military occupation of the Dominican Republic, fearing intervention by European powers on behalf of their creditors. Two years later the U.S. military personnel managing the country established the Dominican National Guard. Trujillo applied for a commission in the new organization. Upper-class Dominicans had refused to apply for openings since they resented the imposition of American occupation forces on their country. On the other hand, the young Trujillo saw the establishment of the new military structure as a career opportunity. Under U.S. supervision, he advanced to the rank of general in what became the Dominican National Army in a matter of only ten years. When the United States ended its occupation in 1924, Trujillo was on his way to securing command of the most powerful force within the country, the army. In 1928 he became chief of the army.

Dictatorship

Taking advantage of a weak presidential administration, Trujillo began to undermine it with a combination of guile and civil disorder, launched surreptitiously by his army subordinates. The U.S. legation suspected that he was behind the turmoil, but Trujillo managed to convince them otherwise. Throughout his political life he sought to maintain good relations with the United States.

By literally terrorizing his political opposition, Trujillo launched a campaign for the presidency and won the office without any opposition. He began his thirty-one years of totalitarian rule in 1930. His first action was to secure recognition of his administration by the United States. He informed the local legation that he would seek its assistance in every matter of importance and be guided by it throughout his administration. Internally, he began a ruthless campaign of eliminating any Dominican whom he saw as an enemy. Some were killed out of hand; others fled the

Rafael Trujillo *(Archive Photos)*

The Assassination of Trujillo

Generalissimo Rafael Leónidas Trujillo Molina died in a hail of gunfire on May 30, 1961. Trujillo was riding in the back seat of a Chevrolet BelAir, accompanied only by his driver, Captain Zacarías de la Cruz. The dictator was armed with both machine guns and revolvers, his customary practice. The four assassins, all members of or allied with prominent Dominican families, drove alongside the Trujillo vehicle and opened fire. Both the driver and Trujillo, though wounded, returned fire. The conspirators were hit as well. Finally, one of the assassins, Antonio de la Meza, managed to crawl up to the dictator's vehicle and fired a shotgun blast directly into Trujillo's chest. Trujillo died immediately, a pistol still clutched in his hand. So ended the life of the tyrant who had controlled the destiny of his country for more than thirty-one years.

country. Trujillo maintained absolute control in a manner practiced by Adolf Hitler and Joseph Stalin. He dominated the country's economy as well, and he regarded all economic activity as an opportunity to enrich himself, his family members, and his political supporters.

Although the paternal side of his family had come to the Dominican Republic from Haiti, Trujillo despised the Haitians. On October 2, 1937, he used supposed border violations to unleash a massacre along the border that resulted in the deaths of an estimated fifteen thousand to twenty thousand Haitians. He managed to conceal the enormity of the crime from the outside world and paid half a million dollars to Haiti as compensation. Trujillo was able to maintain his excellent relations with the U.S. government despite the horrendous crime. In subsequent years the dictator allowed selected followers to assume the country's presidency, but he never relinquished his tight hold over the country's politics, economy, and army.

Trujillo's rule finally ended in 1961 in the only way that his power could be broken: A group of political opponents formed a conspiracy and managed to waylay and kill him. Most paid for their participation in the assassination with their lives at the hands of the dictator's survivors. The country, however, was finally freed from the shackles of the Trujillo dictatorship.

Dominican Republic head of state Rafael Trujillo being hugged by a woman whose son he ordered released from prison. (*Archive Photos*)

Bibliography

Crassweller, Robert D. *Trujillo: The Life and Times of a Caribbean Dictator*. New York: Macmillan, 1966.

Diederich, Bernard. *Trujillo: The Death of the Goat*. Boston: Little, Brown, 1978.

Carl Henry Marcoux

Harry S Truman

Born: May 8, 1884; Lamar, Missouri
Died: December 26, 1972; Kansas City, Missouri

President of the United States (1945-1953)

The father of Harry S Truman (HEH-ree EHS TREW-muhn), John Truman, followed a number of vocations ranging from farming to speculating in grain to being a night watchman. His mother, Martha, was a bright, college-educated woman from a prosperous family. Harry, his brother, and his sister, were raised in Independence, Missouri. In 1919, Truman married Elizabeth "Bess" Wallace, a marriage that produced one daughter, Margaret. Truman served in the Army during World War I and, in 1922, was elected a judge in Jackson County, Missouri. In 1934 he became a U.S. senator. In 1944 Truman was selected as Franklin D. Roosevelt's running mate in Roosevelt's bid for a fourth term as president. Upon Roosevelt's death on April 12, 1945, Truman became president of the United States. He was reelected in 1948.

Before the Presidency

Harry Truman was not college educated, but he had an uncommon ability to assess difficult situations judiciously and, after weighing the facts and alternatives, act decisively. He and Eddie Jacobson owned a haberdashery in Kansas City before Truman's election to the judgeship, Truman acting as bookkeeper, Jacobson as buyer.

Missouri politics were strongly controlled by Thomas J. Pendergast in the 1920's. Truman became associated with the so-called Pendergast machine, which supported his bid for a judgeship. When he came up for reelection in 1924, however, Truman was defeated, the only election he ever lost in a career that spanned four decades. In 1926, with substantial help from Pendergast, Truman was elected presiding judge of Jackson County. Truman threw himself into civic projects and, when the Great Depression of the early

1930's created severe economic strife throughout the United States, Truman devised a six-county regional plan that gained him national recognition. In 1934, after Pendergast's two top choices to run for the Senate declined, Pendergast turned to Truman. With a campaign chest of only nine thousand dollars, Truman campaigned vigorously, narrowly won nomination, and in November soundly defeated the Republican candidate.

Despite accepting Pendergast's help and support, Truman, who sought always to be meticulously honest, never profited personally from their association. He did, however, sometimes

Harry S Truman *(Library of Congress)*

1505

U.S. president Harry S Truman (center) at the Potsdam Conference in 1945, at the conclusion of World War II. British prime minister Winston Churchill is at left, Soviet premier Josef Stalin at right. *(National Archives)*

use his position to appoint Pendergast's cronies to political positions, thereby strengthening the Pendergast machine. Truman realized the necessity for political organization and defended machine politics as an efficient way of getting things done. He managed, remarkably, to maintain his integrity while simultaneously being loyal to Pendergast.

As a senator, Truman acted independently, always gathering extensive facts and voting his conscience on the basis of those facts. He served admirably as a member of the appropriations and

Dropping the Atomic Bomb

U.S. Marines captured the Japanese island of Okinawa in June, 1945. The next step logically was to invade the Japanese mainland. Five months earlier, in their defense of Iwo Jima, the Japanese had demonstrated their willingness to fight to the death to maintain their territory. More than twenty thousand Japanese died on Iwo Jima, and nearly seven thousand U.S. Marines were killed. President Harry S Truman had to reach a difficult decision: Was it now best to invade the Japanese mainland and incur enormous American casualties or to unleash nuclear weapons upon the enemy to bring the war to an end? Truman opted to bomb Japan with the recently developed atomic bombs. On August 6, 1945, Hiroshima was bombed, resulting in 140,000 Japanese casualties, mostly civilians. On August 9, a plutonium bomb was dropped on Nagasaki, which suffered 100,000 casualties. Within days, Japan surrendered.

The Truman Doctrine

Harry S Truman requested $400 million in military aid for Greece and Turkey to thwart the spread of communism in those countries. He promised similar aid to other countries in danger of falling under communist domination. The U.S. Congress, with which Truman had a solid relationship, supported the proposal and enacted two policies germane to it. First, it accepted the plan of Secretary of State George Marshall, called the Marshall Plan, to provide up to $22 billion of American aid over a four-year period to help Europe regain its prosperity. This integrated plan affected all of Europe rather than individual nations. Second, on April 4, 1949, Congress approved the United States' entry into the North Atlantic Treaty Organization (NATO), a defense pact involving Belgium, Canada, Denmark, France, Great Britain, Iceland, Italy, Luxembourg, the Netherlands, Norway, and Portugal. The chief goal of the Truman Doctrine was to contain communism.

---

interstate commerce committees and worked tirelessly to create the Civil Aeronautics Board. Although Truman consistently supported President Roosevelt's social reforms, Roosevelt had little respect for the senator from Missouri because he viewed him as a Pendergast puppet. Such reservations did not prevent Truman from winning reelection in 1940. During World War II, he gained increased recognition for his hard work in the Senate and emerged as one of its leaders.

Truman's dedicated efforts led to the establishment of the War Production Board, for which Roosevelt took full credit without even a nod to Truman. When Roosevelt ran for his fourth term in 1944, Harry Truman—quite reluctantly—became his running mate. Roosevelt was in perilous health. Truman served as vice president for only eleven weeks before Roosevelt's death. During that time, he met with the president only twice, and Roosevelt neglected to share with him information about crucial affairs of state.

The Truman Presidency

The United States was still at war when Harry S Truman became the thirty-third president of the United States on April 12, 1945. The war in Europe was winding down, but the Pacific war was still raging. Truman was uninformed about many of the details of national policy during Roosevelt's final months. Truman therefore became the leader of a nation at war but had little notion of what was occurring officially in the conduct of that war. His first job was to gather information. As president, Truman was fond of saying from his desk in the Oval Office, "The buck stops here." Realizing that decisions had to be made, he acted decisively when the need arose. The most crucial decision he had to make in his early days as president concerned the use of nuclear weapons as a means of ending the war with Japan.

The development of the atomic bomb had proceeded in the United States in secret for many years, and the military now had produced operational atomic weapons. Truman gave his approval to the dropping of the atomic bomb on Japan in the hope that it would save American lives and hasten the war's end. On August 6 and 9, 1945, two bombs were dropped on Japanese cities. Japan quickly surrendered, and World War II was over.

With the war at an end, Truman was faced with helping the world return to normal. Lacking Roosevelt's charisma and popular appeal, the new president faced an uphill battle. He realized, nevertheless, what had to be done and, with characteristic zeal, set about doing it. Peace in Europe had brought about a contest between the Soviet Union and the free world, dominated by Britain, France, and the United States. Each controlled parts of Germany and Austria. In war-ravaged Europe, economic recovery was slow. Truman knew that the contest between communism and democracy presented a menacing threat to the West, so on March 12, 1947, he presented Congress with his solution, the Truman Doctrine. The Truman Doctrine included providing military aid and advisers to countries in danger of communist takeover; among the early recipients of aid were Greece and Turkey. Any country in similar danger, according to Truman, could also expect to receive U.S. aid.

Harry Truman ran for reelection against Thomas Dewey in 1948. His margin of victory was so small that some newspapers declared Dewey the winner before all the votes were counted. Truman declined to run for a second full term in 1952. He returned to private life in Independence, Missouri.

Bibliography

Feinberg, Barbara Silberdick. *Harry S. Truman*. New York: Franklin Watts, 1994.

Leavell, J. Perry, Jr. *Harry S. Truman*. New York: Chelsea House, 1988.

McCullough, David. *Truman*. New York: Simon and Schuster, 1992.

Miller, Merle. *Plain Speaking*. New York: G. P. Putnam's Sons, 1982.

Miller, Richard Lawrence. *Truman: The Rise to Power*. New York: McGraw-Hill, 1985.

R. Baird Shuman

Moïse Tshombe

Born: November 10, 1919; Musamba, Katanga, the Belgian Congo (now Congo)
Died: June 29, 1969; near Algiers, Algeria

Katanga secessionist leader (1960-1963), prime minister of the Congo (1964-1965)

Moïse Kapenda Tshombe (moh-EES kah-PEHN-dah SHOM-bay) was born in the traditional capital of the Lunda Empire, in the Belgian Congo's mineral-rich southeastern province of Katanga. His family was related to Lunda kings. His father was a traditional chief who worked closely with Belgian colonial authorities and later became a millionaire. Tshombe received his primary education from Methodist missionaries at Sandoa, then obtained diplomas in teaching and accounting. In the 1950's, he helped found the Lunda-dominated Conakat Party. He led the Conakat delegation to preindependence conferences in 1960. The Congo became independent that same year. In elections that same year, Tshombe was elected to the National Assembly as a delegate from Katanga, but his southern-based supporters failed to obtain enough seats elsewhere in the country to form a majority.

Secessionist Leader

Fighting broke out in the south as the Lunda gradually edged the Luba people out of influence in Katangan politics. Tshombe was angered by what he felt was a lack of Katangan representation in the Congo government of the fervent nationalist Patrice Lumumba. Encouraged by Belgian commercial interests in Katanga, Tshombe declared Katanga independent of the Congo on July 11, 1960. Supported by Belgium, the Katanga secession brought the first mercenaries to independent Africa. It also prompted the United Nations' first police action on the continent.

Lumumba's appeals for aid from the Soviet bloc countries undermined his international reputation. Western governments viewed him as a dangerous pro-Soviet radical. Lumumba's government collapsed in chaos. Captured while at-tempting to escape and join his supporters in Stanleyville, Lumumba was flown to Katanga, where Tshombe's forces murdered him on arrival on January 17, 1961. Lumumba's death has been attributed to a conspiracy between General Joseph Mobutu (Mobutu Sese Seko) and Tshombe, in which the U.S. Central Intelligence Agency (CIA) is also believed to have been involved. The Katanga secession was ended in

Moïse Tshombe *(Library of Congress)*

Moïse Tshombe, Katanga secession leader and future prime minister of the Congo, in 1963 exhorting his followers to continue their fight. *(Archive Photos)*

January, 1963, and Tshombe went into exile in Spain.

Controversial Prime Minister

In 1964, Congolese president Joseph Kasavubu named Tshombe prime minister, with a mandate to end rebellions in Kwilu and the eastern provinces. The Tshombe government was installed on July 6, 1964; Tshombe himself held five cabinet posts. He subsequently infuriated many African leaders and diplomats by hiring mercenaries, many of them veterans of the Katanga secession. He also authorized a Belgian air drop on Stanleyville. Under the 1964 constitution, the prime minister assumed greater powers, and Tshombe's party scored significant gains in elections in 1965.

However, Kasavubu dismissed Tshombe on October 13, 1965, and appointed Evariste Kimba to form a government. Kimba's attempt was blocked by Tshombe's supporters. The situation led to a stalemate that was one of the major reasons for the military coup led by Mobutu on November 24, 1965. Tshombe fled into exile in Spain once again as the Congo descended into

The Katangan Republic

When the Congo gained independence from Belgium on June 30, 1960, Moïse Tshombe's Conakat Party swept local elections in the Congo's southeastern Katanga Province. His Lunda tribe dominated the government of Katanga, an area rich in copper, diamonds, and uranium. Katanga was unhappy with Conakat's minimal representation in the national government and was polarized along ethnic lines. Encouraged by commercial interests and by an organization of European residents called the Union Katangaise, Katanga seceded from the new nation of the Congo only twelve days after independence. Recognized by several foreign governments, the Katanga Republic held world attention for two years as Tshombe stalled mediation efforts. The United Nations (U.N.) attempted numerous approaches to reunification. Congo's first prime minister, Patrice Lumumba, and U.N. secretary-general Dag Hammarskjöld both died: Lumumba was murdered, and Hammarskjöld died in a plane crash. Thousands of Luba and Lunda peoples were killed in ethnic fighting. Only after two U.N. military actions, which were condemned by some members of the international community, was the Katanga secession declared ended on January 14, 1963. Katanga was renamed in the 1970's, becoming known as the Shaba region.

decades of corrupt dictatorship and economic decline under Mobutu, who renamed the country Zaire. Tshombe was condemned to death in absentia for high treason on March 13, 1967. On June 30, he was kidnapped while on a flight over the Mediterranean and placed under house arrest in Algeria. The Algerian government announced that he died of a heart attack on June 29, 1969. To many people, the controversial Tshombe epitomized the destructive tribalism of Congolese politics and the subservience of some postindependence leaders to foreign interests. To others, however, he was a pragmatic leader who attempted to unify the country.

Bibliography

Kanza, Thomas. *The Rise and Fall of Patrice Lumumba*. Rochester, Vt.: Schenkman, 1994.

Lemarchand, René. *Political Awakening in the Belgian Congo*. Berkeley: University of California Press, 1964.

Tshombe, Moïse. *My Fifteen Months in Government*. Plano, Tex.: University of Plano, 1967.

Randall Fegley

William V. S. Tubman

Born: November 29, 1895; Harper, Liberia
Died: July 23, 1971; London, England

President of Liberia (1944-1971)

The paternal grandfather of William Vacanarat Shadrach Tubman (WIHL-yuhm va-ka-NAH-rat SHAY-drak TOOB-mahn) arrived in Liberia in 1837, the freed slave of Richard Tubman of Georgia. His mother's family emigrated from Georgia to Liberia in 1872. William's father, a Methodist preacher and stonemason, served in both the Liberian House of Representatives and the Senate. William was raised in Cape Palmas and educated at a Methodist seminary. In 1914 he became a Methodist lay preacher and taught at the Las Palmas Seminary until 1920. William also studied law, passing the bar exam in 1917. As a lawyer he established a reputation for defending poor clients. This reputation later helped attract grassroots support for his rising political career, which began with his entrance into local government as county attorney for Maryland County. Tubman also became active in a number of Masonic lodges, rising to top positions.

It was a fortuitous welcoming speech in 1920 during a Masonic banquet in honor of a powerful visitor, Liberian president Charles King, that propelled Tubman into national politics. In 1921, when a Senate seat opened because Senator H. Wesley moved to the vice presidency, King supported Tubman for the position. The twenty-eight-year-old Tubman, representing the True Whig Party, a party which had dominated Liberia since the 1870's, became the youngest senator in Liberia's history.

National Leadership

Loyalty to President King, who was accused by the League of Nations of supporting slavery in Liberia through contract labor of tribal Liberians to foreign companies, almost wrecked Tubman's career. He served as adviser to King and defended King's actions. King's resignation in 1930 caused Tubman to resign as well. However, Tubman regained his Senate seat in 1934 and, in 1937, was appointed by President Edwin Barclay as associate justice of the Supreme Court. When Barclay, following the constitution, ended his presidency after completing his second term, Tubman was his hand-picked successor. The election of May, 1943, saw Tubman lead the True Whig Party to victory. Barclay and president-elect Tubman (scheduled to take office in January,

William V. S. Tubman *(Popperfoto/Archive Photos)*

1944) visited U.S. president Franklin D. Roosevelt and became the first black visitors to stay overnight at the White House. During the visit, Tubman negotiated loans for Liberia and the construction of a deep-water port for Monrovia, its capital, in return for rubber-rich Liberia's entry into World War II on the side of the Allies. Three weeks after beginning his presidency, Tubman brought Liberia into the war. A host of other changes were also planned.

One month after taking office, Tubman announced his Unification Policy. He attacked the concept that Americo-Liberians, only 5 percent of the population, were entitled to special privileges. He proposed that universal adult suffrage be initiated. Shortly afterward came another new initiative, the open-door policy: Foreign investors would be invited into Liberia to build a more diversified economy. At the time, Liberia had only one foreign investor,

Liberian president William V. S. Tubman (second from left, front) shakes hands with the pastor of St. Mark's in New York after attending a service in 1954. *(Library of Congress)*

Firestone Corporation, which had gained control of Liberian rubber production in 1926. In the 1950's, Tubman's economic policy led to the development of rich iron-ore deposits in the hill country north of Monrovia. A consortium of Swedish and American investors undertook the

Universal Adult Suffrage

Throughout Liberia's history as a republic, indigenous Liberian Africans—constituting the overwhelming majority of the population—were not permitted to vote. In his election campaign of 1943, William V. S. Tubman advocated the principle of one person, one vote. He promised to extend the vote not only to indigenous Africans over the age of twenty-one but also to women. Tubman kept his promise on the centennial of Liberia's constitution (1947) by passing an amendment to the constitution granting the vote to all Liberians over the age of twenty-one, provided that they owned property and paid taxes.

By the end of 1947, three indigenous Liberians sat in the House of Representatives. In the 1951 national election, women and native Liberians voted for the first time for a national president. Tubman, who had changed the constitution to avoid being limited to two terms, was elected president. He continued to be reelected until he died at the beginning of his seventh term. As indigenous Liberians attempted to form their own political parties, such as the Reformation Party and the United People's Party, they were vigorously suppressed. The extension of voting rights was not intended to bring about true political change.

Liberian Public Expenditures

Public expenditures rapidly increased during the first quarter century of William V. S. Tubman's presidency. Revenues were spent on public projects, including expansion of the University of Liberia, bringing a water system to Monrovia, building a merchant fleet, and developing transportation and communication capabilities. Operation Production was launched in 1963, comprising a series of five-year plans aimed at producing self-sufficiency in rice (Liberia's staple) and in creating small Liberian businesses to replace Lebanese dominance of the retail and wholesale trades.

However, the fall of rubber and mineral prices in the late 1960's, coupled with a rise in the national debt, produced a financial crisis. Government expenditures were dramatically cut, and even the multitude of government workers—on whom Tubman's patronage system rested—saw their salaries cut. Periodically, they went unpaid. Tubman toured the country making austerity speeches, urging both government officials and the public to "watch their pennies." While austerity was imposed at the public level, however, Tubman and his inner circle continued lavish spending on travel and accumulating estates and plantations. In Tubman's austerity program, cracking down on government corruption at the higher levels was not on the agenda.

development. German investors developed rich iron-ore deposits in the Bong Mountains. By 1967, Liberia had become the world's third largest exporter of iron ore. A flood of Lebanese and other foreign merchants came to Liberia to handle the wholesale and retail trade.

Negative Aspects of Tubman's Leadership

Tubman's development policy increased government revenues from $1 million when he took power to $55 million by 1967. However, although he created tens of thousands of low-paying jobs through foreign concessions, his policies did little to encourage a Liberian entrepreneurial class—which might challenge the dominant True Whig Party. Government positions were one existing source of better-paying employment, and the patronage system became a major source of Tubman's political power. Unfortunately, the huge bureaucracy led to inefficiency, incompetence, and corruption. As the years passed, Tubman took charge of appointing people to most important government positions, including the appointment of the entire board of trustees of the

University of Liberia. Loyalty, not ability, was the prime consideration. Only a few small steps were taken after 1963 to encourage Liberian-owned business. Although Tubman encouraged tribal arts, visited reservations, banned racial discrimination (in 1958), and provided some education to rural areas by using U.S. Peace Corps volunteers, he did little to improve the living conditions and political power of indigenous Liberians.

In 1971, while undergoing a prostate operation in a London hospital, Tubman, the president of Liberia for the previous twenty-seven years, died from complications of the surgery. By then he seemed to some to be more like a dictator than the president of a republic, and he had a growing number of enemies, particularly in the army. During previous years he had survived several assassination attempts. Yet Liberians as a whole sincerely mourned the passing of Tubman. Though power still remained with a small group of Americo-Liberians, Tubman had projected to the nation an image of a leader who cared. To the rest of the world he appeared as the leader of a stable, developing nation. There was a smooth constitutional transition of power to Tubman's vice president, William Tolbert. Such was not the case when Tolbert was removed from office in 1980, killed in a bloody coup headed by army sergeant Samuel Doe.

Bibliography

Boley, G. Saigbe. *Liberia: The Rise and Fall of the First Republic*. New York: St. Martin's Press, 1984.

Henries, A. Banks. *A Biography of President William V. S. Tubman*. London: Macmillan, 1967.

Nelson, Harold D., ed. *Liberia: A Country Study*. 3d ed. Washington, D.C.: U.S. Government Printing Office, 1985.

Wreh, Tuan. *The Love of Liberty . . . : The Rule of President William V. S. Tubman in Liberia, 1944-1971*. London: C. Hurst, 1976.

Irwin Halfond

John Napier Turner

Born: June 7, 1929; Richmond, Surrey, England

Prime minister of Canada (1984)

John Napier Turner (JON NAYP-yur TUR-nur), Canada's seventeenth prime minister, arrived in Canada from England in 1932 after the death of his father. With his mother and stepfather, Turner moved to the province of British Columbia in the 1940's, where he attended the University of British Columbia. Reflecting his wealthy background, his education also included Oxford University and the University of Paris. Turner became a lawyer in Quebec in 1954. In 1963 he married Geils Kilgour, with whom he had four children.

John Napier Turner *(Camera Press Ltd./Archive Photos)*

In Power

In 1962 Turner's political career began when he was elected to Canada's federal parliament as a member of the Liberal Party for an electoral riding (district) in the city of Montreal. The ambitious Turner quickly rose through the political hierarchy, joining the cabinet of Prime Minister Lester Pearson in 1965. He achieved his first important cabinet post in 1968 in the government of newly elected Prime Minister Pierre Trudeau when he became the minister of justice. He served in that capacity until 1972, when he was appointed to the most important post in any Canadian cabinet, that of minister of finance. Canada was experiencing high inflation, which Turner was unable to bring under control. His tenure as finance minister marked the end of budgetary surpluses for the next twenty-four years.

Long rumored to have aspirations to be leader of the Liberal Party and prime minister, Turner found his path to the top blocked by Pierre Trudeau, who by the 1970's was entrenched as party leader and prime minister. Turner resigned suddenly in 1975 and returned to private life. He continued, however, to be mentioned as a candidate for the Liberal leadership whenever there was speculation about Trudeau's retirement.

Eighty Days and Beyond

The end of Trudeau's era as Liberal leader and prime minister arrived in 1984. Soon after Trudeau quit, Turner announced his candidacy for the leadership of the party. In June, 1984, he won the leadership on the second ballot, defeating Jean Chrétien. Because the Liberal Party held power, Turner automatically became prime minister of Canada. After governing for a brief period, he announced that an election would be

The Official Languages Act

In 1963 the Canadian government appointed a special commission to tour Canada. Its purpose was to examine Canada's official language policy. The government feared French-Canadian nationalism, centered almost exclusively in the province of Quebec and fueled partially by a fear of the decline of the French language. French-Canadian nationalism was an increasingly potent force in the 1960's. The commission's final report led the government of Prime Minister Pierre Trudeau to enact the Official Languages Act of 1969 during John Napier Turner's tenure as minister of justice. This policy rendered Canada officially bilingual at the federal level. In practice, this meant that French- and English-speaking Canadians could deal with their government in their own language. The new policy proved controversial. Many English-speaking Canadians found the presence of the French language a nuisance. Many French-speaking Canadians argued that the legislation is not sufficient, and they have continued to press for the independence of the province of Quebec.

held on September 4, 1984. On the campaign trail, however, Turner made several mistakes which reflected his long period outside active politics. His worst moment came during the election leadership debate, when Turner was unable to defend patronage appointments he had made after taking office.

Turner's eighty-day era as prime minister ended on election night, when he and the Liberals suffered a crushing defeat at the hands of Brian Mulroney and the Progressive Conservative Party. Turner's political career continued, however, despite criticism. He stayed on as leader of the opposition in the Canadian House of Commons. His next big political moment came during the federal election of 1988, when he focused his campaign against a free trade agreement signed between the Mulroney government and the United States. Turner vehemently opposed the agreement on nationalist grounds, arguing that it would inevitably lead to the absorption of Canada into the United States. Although support for the Liberals grew substantially in the 1988 election, the party finished second. Turner resigned after the 1988 election and was replaced by Jean Chrétien as Liberal leader in 1990. Turner returned to private life as a lawyer. His political legacy is not as prime minister but as leader of the opposition leading a spirited fight against the free trade agreement in the 1988 election. That fight won him a great deal of admiration, although ultimately it proved futile, as he lost the election and free trade with the United States continued unimpeded.

Bibliography

Graham, Ron. *One-Eyed Kings: Promise and Illusion in Canadian Politics*. Toronto: Collins, 1986.

Newman, Peter Charles. *The Canadian Revolution, 1985-1995: From Deference to Defiance*. Toronto: Viking, 1995.

Weston, Greg. *Reign of Error: The Inside Story of John Turner's Troubled Leadership*. Toronto: McGraw-Hill Ryerson, 1988.

Steve Hewitt

Desmond Tutu

Born: October 7, 1931; Klerksdorp, Transvaal, South Africa

Anglican archbishop of South Africa, antiapartheid activist, and winner of 1984 Nobel Peace Prize

The son of a schoolteacher and a domestic worker, Desmond Mpilo Tutu (DEHZ-muhnd ehm-PIH-loh TEW-tew) grew up around Johannesburg, South Africa's largest city. Tutu was baptized a Methodist. However, after an older sister entered an Anglican school, he and the rest of his family became Anglicans. His first career choice was to become a doctor. However, his family could not afford medical school tuition, so he trained to become a teacher.

Tutu graduated from college in 1954 and began teaching high school at a time when South Africa

Desmond Tutu *(The Nobel Foundation)*

was undergoing a fundamental political and social transformation. Since the National Party had taken power in 1948, the government had been tightening its control over the lives of Africans. Under a policy known as "apartheid," the government was restricting the freedoms and movements of African people and enacting increasingly harsh laws to suppress dissent. In 1957 the government implemented the Bantu Education Act. Under this measure the education system for Africans was separated entirely from that for whites and was made almost strictly vocational. (The government officially called Africans "Bantu" because most of them spoke Bantu languages, such as Sotho, Tswana, Xhosa, and Zulu.) The effect was to reduce the amount of money spent on Africans and to greatly lower educational standards.

Religious Calling

Disgusted by this development, Tutu quit his teaching job and began training for the priesthood in an Anglican theological college in Johannesburg. After being ordained in 1961 and graduating from the University of South Africa the following year, Tutu worked part-time as a curate and served as a theology instructor. In 1975 he became the Anglican Church's first black dean in South Africa.

In 1976 Tutu began his career as a public critic of apartheid by writing an open letter to Prime Minister John Vorster, asking him to relieve the sufferings of black South Africans by repealing the "homelands" system, which forced most Africans to make the impoverished rural areas from which their families originated their permanent homes. That same year Tutu was consecrated bishop of Lesotho.

Tutu's public visibility increased in 1977, when

he delivered the oration at the funeral of Steve Biko, a prominent antigovernment leader who had been killed by security police. The following year Tutu was made general secretary of the South African Council Churches, which represented most of the country's Christian denominations. As Tutu's reputation grew, he spoke more forcibly against the government's increasingly oppressive apartheid policies. During a visit to Europe in 1980, he called upon other nations not to buy South African coal in order to put pressure on the South African government. The government responded by confiscating his passport.

Archbishop Desmond Tutu visiting a Cape Town squatters' camp in 1990. The camp had been raided by police a few nights before, and three residents had been shot. *(AP/Wide World Photos)*

Through these years most black South Africans who openly criticized the government were either killed, imprisoned—as Nelson Mandela was—or "banned." (Banning was a punishment that restricted persons to their homes and made it illegal for anyone to mention their names or quote them publicly.) As one of the most prominent South Africans whose voice was still being heard, Tutu stood out as a leading spokesperson for South Africa's oppressed masses. In 1984 he was awarded the Nobel Peace

The Anglican Church and South Africa

Also known as the Church of England, the Anglican Church is a Protestant denomination. Its roots go back to the early sixteenth century, when England's King Henry VIII renounced the authority of Rome's pope and made himself head of an independent English church. After taking over the Catholic Church's properties, the new Church of England abandoned monastic orders but retained many of the beliefs, institutions, and clerical offices of the older church, including a hierarchy of priests, bishops, and archbishops.

The Anglican Church has been the most popular religious denomination among English immigrants to South Africa and their descendants. Moreover, because Anglican missionaries have long worked among African communities, Anglicanism became one of the most popular faiths among nonwhites as well. Under South Africa's apartheid regime, most ordinary means of political dissent were closed to Africans. As a result, many religious leaders, particularly Anglicans, played leading roles in speaking out against the government.

Apartheid

An Afrikaans word meaning "apartness," apartheid was the term applied to the system of total racial segregation that South Africa's government imposed through most of the late twentieth century. After the white-ruled Union of South Africa was created in 1910, racial segregation was the norm in the country. However, it was not until after the Afrikaner-dominated National Party took power in 1948 that segregation took on the severe trappings that eventually characterized apartheid. Under the Population Registration Act of 1950 the government began classifying all South Africans by race. Under the Group Areas Act of the same year the government began the forcible moving of many nonwhites to designated areas. Over the next four decades, the government passed further legislation that expanded and refined segregation to an extent unparalleled elsewhere in the world.

Not only was almost every aspect of daily life rigidly segregated—from separate telephone booths to separate school systems for blacks and whites—but also the government began creating separate regions called "homelands" for each major African community. The National Party's goal was to create separate nations for each group. Ultimately, however, the whole system collapsed in the 1990's. The reality of South African life was that growing economic interdependence among members of all races was making apartheid unworkable. Moreover, because the system was designed to give whites all the advantages, its inherent unfairness and the cruelties it imposed on nonwhites evoked growing internal opposition as well as harsh economic sanctions from the outside world.

Former South African president P. W. Botha shaking hands with Desmond Tutu in 1996. Tutu was chairman of South Africa's Truth and Reconciliation Commission, which collected evidence of rights abuses under the previous apartheid governments. *(AP/Wide World Photos)*

Prize. After Tutu returned home from receiving his Nobel Prize in Norway, he was elected bishop of Johannesburg, a position that made him the second-highest-ranking Anglican cleric in South Africa.

Rising Tensions and Violence

Meanwhile, violent opposition to apartheid within South Africa was rising to such a level that the government called a state of emergency. Tutu continued his criticisms of the government, both at home and abroad. At home, he received yet another honor when he was made archbishop of Cape Town. This position made him the highest-ranking Anglican cleric in South Africa—black or white. Despite his increasingly strong criticisms of the government, Tutu's position as a high-ranking clergyman and his growing international reputation made it difficult for the government to silence him.

Thanks to the unrelenting pressure placed on the South African government by internal critics such as Tutu, armed guerrilla fighters, and international sanctions, the white government finally decided to abandon apartheid and move to a system based on nonracial democracy. In 1994 the country held its first truly democratic elections. In fulfillment of a prediction that Tutu had made a decade earlier, Nelson Mandela was elected president of the country.

Truth and Reconciliation Commission

One of the most difficult challenges faced by the new government was dealing with the abuses—such as Biko's murder—perpetrated against citizens under the former apartheid regime. In order to confront unpleasant truths about the past and put them behind, the government created a Truth and Reconciliation Com-

mission to collect evidence. Mandela appointed Tutu, who had resigned his clerical posts, to head the commission. The appointment reflected Tutu's unchallenged stature as a moral leader.

Bibliography

Bentley, Judith. *Archbishop Tutu of South Africa*. Hillside, N.J.: Enslow Publishers, 1988.

Comerford, Patrick. *Tutu: Black Africa's Man of Destiny*. New York: Veritas IE, 1989.

Du Boulay, Shirley. *Tutu: The Voice of the Voiceless*. Grand Rapids, Mich.: Eerdman's, 1998.

Hendrik, J. C. Pieterse, ed. *Desmond Tutu's Message: A Qualitative Analysis*. Kampen, the Netherlands: Deutscher Studien Verlag, 1995.

Tlhagale, Buti, and Itumeleng J. Mosala, eds. *Hammering Swords into Ploughshares: Essays in Honor of Archbishop Mpilo Desmond Tutu*. Lawrenceville, N.J.: Africa World, 1987.

Tutu, Naomi, ed. *The Words of Desmond Tutu*. New York: Newmarket Press, 1989.

R. Kent Rasmussen

Tz'u-hsi

Born: November 29, 1835; Beijing, China
Died: November 15, 1908; Beijing, China

Empress dowager, dominant Chinese political figure from 1861 to the early 1900's

In the last decades of the nineteenth century, at a time when China was beleaguered by foreign imperialism and in dire need of reform, the effective ruler was a Manchu woman, Tz'u-hsi (TSOO-SHEE), or Cixi. She was the daughter of a junior government official in the Qing (or Ching, also called Manchu) Dynasty. At sixteen, she became a concubine of Emperor Xianfeng. In 1861, she became empress dowager and coregent when her five-year-old son, the only male progeny of Xianfeng, succeeded as Emperor Tongzhi.

Tz'u-hsi *(UPI/Corbis-Bettmann)*

Unlike most women in China, Tz'u-hsi could read and write, although she never received a formal education. For nearly half a century, she ruled China with a dominant will and unabashed power. Despite her literacy, she was profoundly ignorant of the outside world, an ignorance that was compounded by a hatred for the Western powers who, in 1860, had forced the court to flee from the summer palace near Beijing and then looted and burned the palace in retaliation for China's mistreatment of foreign envoys.

Opposition to Reform

In 1875, when Emperor Tongzhi died without an heir, Tz'u-hsi selected her young nephew, the son of her sister and an imperial prince, to be Emperor Guangxu. Thus began her second regency, which ended when Guangxu assumed the throne in 1889 at nineteen years of age.

In 1898, Emperor Guangxu was persuaded by the intellectual Kang Youwei to initiate a radical reform program aimed at modernizing the Chinese economy and instituting a constitutional monarchy. As the reforms directly threatened the power of Tz'u-hsi and her conservative supporters in government, she instigated a *coup d'état* on September 21, 1898. The emperor was imprisoned in the Forbidden City until his death ten years later; six reform leaders were executed, while others escaped by fleeing China. Tz'u-hsi resumed her regency.

The Boxer Rebellion

In June, 1900, thousands of Boxers—members of a secret society—undertook a xenophobic uprising across several provinces in northeastern China. The Boxers had the support and encouragement of Tz'u-hsi and conservative officials

Imperial Reforms

After the suppression of the Boxers by the allied forces, Tz'u-hsi was under domestic and foreign pressure to bring about reform. On January 29, 1901, she issued a reform decree in the emperor's name. Over the course of the next five years, the antiquated civil service examination was abolished, modern schools were established, including Beijing University, and Chinese students were sent abroad to study. In 1906, two official missions to Europe and the United States to study their constitutional governments returned with a recommendation that a constitutional monarchy be established. In 1908, regulations for provincial assemblies and for their elections were proclaimed, followed by a plan for the installation of a national constitution and parliament by 1917.

and princes. Inspired by superstition to believe that they were invincible to bullets, the Boxers destroyed telegraph lines and railways, burned Christian churches, and killed foreign missionaries and their Chinese converts. On June 20, the Manchu regime declared war on the foreign powers and laid siege to their legations as well as a Catholic cathedral in Beijing. Two months later, the Boxers were suppressed by an allied force of eight nations, including the United States, England, Germany, France, and Japan. The victorious allies imposed a severely punitive settlement on the Chinese government in 1901, exacting an indemnity of some $334 million.

In 1908, Emperor Guangxu died of an unknown illness; it has been widely suspected that Tz'u-hsi had him poisoned. A day later the empress dowager herself died from dysentery. The dynasty itself would collapse three years later because of a spontaneous revolution. Tz'u-hsi left a huge personal fortune in gold and silver bullion amassed from the many gifts and bribes collected from her officials. Her diversion of funds that were meant for the modernization of the Chinese navy toward the rebuilding of the summer palace doomed China to defeat by the Japanese in the war of 1894.

A bronze lion guarding the Forbidden City in Beijing, where Tz'u-hsi had Emperor Guangxu held prisoner for ten years. *(Archive Photos)*

Bibliography

Haldane, Charlotte F. *The Last Great Empress of China*. London: Constable, 1965.

Seagrave, Sterling. *Dragon Lady: The Life and Legend of the Last Empress of China*. New York: Knopf, 1992.

Warner, Marina. *The Dragon Empress*. New York: Macmillan, 1972.

Maria Hsia Chang

Walter Ulbricht

Born: June 30, 1893; Leipzig, Germany
Died: August 1, 1973; East Berlin, East Germany

Secretary-general of East German Communist Party (1950-1971)

In 1912 Walter Ulbricht (VAHL-tur EWL-brihkt) joined the German Social Democratic Party, a political party with close ties to German labor unions. In December, 1918, following the collapse of the monarchy, Ulbricht helped establish the German Communist Party. He remained active in the Communist Party until the Nazis gained power in 1933. Ulbricht spent the years between 1933 and 1945 in exile, first in Paris and then in Moscow.

East German Communist Leader

Ulbricht returned to Germany in 1945 as the leader of the so-called Ulbricht Group—the German communist political leaders who returned to Germany following the defeat of Nazi Germany in World War II. He did not vow to create a Soviet Germany. Instead, Ulbricht exhibited a surprising amount of moderation by calling for a parliamentary system for Germany. Ulbricht thereby rejected the Soviet model of communism. However, he did support a proposal which made inevitable the division of Germany and the emergence of a Communist East Germany: a merger between the moderate Social Democratic Party and the Communist Party. Kurt Schumacher, leader of the Social Democratic Party in the Western zones of occupation, steadfastly refused to collaborate with the communists. This refusal in turn led to the merger of the German Social Democratic Party and the Communist Party in Soviet-occupied East Germany.

Heightened tensions between the Soviet Union and the United States transformed Germany into a political battlefield for the superpowers. By 1949 the creation of a noncommunist Federal Republic of Germany (West Germany) and a communist German Democratic Republic (the GDR, or East Germany) had formalized the political division of Germany. Ulbricht became the head of the GDR and was forced to deal with the consequences of Germany's division. First, Ulbricht's regime was weak internally. The Soviet Union demanded reparations from the GDR, and this fact contributed to economic trouble in East Germany. In 1953 the Soviet Union used military force to suppress rioting in the GDR. Germany's division, the weakness of the GDR, and a possible negotiated settlement of the unity question forced Ulbricht to discuss the

Walter Ulbricht *(National Archives)*

German national question. Many of his speeches during the 1949-1953 period focused on German unity and how to achieve it.

After 1953 the Soviet Union decided against a negotiated settlement and sought to bolster the strength of the GDR. The maintenance of a communist East Germany became a cornerstone of Soviet foreign policy. This path led to serious clashes between the Soviet Union and the United States. The poor conditions inside the GDR undermined the Soviet goal of a communist East Germany. In 1958 and 1961 the Soviet Union made demands that, if accepted by the United States, would have transferred control over non-communist West Berlin to the GDR. Ulbricht could then claim Berlin as the capital of the East German state.

Impact of Ulbricht's Career

Walter Ulbricht remained in power until May, 1971, when he lost the office of party leader, although he retained a ceremonial post. Ulbricht's strict adherence to Communist Party principles influ-

East German Communist Party leader Walter Ulbricht speaking in front of a statue of Soviet leader Josef Stalin. *(National Archives)*

Building the Berlin Wall

In 1961 Soviet leader Nikita Khrushchev met with U.S. president John F. Kennedy in Vienna and threatened to sign an agreement with East Germany settling the remaining issues from World War II. This action by the Soviet Union was designed to force the United States and its allies from West Berlin and to transfer control of Berlin to Walter Ulbricht. During the summer of 1961, tensions between the superpowers over this question were particularly acute. To avoid a military confrontation, the Soviet Union and East Germany constructed the Berlin Wall, dividing East and West Berlin.

The Berlin Wall stabilized Ulbricht's GDR and reduced the numbers of East Germans fleeing to the West. Still, the wall presented Ulbricht with a major political dilemma: How could he address the issue of German unity when his regime had contributed to Germany's division? The East German policy after 1961 tried to define an identity for the GDR by using historical figures from Germany's past to lend legitimacy to the East German state.

Walter Ulbricht (with flowers) arriving in Prague, Czechoslovakia, for an Eastern European summit in 1968. At left is Alexander Dubček, head of Czechoslovakia's Communist Party. *(Archive Photos/Paris Match)*

enced his successors, and East Germany developed a reputation for being an orthodox communist state.

Bibliography

McCauley, Martin. *The German Democratic Republic Since 1945*. Hampshire, England: Macmillan, 1983.

Stern, Carola. *Ulbricht: A Political Biography*. New York: Praeger, 1965.

Ulam, Adam B. *Expansion and Coexistence: Soviet Foreign Policy 1917-1973*. New York: Praeger, 1974.

Windsor, Phillip. *German Reunification*. London: Elek Books, 1969.

Michael E. Meagher

Georges Vanier

Born: April 23, 1888; Montreal, Quebec, Canada
Died: March 3, 1967; Ottawa, Ontario, Canada

Canadian statesman, first French Canadian governor-general (1959-1967)

Georges Philias Vanier (ZHOHRZH fee-lee-AHS vah-NYAY) was a true Canadian, born of an English mother and a French father. He attended English schools in Montreal until age eighteen, then continued his studies in Quebec City in French at the University of Laval. He eventually received his law degree from Laval, and was admitted to the Quebec bar in 1911. His efforts to continue his education traveling in the United States and Europe were interrupted by World War I.

Early Military Career

In 1914 Georges Vanier became an original member of the Twenty-second French Canadian Battalion, soon to win glory as the Royal Van Doos. He won the Military Cross for conspicuous gallantry in 1915 and the French Cross of the Legion of Honor in 1917. In 1916, he was named a commander of the U.S. Order of Merit. His active duty ended, however, when he was wounded in 1918 and one of his legs had to be amputated.

Upon returning to Canada, Vanier became an aide to Lord Byng, who was then the governor-general of Canada. A lifelong friendship formed; following Byng's advice, Georges continued his military studies at the Staff College in Chamberley, England. In 1925 he became the commanding officer at the Citadel in Quebec City. Then he moved back to Europe to represent the Canadian delegation to the League of Nations from 1927 to 1930.

Diplomatic Service

Georges married Pauline Archer in 1921, and together they raised four children: Therese, Georges, Jean, and Michel. Pauline also had a dual English and French heritage and became a valuable diplomatic asset. Throughout the 1930's Vanier continued to represent Canada, serving on the Disarmament Commission, attending the Naval Conference in London, and serving under Vincent Massey as secretary of the Canadian High Commission in London. He was appointed minister to France in 1939 but had to flee the country soon after when it fell to Nazi control.

During World War II, Vanier was active in recruiting support for the war effort in the United

Georges Vanier *(Archive Photos)*

Vanier and de Gaulle

During World War II, Georges Vanier was an early supporter of General Charles de Gaulle as the head of the provisional French government. Vanier remained somewhat discreet in this support, however, because neither Britain's Winston Churchill nor Canada's Mackenzie King had voiced support for the somewhat controversial de Gaulle. Finally, de Gaulle traveled to the United States in the summer of 1944. His meetings with President Franklin D. Roosevelt turned the tide toward official recognition of de Gaulle as the head of the provisional French government. Vanier and de Gaulle remained friends, but after the war Vanier was less enthusiastic about him as a politician than as a military leader. De Gaulle invited Vanier for a private farewell lunch in 1953 when both found themselves in temporary retirement, but there was little contact after that. However, de Gaulle visited the grave of Vanier on July 24, 1967, only hours before delivering his famous "Vive le Quebec libre" speech in Montreal. It was received as a rousing endorsement of Quebec independence. De Gaulle's reverence for such a symbol of Canadian unity, however, would seem to cast doubt on this interpretation of his words.

States. Later, he represented Canada to the provisional French government in Algiers. In this position he became an important link to the French resistance and an early supporter of General Charles de Gaulle. He continued to serve as Canadian ambassador to France until 1952.

Governor-General of Canada

Living in retirement in Montreal after his diplomatic career, Vanier became a member of the boards of directors of the Bank of Montreal and the Credit Foncier. He also served as honorary commander of the Royal Van Doos. In 1959 the Conservative Party prime minister asked him to become the first French Canadian governor-general. The governor-general is the essential constitutional link between Canada and the English crown. The offer coincided with the two-hundredth anniversary of the battle on the Plains of Abraham, near Quebec City, which established English domination in the territory later to become Canada.

Vanier accepted the appointment and did his best as governor-general until 1965 to promote Canadian unity against growing separatist sentiment in Quebec. Vanier saw Canada as "the union of two intellectual cultures, those of Great Britain and France, which owe everything to each other, so that to understand the one is to love the other."

Bibliography

Cowley, Deborah, and George Cowley. *One Woman's Journey: A Portrait of Pauline Vanier*. Ottawa: Novalis, 1992.

Hubbard, R. H. *Rideau Hall*. Montreal: McGill-Queens University Press, 1977.

Speaight, Robert. *Vanier: Soldier, Diplomat, and Governor General*. Toronto: Collins, 1970.

Steven Lehman

Getúlio Vargas

Born: April 19, 1883; São Borja, Brazil
Died: August 24, 1954; Rio de Janeiro, Brazil

Dictatorial president of Brazil (1930-1945, 1950-1954)

As president and dictator of Brazil for more than a generation, Getúlio Dorneles Vargas (zheh-TEW-lyew dewr-NEH-lehs VAHR-gahs) was the dominant figure of modern Brazilian political history. He was born in the south of Brazil, in the state of Rio Grande do Sul, which borders both Uruguay and Argentina. The state was dominated by elements of Spanish American culture, such as gaucho cattle ranching and the authoritarian caudillo, or political boss.

Early Career

The son of a general, Vargas rejected a military career, instead becoming a lawyer; he graduated from law school in 1907. He first entered politics as a member of the state legislature. In 1922 he was elected to the national congress, in Rio de Janeiro. He became finance minister in 1926, and two years later was elected governor of his state. Although a member of the established political order, Vargas sought improvements and reforms in his state by investing in its economic development. On the national level, he fought against the dominance of Brazilian politics by politicians from the wealthier or more traditional states.

In 1930 he was nominated as a candidate for the presidency by an alliance of liberal political elements. In a rigged election, he was defeated by the government candidate. Initially accepting this defeat, he reversed himself when his former vice presidential candidate was assassinated. Leading a successful revolution to overthrow the government, he became provisional president at the end of the year. He thereby ended the political regime known as the Old Republic (1889-1930), dominated by rich coffee growers and exporters, principally from the state of São Paulo.

Leader of Brazil

With the unsettling of Brazilian political life because of his revolution, and in the midst of the economic trauma of the Great Depression, Vargas asserted the power of the federal government over the states. This repression attracted strong opposition from São Paulo, which rose in rebellion and was defeated by the federal government in 1932. With the constitution of the Old Republic no longer in effect, a new constitution was written in 1934. Vargas was elected by the constituent

Getúlio Vargas *(Library of Congress)*

The "New State"

Following the fascist models of Portugal, Spain, and Italy, Vargas consolidated his power over Brazil beginning in 1937 with the declaration of the "New State" (*Estado Novo* in Portuguese, the language of Brazil). He closed the congress and abolished political parties, governing by decree. In the midst of economic depression and the threat of international conflicts based on hostilities between Left and Right, a majority of the Brazilian population accepted his dictatorship as a means of maintaining stability amid widespread uncertainty.

Newspapers, films, and radio were under the control of government censors. Through police spying, political critics were jailed and persecuted. Nationalism was a tool of the authoritarian regime because the federal government was considered the expression of Brazil as a nation. The regime functioned through manipulation of various corporate bodies controlling industry, labor, communications, and education. The Brazilian New State ended when Vargas was ousted in 1945.

Getúlio Vargas, president of Brazil, a few months before his death in 1954. *(Archive Photos)*

assembly as president for a four-year term.

Seeking to develop Brazil economically by emphasizing the federal government's stimulus and regulation of industry, he strengthened his hand over the national economy. His authority increased as he suppressed uprisings in 1935 and 1937. In 1937, and in accord with the development of fascist regimes in Europe, Vargas abrogated the constitution of 1934 and established himself as the head of a new, authoritarian regime known as the "New State." This government lasted until the end of World War II. In 1942, Brazil entered the war on the side of the Allies, its troops fighting primarily with the United States in Italy.

With the Allied victory, it became glaringly apparent that Brazil, having victoriously fought for democracy in Europe, could not continue an authoritarian regime at home. Vargas was ousted by a military coup in 1945. However, in 1950 he returned to the presidency, elected in a campaign that brought together populist labor forces stirred by a rhetoric of fervent nationalism. As political and economic scandals mounted in his government, however, the military organized to oust him again. In order not to suffer this humiliation again, Vargas committed suicide in the presidential palace, tragically ending his role in Brazilian history.

Bibliography

Dulles, John W. F. *Vargas of Brazil: A Political Biography*. Austin: University of Texas Press, 1967.

Levine, Robert M. *Father of the Poor? Getúlio Vargas and His Era*. New York: Cambridge University Press, 1998.

Skidmore, Thomas J. *Politics in Brazil, 1930-1964: An Experiment in Democracy*. New York: Oxford University Press, 1967.

Edward A. Riedinger

José María Velasco Ibarra

Born: March 19, 1893; Quito, Ecuador
Died: March 30, 1979; Quito, Ecuador

Five-time president of Ecuador between 1934 and 1972

José María Velasco Ibarra (hoh-ZAY mah-REE-ah vay-LAHS-koh ee-BAH-rah) had one of the most extraordinary political careers in Ecuadorean history. He occupied the presidency five times, and all but one of his administrations ended with him being forcibly removed from office. Although outwardly espousing democratic values, he ruled in an authoritarian and personalist manner, thereby leading to his overthrow and his eventually being forced into exile. Consequently, Velasco Ibarra left no lasting political organization in the country.

Early Political Career

Velasco Ibarra trained as a lawyer in Quito. Elected to Congress in 1932, the following year he became president of the Chamber of Deputies. After a military coup in 1934, he was made provisional president of the country but was ousted a year later in another coup. Government in Ecuador has historically been unstable and authoritarian. The decade of the 1930's was one of exceptional instability. In the midst of a worldwide depression, power was moving from Ecuador's liberal, commercial interests, centered in the Pacific port of Guayaquil, to the traditional center of power—the mountain-ringed capital, Quito. The instability of Ecuadorean politics is reflected in the fact that since its independence in 1830 it has had seventeen constitutions.

In 1944 Velasco Ibarra returned to Ecuador from exile in Colombia. He reentered the coun-

José María Velasco Ibarra *(Corbis/Bettmann-UPI)*

The Military in Ecuadorean Politics

The Andes Mountains divide Ecuador both physically and socially. Since the end of Spanish colonial rule, Ecuador has had difficulties in maintaining a cohesive national authority. From the 1830's to the 1880's, four generals ruled the country, interspersed with civilians who also used force to acquire and maintain power.

The first half of the twentieth century witnessed instability among civilian regimes trying to govern the country. There were only brief periods of peace; these occurred during periods of increased export revenue in the early 1920's and during the 1950's. The armed forces established military regimes several times in the second half of the twentieth century, between 1963 and 1966 and between 1972 and 1979. The latter was an exceptional period of revenue increase because of oil exports. These regimes tried to maintain a character of modified populism, favoring economic reforms and social equality. In 1979 civilian government returned to Ecuador.

try at a historic moment. After a border conflict with Peru, Ecuador was forced to surrender most of its territory in the Amazon region. Velasco Ibarra led a coalition of parties to overthrow the president who had made this surrender of the country's territory. (Maintaining the integrity of Ecuador's border with Peru has been a constant point of conflict in its history.) Backed by a coup, Velasco Ibarra became president again. Abandoning his affiliations with other parties, his administration became increasingly authoritarian and personalist. In 1947 he was again forcibly removed from office and went into exile in Argentina.

Although Velaso Ibarra was essentially conservative, he did not have a formal party organization. It was his populist rhetoric that most attracted and maintained his following. He always presented himself as a supporter of the poor and downtrodden. Through patronage and the spoils of office, he was able to support his followers. While politically astute, his governments were inefficient and corrupt.

Later Career

In 1952 Velasco Ibarra's populist appeals attracted sufficient votes to elect him to the presidency. He served his full four-year term and passed the office on to his legally elected successor. During the 1950's, Ecuador enjoyed an exceptional period of political stability because of the increased revenue the country was acquiring from its exports, particularly bananas.

The situation worsened, however, in the 1960's. Velasco Ibarra was briefly president again, from 1960 to 1961. Overthrown by a military coup, he went into exile in Argentina. A military regime controlled the country from 1963 to 1966. With the overthrow of the military, Velasco Ibarra returned to Ecuador and was elected president for the last time in 1968. He returned to his authoritarian habits of ruling and was once more forcibly removed in 1972. His final years were spent in exile in Argentina.

Bibliography

Cueva, Agustin. *The Process of Political Domination in Ecuador*. New Brunswick, N.J.: Transaction Books, 1982.

Hurtado, Osvaldo. *Political Power in Ecuador*. Albuquerque: University of New Mexico Press, 1980.

Maier, Georg. *The Impact of Velasquismo on the Ecuadorean Political System*. Doctoral dissertation, Southern Illinois University, 1965.

Edward A. Riedinger

Eleuthérios Venizélos

Born: August 23, 1864; Mourniés, Crete, Ottoman Empire
Died: March 18, 1936; Paris, France

Five-time prime minister of Greece between 1910 and 1932

Eleuthérios Kyraiakos Venizélos (ay-lyehf-THAY-ree-os kyee-ryah-KOS veh-nee-ZEH-los) was Greece's most charismatic statesman in the early twentieth century. He was prime minister five times (1910-1915, 1915, 1917-1920, 1924, 1928-1932), and his nationalist vision brought territorial, population, and diplomatic gains.

Early Influences

Eleuthérios's father was a Cretan revolutionary deported by the Ottomans to the island of

Eleuthérios Venizélos *(Library of Congress)*

Síros, where Eleuthérios lived with his family from age two. A student leader, he graduated with a law degree from Athens University. After law school, Venizélos returned to Crete as a lawyer, journalist, member of the National Assembly, and leader of the new Liberal Party of the Cretan parliament.

Intervention by European powers secured autonomy for Crete. When Prince George was made high commissioner of Crete, Venizélos became his minister of justice. He came into conflict with George, however, and organized an armed insurrection against his rule, forcing him to leave Crete. Venizélos later joined the Cretan government under the new high commissioner.

Prime Minister

The Military League formed a revolutionary movement in Greece, inviting Venizélos to lead it. The league and King George revised the constitution at Venizélos's urging. He won a seat as deputy in the August, 1910, elections, and in October he became prime minister of Greece. He instituted wide-ranging reforms, reorganized the armed forces, created the Balkan League of Christian peoples, and, in the Balkan Wars of 1912-1913, participated in expelling the Ottoman Empire from the Balkans. Greece doubled its territory and population, acquiring southern Macedonia, southern Epirus, Crete, and islands in the Aegean.

World War I began in 1914. Prime Minister Venizélos strongly advocated joining the Allies against the Central Powers, especially the Turks, allies of Germany. However, King Constantine, because of family connections with German royalty, was sympathetic with the Central Powers and refused. When Germany, Austria, and Bulgaria invaded Macedonia in 1916, Venizélos led an antiroyalist insurrection. His army, with Franco-British support, forced Constantine into exile in 1917. Greece, united under Venizélos and Constantine's second son, Alexander, declared war against the Central Powers. After the 1918 armistice, Venizélos participated in the Paris peace conference, staying almost two years. He gained a reputation as an international statesman, convinced Italy to cede the Dodecanese Islands, and extended Greek occupation in Anatolia. He successfully negotiated the Treaties of Neuilly and Sèvres with Bulgaria and Turkey in 1919-1920 and returned to Greece in triumph.

However, after King Alexander's death in October, 1920, the Greeks elected a monarchist majority and recalled King Constantine by plebiscite. With Venizélos in exile in Paris, the disastrous defeat of the

During Venizélos's prime ministership, Montenegrin fighters allied with Greece against Turkey in the First Balkan War. *(Library of Congress)*

The Invasion of Turkey

Sometimes called the Anatolian adventure, the Greek invasion of Anatolia after the defeat of the Ottoman Empire in World War I proved how dreams of empire can turn an illusion into a nightmare. For the Greeks, the loss of Constantinople to the Turks in 1453 signaled the end of the Greek state, although many Greeks remained in Anatolia under Ottoman hegemony. Other Greeks were under Ottoman domination in the Balkans. The nineteenth-century Greek independence movement prompted Greek dreams of reuniting all Greeks in one state. Greece saw Orthodox Russia as a possible guar-

antor of this reunion; Europe's Great Powers viewed the prospect of such a reunion with alarm. The collapse of the Ottoman Empire in World War I excited Greek hopes of recapturing lost territories in Asia Minor, and they invaded the Turkish mainland. They hoped to recover, at the least, Constantinople, Black Sea settlements, and Smyrna. This attempt was thwarted by Atatürk's strong resistance. The end result was that the Greeks were pushed out of Anatolia in 1922 and Smyrna was burned. Further, an exchange of populations forced hundreds of thousands of Greeks to leave Anatolia forever.

Greek army by Atatürk in 1922, as well as armed insurrection led by Generals Nikólaos Plastíras and Stilianos Gonatas, occurred. Constantine was dethroned, succeeded by his eldest son George, and six royalist leaders were executed. Recalled to service, Venizélos led the Greek delegation negotiating the peace treaty of Lausanne with the Turks in 1923. A second insurrection, led by General Metaxas, forced George into exile, and Venizélos returned to Greece. He clashed this time with antimonarchist Republican leaders, exiling himself again in 1924. During the Second Republic of 1924-1935, he returned and again led the Liberal Party. In the 1928 election, he won a majority, forming his last cabinet. He restored normal relations with Greece's Balkan neighbors, but the Great Depression of the 1930's weakened his position at home, and he was defeated in 1932. Venizélos continued to lead the Liberals, but his political career ended in March 1935, when he went to Paris, where he died in 1936.

Bibliography

Alastos, Doros. *Venizélos: Patriot, Statesman, Revolutionary.* London: Humphries, 1942.

Chester, Samuel Beach. *Life of Venizélos.* London: Constable, 1921.

Gibbons, Herbert Adams. *Venizélos.* 2d ed. New York: Houghton Mifflin, 1923.

Kerofilas, C. *Eleftherios Venizélos: His Life and Work.* London: Murray, 1915.

Gloria Fulton

Pancho Villa

Born: June 5, 1878; Hacienda de Río Grande, San Juan del Río, Durango, Mexico
Died: July 20, 1923; near Parral, Chihuahua, Mexico

Mexican bandit and revolutionary

Pancho Villa (PAHN-choh VEE-yah), born Doroteo Arango (doh-roh-TAY-oh ah-RAHN-goh), was born during Porfirio Díaz's dictatorial Mexican presidency. Fatherless early, Villa helped support his mother and four siblings as a peon under a cruel hacienda owner. According to tradition, about 1894 Villa killed the hacienda owner, or the man's son, for raping his sister. Fleeing to the Chihuahua mountains, he joined an outlaw band, adopted the name Francisco "Pancho" Villa (from that of a famed Mexican bandit), and moved to Parral, a Chihuahua mining town. By 1908 he was popular with peons as a leader of a band of rustlers, since regional villages were heavily taxed by hated cattle barons.

Guerrilla Fighter

In 1910 Villa, an expert horseman and marksman, joined prodemocracy Francisco Madero in rebelling against Diaz. Villa was given the rank of colonel. With Pascuál Orozco, he captured Ciudad Juárez, contributing to Diaz's abdication and exile in 1911. Once Madero declared himself provisional president, his family bankrolled a meat-packing business for Villa, who also owned a hotel and ran casinos. Resuming his military career in 1912, Villa conducted attacks against Orozco's counter-revolution, which supported Victoriano Huerta. Huerta captured Villa and ordered his execution. Madero commuted the sentence to a term in prison, from which Villa escaped to Texas.

When Huerta made himself dictator of Mexico and assassinated Madero, Villa formed his hard-charging "Division of the North" in 1913. He allied himself with Venustiano Carranza and Emiliano Zapata. Backed by peasants, cowboys, and miners, Villa seized land from Chihuahua aristocrats and delivered the state to supporters of the constitutional movement. He became Chihuahua's governor in 1913. He joined Zapata against Carranza, now distrusted as autocratic, and occupied Mexico City in 1914. After Villa opposed Carranza at a convention of generals, constitutionalist Álvaro Obregón emerged from the south, entered Mexico City, forced Huerta into exile, and proclaimed Carranza "first chief" (1914).

Pancho Villa *(Library of Congress)*

The Columbus Raid

Pancho Villa felt insulted when President Woodrow Wilson officially recognized Venustiano Carranza as Mexican president in October, 1915. He retaliated by crossing the border and raiding Columbus, New Mexico, on March 9, 1916. Villa planned to seize American weapons and ammunition. However, nearby American soldiers, though taken completely by surprise, defended the town valiantly. Guerrillas killed eighteen Americans and wounded eight; ninety *Villistas* were killed and twenty-three wounded. From a hill southeast of town, Villa retreated with American materiel and many horses and mules. Wilson ordered General John J. Pershing to pursue Villa into Mexico, but without success. Not only Villa's neighbors but also Carranza's own military forces were thoroughly anti-American and provided no cooperation to the hated *gringos*.

Retreat

Villa's and Zapata's forces never coordinated effectively, and Villa fled Mexico City. Allied with Carranza, Obregón killed, wounded, or captured three-fourths of Villa's army at Celaya, Querétaro in April, 1915. Pro-Carranza Plutarco Elías Calles then defeated Villa at Agua Prieta, Sonora, in November. In 1916 Villa resumed guerrilla tactics in Chihuahua against pro-Carranza towns and cohorts. To highlight Carranza's inability to control northern Mexico, Villa executed sixteen American mine employees in Santa Isabel, Son-

Pancho Villa (center) leading his forces. Villa was part revolutionary, part bandit, and part folk hero. *(Library of Congress)*

ora. He also raided Columbus, New Mexico, on March 9, 1916, to seize arms and dramatize his displeasure at President Woodrow Wilson's recognizing Carranza's provisional presidency. American soldiers drove Villa and his guerrillas back into Mexico.

Aftermath

President Wilson ordered General John J. Pershing to pursue Villa into Mexico and capture him. Villa knew the Chihuahua terrain well, however, and was popular with its people. Furthermore, Pershing's presence on Mexican soil insulted Carranza and his fellow anti-Americans. Therefore, the punitive expedition of Pershing came to naught while costing an estimated $130 million. Villa continued to harass the forces of Carranza, who opposed labor unions and land reform, and even had Zapata murdered (in 1919). Obregón overthrew Carranza, who looted the treasury and fled but was soon assassinated (1920). Succeeding as president, Obregón granted a general amnesty and gave Villa a hacienda in Durango and a substantial pension. Unidentified Obregón followers, however, fearing Villa's opposition to pro-Obregón Calles's candidacy, ambushed and murdered Villa near Parral.

Pancho Villa remains a controversial figure. Martin Luis Guzmán, his friend and early biographer, aptly calls him "eagle and serpent." Illiterate until adulthood, always racist, murderous, and self-serving, Villa only intermittently sought land reform. He was a brilliant guerrilla tactician but often outraged his fellow strategists. Nevertheless, he has become enshrined as a hero of the Mexican Revolution.

Bibliography

Braddy, Haldeen. *Pancho Villa at Columbus.* El Paso: Texas Western College Press, 1965.
Clendenen, Clarence C. *The United States and Pancho Villa: A Study in Unconventional Diplomacy.* Ithaca, N.Y.: Cornell University Press, 1951.
Lansford, William Douglas. *Pancho Villa.* Los Angeles: Sherbourne Press, 1965.
Ruiz, Ramón Eduardo. *Triumphs and Tragedy: A History of the Mexican People.* New York: W. W. Norton, 1992.

Robert L. Gale

Vo Nguyen Giap

Born: 1911 (or 1912, possibly September 1); An Xa; Quang Binh Province, Vietnam, French Indochina

Vietnamese guerrilla leader, defense minister of North Vietnam (1945-1975), defense minister of united Vietnam (1975-1980)

From a poor family with strong anti-French sentiments, Vo Nguyen Giap (VOH NEW-yehn ZYAHP) joined the Vietnamese Communist Party in his early teens. Well-educated, Giap earned a bachelor of law degree at Hanoi University. He also studied history and military strategy and began writing political tracts, including *The Peasant Problem* (1938) and *The Question of National Liberation in Indochina* (1939). In 1939, Giap was forced to flee to China after French crackdowns on insurgent political parties. Giap

quickly attached himself to other key Vietnamese communist-nationalist leaders and was soon a close confidant of Ho Chi Minh. Giap organized the Vietminh guerrilla forces and fought against Japanese occupation of Indochina during World War II. After the August Revolution of 1945, Giap became a top official of the new government of the Democratic Republic of Vietnam.

Early Military Career

Giap's military prowess came to the forefront during the French Indochina War of 1946-1954. Placed in charge of organizing the new People's Army of Vietnam (PAVN), Giap built a formidable armed force. He utilized the three-phase strategy of revolutionary warfare, based upon the Chinese communist model. Using Vietnam's meager national resources with great efficiency and accepting aid from the Soviet Union and China, Giap's PAVN overcame early defeats to gain the upper hand against the French colonial forces.

Giap learned quickly, but at great cost in men and matériel, that Vietnamese forces could not directly engage the military forces of industrialized powers—in this case, France—in conventional warfare. Instead he pursued guerrilla warfare, which ultimately proved effective against the French and later the Americans. His great victory at Dien Bien Phu in May, 1954, helped force the Geneva Accords, drawn up at the Geneva Conference of 1954. The accords partitioned Vietnam into two states, North and South, and ended French domination in Indochina.

Giap's fear of conventional warfare led him to support seeking a political solution to achieve national unification of North and South Vietnam. His opponents in the government impatiently

Vo Nguyen Giap *(Library of Congress)*

urged a great conventional-style war. With the United States replacing France as South Vietnam's major supporter, Giap realized that conventional war with the United States had to be avoided at all costs. In that light, Giap supported continuing guerrilla warfare tactics and expanding the communist political base in the rural areas of South Vietnam. This policy was followed from the late 1950's through the mid-1960's, when the United States began its massive military buildup in South Vietnam, leading to the most intense phase of the Vietnam War.

War Against the Americans

Giap took complete strategic command of the PAVN in 1967, after several conventional-style defeats by American forces. During this time Giap designed the famous Tet Offensive of 1968. This offensive represented the great push to end the war with a North Vietnamese victory. A crucial element of the plan was a popular uprising in the South,

North Vietnamese general Vo Nguyen Giap (right) with members of the People's Army of Vietnam. *(National Archives)*

Dien Bien Phu

The French outpost at Dien Bien Phu, located in northwestern Vietnam, was taken on May 7, 1954, after a two-month siege by Vietminh forces under the command of General Vo Nguyen Giap. As part of a plan to lure the Vietminh into a conventional battle and to interdict supply and infiltration routes, French general Henri Navarre commanded French forces as they garrisoned the Dien Bien Phu valley. Giap slowly surrounded the valley, using the human labor of thousands of men and women, who carried everything from food to artillery shells through the steep hills surrounding the French position.

This incredible show of human will caught the French completely off-guard in their supposedly impregnable position. Despite several calls for assistance, the United States refused to save the beleaguered garrison. In France, news of the fall of Dien Bien Phu caused riots. The Geneva peace agreement was subsequently signed in July, 1954, ending French involvement in Indochina and dividing Vietnam into southern and northern halves. Elections were to be held in 1956 to decide unification, but they never took place. Instead, war in Vietnam continued for almost twenty years.

The People's Army of Vietnam

The People's Army of Vietnam (PAVN), the military forces of the Democratic Republic of Vietnam, evolved through experience, determination, foreign aid, and efficient use of resources to become one of the best Third World fighting forces in the world. The PAVN defeated both France (1946-1954) and the United States (1964-1973) in brutal, costly wars. Principally under the command and organizational skills of General Vo Nguyen Giap, the PAVN specialized in small unit warfare, guerrilla tactics, and infiltra-

tion. It was perhaps best known to Americans as the North Vietnamese Army, or NVA. The PAVN excelled at logistics and is most famous in this regard for the Ho Chi Minh Trail, which provided supplies and men through miles of jungle trails, footpaths, and highways into South Vietnam. Casualty estimates for the PAVN during the war with the United States stand at approximately 500,000 killed, compared with the 58,159 American military personnel killed in Vietnam.

which would pave the way for PAVN forces. This necessary part of the plan failed, defeating the entire offensive. Casualties were heavy, especially among the political cadres of the South. Despite

the military setback, Tet proved a political victory for the North Vietnamese: It helped galvanize antiwar sentiment in the United States. By 1969, American forces had begun to pull out of Vietnam. Giap now realized that if the North could hang on until the Americans left, then a defeat of South Vietnamese forces was entirely probable.

After Tet, Giap continued to command guerrilla operations against U.S. and South Vietnamese forces. In 1973, Giap retired from command, probably for health reasons. North Vietnam defeated South Vietnam in 1975, unifying the country as the Democratic Republic of Vietnam. Giap was minister of defense, a position he resigned in 1980. He gave up his Politburo (executive committee) seat in 1982. His power base in party politics continued to erode as ambitious younger men gained control of the party. The Vietnamese people, however, supported the war hero, honoring him with the Gold Star Order, Vietnam's highest accolade, in 1992. As a tactician and leader, Giap is admired among armed services worldwide, and his tactical and strategic doctrine is studied in many military service schools, including those in the United States.

Vo Nguyen Giap and the People's Army of Vietnam used guerrilla tactics to fight against the French. Here French soldiers interrogate an apprehended Vietnamese man they suspect of being a guerrilla. *(National Archives)*

Bibliography

Colvin, John. *Giap: Volcano Under the Snow.* New York: Soho, 1966.

Currey, Cecil B. *Victory at Any Cost: The Genius of Viet Nam's General Vo Nguyen Giap.* Washington, D.C.: Brassey's, 1997.

Macdonald, Peter G. *Giap: The Victor in Vietnam.* New York: W. W. Norton, 1993.

Vo Nguyen Giap. *How We Won the War.* New York: Recon Publications, 1976.

William Allison

Kurt Waldheim

Born: December 21, 1918; Sankt Andrä-Wördern, Austria

Austrian diplomat, secretary-general of the United Nations (1972-1982)

Kurt Josef Waldheim (KEWRT YOH-sehf VAHLT-him) was born to a devout Catholic family during a time of great national instability and economic hardship in Austria. After graduating from high school, he enlisted in the compulsory Austrian army as a "one-year volunteer." He later received elite diplomatic training at the Vienna Consular Academy but was drafted into the German army in 1938 at the onset of World War II. A war injury in 1941 relieved him of further military duty and enabled him to continue his studies. In 1944 he received his doctoral of law degree from the University of Vienna shortly after marrying Elisabeth Ritschel. Together they had three children.

Rising Diplomat

Waldheim's youth was shaped partly by the massive political upheavals of central Europe prior to World War II. His family suffered greatly in poverty-stricken Austria as Adolf Hitler's Germany invaded the country and assumed control in 1938. The impact of such international turmoil intrigued Waldheim and fostered his interest in politics and foreign diplomacy. His tall, stately appearance and calm, patient demeanor aided his ambitious career endeavors. Decades later, however, in the 1980's, accusations concerning the nature of Waldheim's military service and his involvement with the German Reich surfaced and created considerable controversy.

In 1945 Waldheim was appointed to his first departmental position with Austria's diplomatic foreign ministry. As a young man making a strong impression, he was promoted rapidly, first assisting the secretary-general of the foreign ministry, then being named Austrian ambassador to France.

In 1951 Waldheim returned to Austria as the head of the ministry's personnel department. He played a crucial diplomatic role in negotiations to reclaim Austria's independence from Allied occupation. Negotiations proved fruitful when on May 15, 1955, Austria's State Treaty was signed, granting Austria permanent military neutrality. That same year, Waldheim led the Austrian delegation to the United Nations.

Controversial World Statesman

Waldheim served the United Nations in various capacities, promoting Austria's interests. He

Kurt Waldheim *(Library of Congress)*

also held other positions; he was ambassador to Canada from 1958 to 1960 and was appointed Austrian foreign minister in 1968. In early 1971, Waldheim ran for the Austrian presidency but lost to incumbent Franz Jonas.

This defeat lost much of its sting when, on December 21, 1971, Waldheim was elected secretary-general of the United Nations, a great diplomatic honor. Although the position carried no executive power, Waldheim supported nuclear disarmament and traveled the world negotiating peace. He was often

Austrian president Kurt Waldheim after an address to the nation in 1987. *(Archive Photos)*

known to make cultural blunders, however, especially in Third World countries. In 1982 Waldheim's tenure as secretary-general ended when China vetoed his bid for a third term.

In 1986 Waldheim's second run for the Austrian presidency was supported by the conserva-

tive People's Party, and he won the election. His campaign and succeeding governance were seriously marred, however, by an international examination into his military past. Allegations as well as supporting documentation surfaced that Waldheim had facilitated criminal warfare for the

Waldheim and the Nazis

During Kurt Waldheim's 1986 presidential campaign, rumors surfaced that he was a Nazi participant in World War II. Details of his military career had previously been left to his own biographical account—at times vague and inconsistent. Recovered records revealed Waldheim's association with Nazi youth organizations and his service as lieutenant under General Alexander Löhr. Löhr was executed after the war for his massive kidnapping and deportation of Jews to German concentration camps. In 1947 a Yugoslav war commission report provided evidence that Waldheim had facilitated the war crimes and possibly helped carry out orders for

the murders. Waldheim avoided repercussions from that report.

In 1987 the World Jewish Congress persuaded the U.S. Department of Justice to put Waldheim on an immigration "watch list" prohibiting him from entering the country. Other countries followed suit. An international debate ensued regarding the liability of those responsible for the atrocities of the Holocaust. Throughout the ordeal, Waldheim maintained his innocence, admitting only to doing what was necessary to survive Nazi influence during the war. A 1987 invitation to the Vatican by Pope John Paul II symbolized the pope's excusing him of any wrongdoing.

Kurt Waldheim signs a copy of his autobiography in 1996 for the leader of Austria's Freedom Party. In the book Waldheim admits that it was a mistake to conceal his Nazi war record but maintains that his behavior in World War II was honorable. *(Reuters/Contrast/Archive Photos)*

Nazi regime. There was a public outcry calling for his prosecution. Under Waldheim's leadership, therefore, many Austrians felt humiliated, and he lost his bid for reelection in 1992.

Bibliography

Bassett, Richard. *Waldheim and Austria*. London: Penguin Books, 1988.

Cohen, Bernard, and Luc Rosenzweig. *Waldheim*. New York: Adama Books, 1987.

Finger, Seymour Maxwell. *Bending with the Winds: Kurt Waldheim and the United Nations*. New York: Praeger, 1990.

Herzstein, Robert Edwin. *Waldheim: The Missing Years*. New York: Paragon House, 1989.

International Commission of Historians. *The Waldheim Report*. Copenhagen: University of Copenhagen and Museum Tusculanum Press, 1993.

Mitten, Richard. *The Politics of Antisemitic Prejudice: The Waldheim Phenomenon in Austria*. Boulder, Colo.: Westview Press, 1992.

Waldheim, Kurt. *In the Eye of the Storm: A Memoir*. Bethesda, Md.: Adler and Adler, 1986.

Caralee Hutchinson

Lech Wałęsa

Born: September 29, 1943; Popowo, Poland

Polish labor leader and president of Poland (1990-1995), winner of 1993 Nobel Peace Prize

Lech Michal Wałęsa (LEHK MEE-kahl vah-WEHN-zeh) was raised on a small four-acre farm in Popowo with his six brothers and sisters by his mother and stepfather. His father, a carpenter, had been arrested by the Nazis in 1943 and sent to a work camp. He developed a serious lung ailment and died two months after the war. Lech found it increasingly difficult to accept his stepfather and left home to pursue a vocational education in Lipno. In 1967 he obtained a position as an electrician at the shipyards at Gdańsk and quickly became involved in trade-union activity.

Solidarity and Martial Law

Wałęsa established himself as a labor leader during the 1976 strikes at the Gdańsk shipyard. Although he was fired for his activity, he initiated contact with various Polish radical intellectuals and continued to pursue a working-class reform agenda. When price increases in 1980 pushed workers to the brink of starvation, Wałęsa launched the Solidarity movement and called for a shipyard workers' strike in July. His movement rapidly gained international attention, and in August the government was forced to recognize Solidarity's right to serve as an independent trade union. Its power soon spread to agricultural and industrial workers as Solidarity gained millions of members almost overnight.

Wałęsa, however, immediately encountered a number of difficulties. While Solidarity called for reform, it lacked an overall cohesive plan of action. Members differed over the pace and style of reforms, what role Poland should play in the international system, and how much authority should be granted to the working-class rank and file. Wałęsa opened countless offices and continuously recruited new members, but with procedures and policies still in the formative stage, controversies and conflicts were commonplace.

Throughout 1980 and 1981, Wałęsa campaigned extensively throughout Poland and attempted to generate greater support for Solidarity's reforms. He met with the head of the Polish Catholic Church, Cardinal Stephan Wyszynski, and in 1981 he visited Pope John Paul II at the Vatican. Following this meeting, the pope publicly endorsed Solidarity and called for change within the communist world. Touring throughout the Polish countryside in his automobile with his wife and children, Wałęsa visited numerous villages, factories, and farms and gained significant recognition among the Polish people.

Lech Wałęsa *(The Nobel Foundation)*

Solidarity leader and future Polish president Lech Wałęsa at a press conference during a visit to Paris. *(Archive Photos/Imapress)*

Communist officials, however, were preparing countermeasures that would undermine Solidarity's reform efforts. In November, 1980, the Warsaw courts ruled that Solidarity must adhere to the "preponderant role of the Party" in all affairs. In February, 1981, communist hardliner General Wojciech Jaruzelski was appointed prime minister. He became Communist Party leader in October. With Poland's economy suffering from strikes and social unrest, Jaruzelski imposed martial law on December 12, 1981. He banned Solidarity, arrested Wałęsa, and initiated a series of reprisals against union organizers. By the end of 1982, with communist control firmly reentrenched and Solidarity dismantled, he released Wałęsa from prison. Wałęsa, however, later received the Nobel Peace Prize for his efforts in 1993 and emerged from the conflict as a leading figure for reform in the communist bloc.

The Solidarity Movement

Solidarity originated as a general strike by shipyard workers in Gdańsk when wages failed to keep pace with price increases in Poland in 1980. Polish workers had gained considerable experience during the strikes of 1970, and the election of Pope John Paul II, the first Polish pope, had inspired Polish nationalists. Lech Wałęsa forced the Communist Party to sign the August Accords, which legalized trade-union activity in Poland. Solidarity quickly attracted millions of members and attempted to use its clout to enact reforms within the communist system. Although Solidarity was outlawed in 1982 by General Wojciech Jaruzelski, it resurfaced in the late 1980's and served as the catalyst that ultimately ended communist rule in Poland.

The Presidential Election of 1995

By the mid-1990's, Polish president Lech Wałęsa's popularity had plummeted. The president had extreme difficulties working with Parliament on budget concerns. The Left feared that the pace of privatization would produce economic chaos. Young voters resented Wałęsa's strict Roman Catholic position on abortion. Former Communist Party members disagreed with his pro-Western stance on foreign-policy issues and advocated more traditional eastern European ties. Polls indicated that by September, Wałęsa's popular support had fallen to 16 percent. Yet Wałęsa embarked on a strong campaign appealing to the conservative anticommunist Right and the political center. He accused his chief rival, Aleksander Kwasniewski of the Democratic Left Alliance and a former Communist Party official, of plotting Poland's return to communism. Several candidates vied for power in the November 5 election, but only Wałęsa (with 33 percent) and Kwasniewski (35 percent) qualified for the November 19 runoff election. In a record voter turnout, Kwasniewski earned a narrow victory, winning 52 percent of the vote, and became Poland's second president.

From Communism to Democracy

Government price increases in 1988 sparked a new wave of labor unrest in Poland. In April a one-day transportation strike paralyzed the nation, a strike erupted at the Lenin Steelworks near Cracow, and the shipyard workers walked out at Gdańsk. Riot police helped squelch the disturbances by using tear gas, small explosives, night-

Lech Wałęsa in May, 1988, sharing bread with striking workers at a Gdansk shipyard. He called for a "decisive protest" against Poland's communist government. *(Reuters/Archive Photos)*

sticks, and clubs, but a general wave of dissatisfaction was sweeping through Poland.

During this period, Wałęsa worked toward securing negotiations that would resurrect Solidarity's rights as an independent trade union. His performance in a televised debate against Alfred Miodowicz, president of the pro-government unions, helped reaffirm his popularity among working-class Poles. He introduced a new platform calling for Solidarity to play an active role in local elections, and he benefited from another visit to the pope.

Jaruzelski realized that Poland's Communist Party was falling prey to the same pressures of democratization that were sweeping the rest of the communist bloc in 1989, and he helped facilitate a peaceful democratic transition in Poland. Wałęsa's campaign skills and popularity ensured Solidarity's dominance in Poland's first democratic government. It secured control of both upper and lower houses. Solidarity's parliamentary success had a profound impact upon Wałęsa's political aspirations and significantly increased his importance to the United States and western investors. Wałęsa conducted a meeting with U.S. president George Bush during a brief Bush stay in Poland.

By the time Poland's first presidential elections occurred in 1990, Wałęsa was the most popular figure in Poland and could boast of a favorable relationship with several global leaders. General Jaruzelski finally resigned in October, paving the way for Wałęsa's victory. In the December presidential election he captured 73 percent of the vote on the second ballot and became the first president of Poland.

President Wałęsa

From 1990 through 1995, Wałęsa's administration tried to reestablish Poland's historic role as a powerful actor in eastern Europe. He sought amicable relationships with both Germany and Russia. He hoped to create trade networks connecting Poland with all European markets. Wałęsa also insisted on widespread protection for workers' rights and eliminated rampant human rights abuses by the police and the military. Overall, however, despite attracting considerable investors from Western nations, Poland's economy struggled during its transition from state-run communism to democracy and market capitalism. When Solidarity failed to generate immediate economic success, more radical solutions surfaced that advocated either a return to communism or a more militant pace of democratization. Thus, as Wałęsa's first term came to an end, his approval rating had considerably declined, and he lost his bid for reelection in 1995.

Some analysts attributed Wałęsa's defeat to his relationship with the Roman Catholic Church, since his major opponent, Aleksander Kwasniewski, promised a greater separation of church and state. Young voters were extremely critical of Poland's rigid antiabortion laws. Yet despite his personal defeat, the 1995 election represented an overall ideological victory for Wałęsa and the principles of Solidarity. Kwasniewski continued Wałęsa's policies of democratic reform, privatization of government-owned industries, and entrance into the North Atlantic Treaty Organization (NATO). He continued to distance Poland from its communist past.

Bibliography

Ash, Timothy Garton. *The Magic Lantern: The Revolution of '89 Witnessed in Warsaw, Budapest, and Prague*. New York: Random House, 1990.

Gati, Charles. *The Bloc That Failed: Soviet-East European Relations in Transition*. Bloomington: Indiana University Press, 1990.

Wałęsa, Lech. *The Struggle and the Triumph*. New York: Arcade Publishing, 1991.

———. *A Way of Hope*. New York: Henry Holt, 1987.

Robert D. Ubriaco, Jr.

George C. Wallace

Born: August 25, 1919; Clio, Alabama
Died: September 13, 1998; Montgomery, Alabama

Four-term Alabama governor (elected 1962, 1970, 1974, and 1982) and U.S. presidential candidate (1968)

George Corley Wallace (JOHRJ COHR-lee WAH-lihs) was the first child born to George C. Wallace, Sr., and Mozelle Smith Wallace in the small southeastern Alabama town of Clio. His father, a farmer, suffered from chronically poor health. Even though the family was fairly prominent in Barbour County, money was always hard to come by.

Early Life

The younger Wallace spent much time going on rounds with his grandfather, Dr. Oscar Wallace. He very early developed an intense interest in people and determined that he would have a political career. He first successfully campaigned to be a page in the Alabama state senate. His primary athletic interest was boxing, and he won the Alabama Golden Gloves bantamweight championships in both 1936 and 1937.

Wallace entered the University of Alabama in 1937 with the goal of getting the law degree he believed to be essential for his contemplated political career. His father's death soon after he began college required that Wallace personally raise all of the funds needed to earn his diploma. He did so and graduated in May, 1942. That summer he met Lurleen Burns. They were married in May, 1943, while Wallace had a brief leave from the Army air corps, which he had joined in October, 1942. They had four children, Bobbi Jo, Peggy Sue, George, Jr., and Lee. After Lurleen Wallace's death, George Wallace married and divorced Cornelia Ellis Snively and Lisa Taylor.

Political Career

Following World War II and his discharge from the military, Wallace got an appointment as an assistant state attorney general. He served in this position only briefly, however, before launching a campaign in 1946 for the state House of Representatives. As a young legislator he was generally on the progressive side of issues (including race) and was a close ally of then-Alabama governor James E. Folsom, Sr. Although reelected in 1950 for another four-year term, he ran successfully for a circuit judgeship in 1952. It was in this position that he first began to attract statewide, regional, and even national attention in disputes related to black voting rights. His most notable confrontation was with federal Judge Frank Johnson, Jr., to whom he surrendered voting records following a highly publicized confrontation in 1959.

George C. Wallace *(Library of Congress)*

Fellow southern segregationist Lester Maddox, governor of Georgia, pouring a cup of coffee for former Alabama governor George Wallace in 1967. *(Library of Congress)*

paign in 1962 he won a decisive victory. His most spectacular stand in behalf of segregated education took place in June of 1963 at the University of Alabama.

In 1964 Wallace entered several presidential primaries in northern states and garnered a surprising number of votes. To be permitted another successive gubernatorial term, Wallace attempted to amend the Alabama state constitution. When he failed, Lurleen Wallace ran in her husband's stead in 1966 and was elected. She died of cancer in May, 1968. That year Wallace made another bid for the presidency. In the November election, running as the candidate of the American Independent Party, he won 13.5 percent of the

Wallace ran for governor the first time in 1958 and lost. He believed that he had been insufficiently forceful in defense of racial segregation in the face of hostile U.S. Supreme Court decisions. Abandoning moderation, in his second cam-

popular vote and the electoral votes of five southern states. Wallace was elected again to the Alabama governorship in 1970. He resumed his presidential bid within the Democratic Party in 1972 and was having considerable primary suc-

School Integration

When George C. Wallace ran successfully for the governorship of Alabama in 1962, he promised to make a dramatic stand for racial segregation and states' rights. The act of defiance with which his name will always be associated, the infamous "stand in the schoolhouse door," occurred at the University of Alabama on June 11, 1963. Wallace attempted forcibly to bar the admission of two black students, Vivian Malone and James Hood, by his appearance at the regis-

tration building. The confrontation was between Wallace and Nicholas Katzenbach, a deputy U.S. attorney general who represented the federal government. After Wallace made a speech on behalf of state sovereignty, he waited at the auditorium until he was informed by a general in the Alabama National Guard that President John F. Kennedy had federalized the Guard to ensure the peaceful integration of the university.

George Wallace on the presidential campaign trail in 1968; here he greets a crowd in Pittsburgh, Pennsylvania. Wallace received 13.5 percent of the popular vote. *(National Archives)*

cess when he was shot on May 15, 1972. Although he survived the assassination attempt, he was paralyzed following the attack.

Wallace's popularity continued virtually unabated in Alabama, and he was reelected to additional gubernatorial terms in 1974 and 1982. He remained in political retirement after leaving office in January, 1987. In his later years he attempted to rehabilitate his image, insisting that he was not a racist and did not hate anyone. He even publicly apologized to blacks for his hostility to integration and the Civil Rights movement. Having long been in declining health, Wallace died in 1998.

Bibliography

Carter, Dan T. *The Politics of Rage: George Wallace, the Origins of the New Conservatism, and the Transformation of American Politics.* New York: Simon & Schuster, 1995.

Frady, Marshall. *Wallace.* New York: New American Library, 1972.

Jones, Bill. *The Wallace Story.* Northport, Ala.: American Southern, 1966.

Lesher, Stephan. *George Wallace: American Populist.* Reading, Mass.: Addison-Wesley, 1994.

Wallace, George, Jr., with James Gregory. *The Wallaces of Alabama: My Family.* Chicago: Follett, 1975.

William H. Stewart

Wang Jingwei

Born: 1883; Canton (Guangzhou), Guangdong Province, China
Died: November 10, 1944; Nagoya, Japan

Chinese revolutionary leader, collaborator with Japan during World War II

Wang Jingwei (WAHNG JEENG-WAY), also rendered as Wang Ching-wei, Wang Zhaoming, and Wang Jixin, was a Chinese politician who distinguished himself with bravery in the republican revolution in China but collaborated with the Japanese against his own country in World War II. An extremely gifted young man, Wang took the civil service examination and obtained the degree of *xiucai* (budding scholar) at the age of eighteen. In 1905, Wang went to Japan, where he was impressed by the successful modernization under the Meiji regime. He joined the

Wang Jingwei *(Library of Congress)*

Tongmenghui (revolutionary alliance) under Sun Yat-sen, an organization dedicated to China's national liberation from the Qing (or Ching, also known as Manchu) Dynasty.

In 1910, Wang Jingwei was arrested by the Qing government in China after a failed attempt to assassinate the regent of the Qing emperor. After the revolution of 1911, Wang was released from prison and participated in the agreement between the revolutionaries and Yuan Shi-kai, a powerful figure in the old regime who became the first president of the Chinese Republic. Between 1922 and 1926, Wang served in the Guangzhou revolutionary regime under Sun Yat-sen.

Wang and the Kuomintang

A superb orator and organizer, Wang became the ideological heir to Sun and was expected to assume leadership in the Nationalist Party, the Kuomintang (KMT), upon Sun's death in 1925. However, he resigned his office as chairman of the military committee in the Guangzhou regime in 1926 and went abroad after a coup by Jiang Jieshi, his political rival in the KMT.

In 1927, Wang returned to China from Europe to take charge of a left-wing Nationalist regime in the city of Wuhan after Jiang Jieshi's bloody purge of the Communists in Shanghai in April. In July, however, Wang and his followers turned against the Communists as well when he felt threatened by the Russian-based Comintern (the Third Communist International in Moscow). The July 15 coup marked the end of the "first united front" between the Nationalists and Communists. Although he reconciled with Jiang Jieshi temporarily, Wang continued to challenge Jiang in vain between 1928 and 1931.

The Wuhan Government

In April, 1927, Jiang Jieshi turned against his Communist allies in Shanghai during the Northern Expedition. Wang Jingwei, then chairman of the Nationalist Party, condemned Jiang's atrocities and reiterated his commitment to the united front between his party and the Chinese Communists. He established a government in Wuhan with some left-wing leaders of the Nationalist Party, including Mme. Sun Yat-sen. In private, however, Wang distrusted both the Russians and the Communists. In mid-July, Wang Jingwei gave in to the anticommunist generals in his government who feared for their lives when the Comintern ordered the Communists to purge the Wuhan government of the "reactionary generals." A coup was carried out in which thousands of Communists and their supporters were killed, jailed, or forced to go underground. The Wuhan government came to an end in September, when Wang was forced by his rivals in the Kuomintang to resign his chairmanship of the party.

Collaborating with the Japanese

After the outbreak of the second Sino-Japanese War in 1937, Wang served in the Nationalist government in such capacities as vice chairman of the central political committee and vice chairman of the KMT. After the Nationalist government retreated to Chongqing, the wartime capital of China, Wang tried to talk Jiang Jieshi into negotiating with the Japanese to obtain a peace settlement. In December, 1938, Wang left Chongqing after his pleas for a settlement proved futile. He went to Japan via Hong Kong. In 1940, Wang returned to China and, with the support of the Japanese, organized a puppet regime in Nanjing. This action, apparent political suicide, was prompted by his belief that it was a waste of lives and resources to fight the Japanese when the real threat to China was Soviet Russia.

This belief was never shared by his countrymen, and he was condemned by both the Nationalists and Communists. Despite Wang's repeated appeals to Chongqing to negotiate with the Japanese for peace, Jiang Jieshi refused to capitulate. Wang's unrealistic dream of a Sino-Japanese alliance against Soviet Russia was thus never realized. In November, 1944, Wang Jingwei died in Nagoya, Japan. The Nanjing puppet regime collapsed upon Japan's surrender in August, 1945, at the end of World War II. Its top leaders were tried and executed for treason. Regardless of his intentions in cooperating with the Japanese, Wang Jingwei has been remembered as a traitor by the Chinese people.

Bibliography

Bates, Don. *Wang Ching Wei: Puppet or Patriot.* Chicago: R. F. Seymour, 1941.

Bunker, Gerald E. *The Peace Conspiracy: Wang Ching-wei and the China War.* Cambridge, Mass.: Harvard University Press, 1972.

So, Wai-Chor. *The Kuomintang Left in the National Revolution, 1924-1931.* New York: Oxford University Press, 1991.

Peng Deng

Earl Warren

Born: March 19, 1891; Los Angeles, California
Died: July 9, 1974; Washington, D.C.

Chief justice of the United States (1953-1969)

Earl Warren (URL WAH-rehn) was the son of Scandinavian immigrants who settled in Bakersfield, California. His father was a railroad worker, and the family had little money. As a young man, Warren worked as a manual laborer for the railroad and performed other jobs as he worked his way through the University of California at Berkeley. He received his bachelor's degree in 1912 and his law degree in 1914. After briefly working for an oil company and a law firm, in 1917 Warren enlisted in the U.S. Army.

Earl Warren *(Library of Congress)*

Public Life

At the end of World War I, Warren began his career in public service. After working as a legislative and municipal assistant in Oakland, California, he joined the Alameda County district attorney's office. In 1925 Warren himself became the district attorney. In 1925 Warren also married Nina Palmquist Meyers, with whom he had two sons and three daughters. In addition, Warren adopted his wife's son born of an earlier marriage. Warren's handsome, all-American looking family proved to be a helpful public-relations aid. Warren hardly needed such assistance, however: In 1931 he was voted "the best district attorney in the United States." In 1938 Warren was elected as California's attorney general, a position he held for only one term. In 1942 he was elected governor of California by a landslide, and he would be reelected to a record three terms.

Warren's exact political affiliation was unclear, as he had often registered—and run—as the candidate of more than one party. He remained, nonetheless, a favorite of Republicans, who saw him as a candidate for national office. In 1952 Warren was in fact a serious presidential aspirant, but he threw his support to Dwight D. Eisenhower, thus securing a political favor.

Chief Justice

After Eisenhower was elected, he nominated Warren to replace U.S. chief justice Fred Vinson, who had died unexpectedly. Later, Eisenhower would declare that appointing Warren to the Supreme Court was "the biggest damn-fool mistake I ever made."

Warren, who had given every indication of being a middle-of-the-road conservative, in fact presided over the most liberal Supreme Court the

U.S. chief justice Earl Warren and his wife at a 1963 White House reception for the Supreme Court justices. At left are President John F. Kennedy and First Lady Jacqueline Kennedy. *(Library of Congress)*

Brown v. Board of Education

Oliver Brown, the father of a seven-year-old African American Kansas schoolgirl, brought suit against his local school board when it refused to allow his daughter to attend the nearest elementary school because of state-mandated racial segregation. He was aided in his suit by the National Association for the Advancement of Colored People (NAACP). The NAACP took his case, together with several other similar cases from other states, all the way to the Supreme Court. The aim of the NAACP was to force the Court to overrule the principle that "separate but equal" facilities for blacks and whites were acceptable under the Constitution. The "separate but equal" doctrine had been the law of the land since the Supreme Court's *Plessy v. Ferguson* decision of 1896. Largely because of the leadership and diplomacy of Chief Justice Earl Warren, on May 17, 1954, the Court announced a unanimous decision in favor of Brown and his fellow plaintiffs. Perhaps no other decision has had as great an impact on American society as *Brown v. Board of Education*, which sparked a revolution in civil rights.

In September, 1964, U.S. chief justice Earl Warren presents President Lyndon B. Johnson with the first copy of the Warren Commission's report on the assassination of John F. Kennedy. *(Archive Photos)*

tionment, separation of church and state, free speech, and the reform of criminal procedure. Many blamed him personally for the social unrest that beset the United States in the 1960's, and he was often the target of impeachments attempts. He would serve as chief justice, however, for nearly sixteen years.

In 1963 Warren also served, at the request of President Lyndon B. Johnson, as head of a commission investigating the assassination of President John F. Kennedy. The experience was not a happy one for Warren, who believed that it violated the principle of separation of powers. He was also uncomfortable with the Warren Commission's final report, which concluded on the basis of less than complete evidence that Kennedy's death was not the product of a conspiracy.

In 1968 Warren informed President Johnson that he intended to retire, but he stayed on for another year when Abe Fortas, whom Johnson had nominated as Warren's replacement, was forced to withdraw because of a financial scandal. Warren finally stepped down on June 23, 1969. He died five years later.

Bibliography

Cray, Ed. *Chief Justice: A Biography of Earl Warren.* New York: Simon & Schuster, 1997.

Schwartz, Bernard. *Super Chief: Earl Warren and His Supreme Court, a Judicial Biography.* Unabridged ed. New York: New York University Press, 1983.

_____, ed. *The Warren Court: A Retrospective.* New York: Oxford University Press, 1996.

Lisa Paddock

country has ever known. Almost his first task after joining the Court in 1953 was hearing the reargument of *Brown v. Board of Education,* which had been held over from the previous year. Largely because of Warren's strong and skillful leadership, the Warren Court often reached a consensus favoring progressive social changes such as desegregation, voting rights, reappor-

Chaim Weizmann

Born: November 27, 1874; Motol, Poland, Russian Empire (now Belarus)
Died: November 9, 1952; Rehovot, Israel

Zionist leader and first president of Israel (1948-1952)

Chaim Azriel Weizmann (KI-yihm ahz-ree-EHL VITZ-mahn) was the third of fifteen children born to Ozer and Rachel Weizmann amid impoverished circumstances in the Pale of Settlement, the only region along Russia's western frontier where Jews could reside legally. Weizmann grew up in an enlightened atmosphere, surrounded by books written in Yiddish, Hebrew, and Russian. Zionist periodicals also found their way into the home and influenced young Weizmann.

While attending secondary school in Pinsk (a center of Zionist activity in the Russian Empire), Weizmann increasingly absorbed the ideas of the Zionist movement. Upon his graduation in 1891, he had decided upon two things: that he wanted a career in chemistry and that he was a committed Zionist. Weizmann left Russia for Germany and then Switzerland to continue his education, since his own country enforced university quotas restricting the admissions of Jewish students. In 1896, he came under the influence of Asher Ginzberg, better known as Ahad Ha'am, a Hebrew essayist and an early Zionist theoretician who advocated a slow and careful Jewish settlement process, making Palestine first a spiritual and cultural center for world Judaism. In 1900 Weizmann received his Ph.D. magna cum laude and shortly thereafter was appointed lecturer in organic chemistry at the University of Geneva. The pattern of Weizmann's adult life was set. He would blend a love of science with a passion for Zionism.

Zionist Leader

By the beginning of the twentieth century, Weizmann was becoming a well-known member of the World Zionist Organization. This group had been created in 1897 by the First Zionist Congress, which Theodor Herzl had convened to bring about the establishment of a Jewish home in Palestine. In 1901, however, Weizmann found himself at odds with Herzl's ideas, so he formed the first opposition group in the Zionist movement. Upon the death of Herzl in 1904 (which left the Zionist movement in a state of shock), Weizmann, Herzl's as-yet-unrecognized heir, went to Great Britain to assume an academic position at the University of Manchester.

Between 1904 and 1914, Weizmann devoted most of his time to his scientific career and personal life, though he remained an active Zionist. In 1905, in Manchester, he met Arthur Balfour

Chaim Weizmann *(Library of Congress)*

(then Great Britain's prime minister) and convinced him that Palestine was the only proper national homeland for Jews. Their meeting established a working relationship that eventually resulted in the Balfour Declaration of 1917. In 1906 Weizmann married Vera Chatzman. Two sons were born to them, and, though the marriage would be marked by many work-related separations, they shared a love that bridged these gaps.

In 1907 Weizmann took an important step toward assuming Herzl's mantle of leadership. At the Eighth Zionist Congress, he delivered a major speech on what he termed synthetic Zionism, an attempt to reconcile the two major schools of Zionist thought: political Zionism (advocated by Herzl), which aimed at securing political guarantees for the establishment of a Jewish home in Palestine, and practical Zionism, the actual establishment of settlers in the land of Palestine. Shortly after the speech, Weizmann made his first

visit to Palestine. There he helped to found the Palestine Land Development Company, which stepped up his campaign for the Jewish settlement of Palestine. In 1910 Weizmann became a naturalized British subject.

Recognized Spokesman

During World War I (1914-1918), Weizmann focused his attention on helping England win the war effort through scientific research. He created a process for synthesizing acetone that aided in the manufacture of explosives, and he held an important governmental post to oversee production of war-related chemicals. After the war, he turned again to Zionism.

Not satisfied with the direction taken by the secret Sykes-Picot Agreement of May, 1916 (a pact between the French and British that divided up the Middle East), Weizmann used his diplomatic talents to persuade the British to reconsider

The Zionist Movement

The Zionist movement was an outgrowth of the deeply felt nationalist attachment that the Jewish people have always had to the region called Palestine. Its origin in modern times can be traced to 1894, when journalist Theodor Herzl, an assimilated Jew from Vienna, attended the treason trial of Alfred Dreyfus, a Jewish French army captain wrongly accused and condemned. In the face of blatant anti-Semitism, Herzl produced a small book, *The Jewish State* (1896), arguing for the creation of a Jewish national homeland. In 1897 he convened the first in a series of Zionist Congresses, or conferences, which drew up the program of the movement (the creation of a home in Palestine for the Jewish people, secured by law).

After the death of Herzl in 1904, and with the outbreak of World War I in 1914, the leadership of the Zionist movement effectively passed to

Chaim Weizmann, a Russian Jew living in England. Weizman was instrumental in obtaining a British promise of support for a homeland in Palestine called the Balfour Declaration (November 2, 1917). Through the early decades of the twentieth century, a steady stream of Jews immigrated to Palestine, forming the *Yishuv*—the Jewish community or settlement in the region. Zionists built both urban and rural Jewish centers there. The Nazi Holocaust led more Jews to adopt the ideas of the Zionist movement and to support the establishment of a Jewish national state. The state of Israel was finally proclaimed on May 14, 1948. With its establishment, some Zionists adopted other goals, including the strengthening and expansion of the state and its influence. The name of the Zionist movement comes from one of the ancient names for Jerusalem—Zion.

The Weizmann Institute of Science

The Weizmann Institute of Science is located at Rehovot, Israel, fourteen miles (22 kilometers) south of Tel Aviv). It was originally founded as the Daniel Sieff Research Institute on April 3, 1934, by Chaim Weizmann, a chemist, Zionist leader, and the first president of the state of Israel. Weizmann originally conceived it to be a School of Agriculture of the Hebrew University of Jerusalem (which he had also been instrumental in establishing in 1925). It was to have the purpose of fostering pure scientific research in all fields of agricultural and biological chemistry. The funding came from a friend who wanted to memorialize his deceased son. Expanded and renamed for Weizmann in 1949, it became a recognized center of postgraduate research in physics, chemistry, mathematics, and the life sciences. It fulfilled its founder's goal of making Rehovot (Weizmann's second home) a seat of learning for the Jewish people.

the plight of the Jewish people and their desire for a homeland. The result was the Balfour Declaration of November, 1917, a statement that seemed to throw full British support behind the Zionist cause. In 1920 Weizmann was elected unopposed as president of the World Zionist Organization and served for twelve years (1920 to 1931 and again in 1935). From 1921 onward, he

Chaim Weizmann speaking at the 1925 opening of Hebrew University in Jerusalem. *(Library of Congress)*

traveled the world at a dizzying pace, preaching Zionist ideology and raising funds at mass rallies.

Weizmann also returned to his science for a time, founding the Daniel Sieff Research Institute at Rehovot, Palestine, in 1934—renamed the Weizmann Institute in 1949. By 1947 he was appearing before the United Nations as Zionism's most knowledgeable and articulate champion. He was sent to the United States in 1948 to reconfirm to President Harry S Truman the rightness of an independent state of Israel, which was created in May of that year. Weizmann was elected its first president.

After 1949, his work as theoretician accomplished, Weizmann was relegated to a position of bystander in the government of the new state. Prime Minister David Ben-Gurion held all the real authority. Worn out by a demanding cause, arduous strife, and personal frustrations, Weizmann died days short of his seventy-eighth birthday. He had become, in the eyes of many Jews around the world, the great emancipator and promoter of Jewish freedom and the person most responsible for an independent Jewish homeland.

Bibliography

Amdur, Richard. *Chaim Weizmann*. New York: Chelsea House, 1988.

Rose, Norman. *Chaim Weizmann: A Biography*. New York: Viking Penguin, 1986.

Weizmann, Chaim. *The Essential Chaim Weizmann*. Edited and compiled by Barnet Litvinoff. New York: Holmes & Meier, 1982.

Andrew C. Skinner

Ida B. Wells-Barnett

Born: July 16, 1862; Holly Springs, Mississippi
Died: March 25, 1931; Chicago, Illinois

American journalist and antilynching activist

Ida Bell Wells (I-dah BEHL WEHLZ) was born in the South in 1862 in the midst of the violent upheaval of the Civil War. She was the first of eight children of Elizabeth Warrenton, a cook, and James Wells, a skilled carpenter, who had both been slaves. After emancipation, James Wells was involved in civic affairs and was a founding board member of Shaw University (later Rust College). He was concerned with building educational, political, and economic opportunities in the black community.

Early Life

In 1878, at age sixteen, Ida Wells had to begin rearing her five surviving siblings after her parents both died during a yellow fever epidemic. Her parents had stressed the importance of education, and Wells studied at Shaw University, supporting her siblings as a teacher in Mississippi and Memphis, Tennessee. In 1884, when a conductor told Wells that the ladies' coach on a Chesapeake and Ohio train was segregated and asked her to move into the smoking car, Wells refused. She had to be physically removed, and she subsequently filed a suit against the railroad. The court ruled in her favor in the amount of $500 damages, but the finding was reversed by the state supreme court. The story of this case became the basis for Wells's first venture into journalism—and the beginning of a passionate crusade.

Wells's Pen for Justice

Ida Wells was one of few female leaders in an age when women's place was believed to be in the home. Her achievements as a journalist and civic leader sparked the creation of "colored women's clubs" dedicated to racial uplift in the United States. Wells's first writings appeared in 1884 in the *Evening Star* newspaper under the name "Iola." The lynching of three black businessmen in Memphis in March, 1892, crystallized Wells's evolving political philosophy.

She believed that the motive for the lynching was economic: The businessmen had been in competition with a white grocer who feared losing black business. Wells's scathing editorial urging blacks to move out of the county altogether

Ida B. Wells-Barnett *(Library of Congress)*

1563

Lynching

Between 1882 and 1968, there were 4,743 documented lynchings in the United States; most occurred in the South against black Americans. Historians record the year 1892 as the peak of violent lynchings. They sometimes took place in a carnival atmosphere in which white families cheered over picnic lunches. Prior to the Civil War, southern blacks, the vast majority of whom were slaves, were rarely assaulted or killed. Because they were property, their deaths were considered a loss of capital. If the state punished a slave by execution, the owner was reimbursed for the loss.

In *A Red Record*, published in 1895, Ida Wells-Barnett cited evidence of the increase of American lynchings against blacks, which she referred to as "unlawful acts of mob violence." She dismissed the notion that black men were being executed for insulting white women's "virtue." Wells believed that the emancipation of millions of black slaves seeking political, economic, and social equality caused fear in whites unused to competing with blacks in society or in the marketplace. Lynchings, she argued, were meant to keep blacks subservient, or "in their place." The fact that a second peak year of lynchings was 1919, after black men returned from fighting in World War I and sought an equal place in American society, seems to support Wells's conclusion.

marked the beginning of the campaign for federal antilynching legislation. The editorial was published in *Free Speech*, a Memphis weekly in which Wells owned one-third interest. She was out of town at a church conference when the editorial appeared. The office of *Free Speech* was ransacked, and threats against Wells's life made it impossible for her to return to Memphis.

She went to New York, writing for the *New York Age*, whose editor, T. Thomas Fortune, had published Wells's "Iola" columns. About the same time that Wells was becoming known as a journalist, she gained a wider audience for her speaking engagements, both in the United States and in England. She spoke there for the first time in 1893 to gain support for the antilynching campaign. In 1895 Wells's *A Red Record: Tabulated Statistics and Alleged Causes of Lynchings in the United States, 1892-1893-1894* was published. That same year Wells married Ferdinand L. Barnett (bahr-NEHT), a Chicago journalist, and settled in Chicago; the couple had four children. Wells concentrated on her children while they were young, although she continued to write and speak for black equality. Ida Wells-Barnett died of uremic poisoning in 1931.

Bibliography

Wells-Barnett, Ida B. *Crusade for Justice: The Autobiography of Ida B. Wells*. Edited by Alfreda M. Duster. Chicago: University of Chicago Press, 1970.

_____. *The Memphis Diary of Ida B. Wells: An Intimate Portrait of the Activist as a Young Woman*. Edited by Miriam Decosta-Willis. Boston: Beacon Press, 1995.

_____. *Southern Horrors and Other Writings: The Anti-Lynching Campaign of Ida B. Wells, 1892-1900*. Edited by Jacqueline Jones Royster. Boston: Bedford Books, 1997.

Dale Edwyna Smith

Walter Francis White

Born: July 1, 1893; Atlanta, Georgia
Died: March 21, 1955; New York, New York

American civil rights leader and writer

Walter Francis White (WAHL-tur FRAN-sihs WIT) was the son of George W. White, a letter carrier, and Madeline Harrison White, a former schoolteacher. Though his parents were fair-skinned and only fractionally African American, Walter was so horrified by the Atlanta riot of 1906 that he felt he must identify with his black ancestry.

In 1916, after graduating from Atlanta University, White went to work for the Standard Life Insurance Company. That year he helped to organize the Atlanta branch of the National Association for the Advancement of Colored People (NAACP). In 1918 White was brought to the NAACP headquarters in New York to serve as assistant secretary of the organization. White married Leah Gladys Powell in 1922; they had two children, Jane and Walter Carl Darrow.

The Power of Print

One of the NAACP's primary targets was mob violence against blacks and, specifically, lynching. Posing as a white reporter, the new NAACP staff member traveled throughout the South and published his observations in newspaper and magazine articles. He also wrote a novel about lynching, *The Fire in the Flint* (1924). A second novel, *Flight* (1926), dealt with light-skinned blacks' "passing" as white.

After winning a Guggenheim Award for creative writing, White went to France to write another novel. Instead, he produced *Rope and Faggot: A Biography of Judge Lynch* (1929). Through his writing, White is believed to have helped reduce the incidence of lynching. Later, the reports that White wrote as a war correspondent in World War II for the *New York Post* and his book *A Rising Wind: A Report of the Negro Soldier in the European*

Theater of War (1945) provided a factual basis for President Harry S Truman's executive order desegregating the armed forces.

Politics and Controversy

After becoming executive secretary of the NAACP in 1931, White focused on practical politics. Over the years, he and his staff systematically lobbied Congress to pass laws that would assure voting rights, stop lynching, end discrimination in hiring and housing, and integrate the armed forces and the public schools. White himself also worked through the executive branch, acting as

Walter Francis White *(Library of Congress)*

1565

An African American battalion training in 1942. Walter Francis White's war reporting during Wold War II was influential in the postwar desegregation of the military. *(Archive Photos)*

an adviser both to President Franklin D. Roosevelt and to President Truman. Frequently White made his influence felt in foreign affairs, for instance, serving in 1945 and in 1948 as consultant to the U.S. delegation to the United Nations.

Within the NAACP White was perceived as an autocrat whose unwillingness to tolerate differences of opinion led, for example, to the ousting of the highly respected W. E. B. Du Bois, longtime editor of the NAACP publication *The Crisis.*

Rope and Faggot

Rope and Faggot: A Biography of Judge Lynch (1929) is Walter Francis White's best-known book. In it, he traces the history of lynching over the course of a century and probes the psychological motivations of those who commit this kind of murder. White cited statistical data and quoted articles in local newspapers in addition to presenting first-hand accounts of survivors. In doing so he produced a work that was far more effective than if it had appealed only to the emotions of its readers. The *New York World* called *Rope and Faggot* a "sound" book that presents "a challenge to our civilization."

White's popularity also suffered when he divorced his wife to marry a white advertising executive, Poppy Cannon. Responding to escalating complaints about White's leadership style, the NAACP board finally reduced his power but permitted him to remain in office until his death.

A Man of Achievement

Although White had his flaws, he also had many admirable qualities. The fact that he chose to claim his black heritage in order to redress wrongs attests to his sense of commitment. He had courage, as proven by his forays into the South and his work as a war correspondent; impressive creative powers, as shown in his publications; and steadfast determination, evidenced by his achievements in the political arena. The work that Walter White did for African Americans also benefited the nation as a whole, which moved closer to its ideal of "liberty and justice for all."

Bibliography

Cannon, Poppy. *A Gentle Knight: My Husband Walter White.* New York: Rinehart, 1956.

McGuire, William, and Leslie Wheeler. *American Social Leaders.* Santa Barbara, Calif.: ABC-Clio, 1993.

Waldron, Edward E. *Walter White and the Harlem Renaissance.* Port Washington, N.Y.: Kennikat, 1978.

Rosemary M. Canfield Reisman

Gough Whitlam

Born: July 11, 1916; Kew, Victoria, Australia

Prime minister of Australia (1972-1975)

Edward Gough Whitlam (EHD-wurd GAWF WIHT-luhm) was the son of a lawyer who held important administrative positions in the Australian government. His mother was the daughter of a judge. During World War II he was a bomber-navigator in the Royal Australian Air Force. Whitlam earned a law degree in 1946 and began practicing law in 1947.

Rise to Power

Whitlam began running for public office in 1947. After losing local elections in 1947 and 1950,

Gough Whitlam *(Library of Congress)*

he won election to the Australian House of Representatives in 1952. During the next fifteen years he rose in the ranks of the Australian Labor Party (ALP) to become its leader in 1967.

As leader of the ALP, Whitlam sought to make the party appear more moderate in its policies. Instead of remaining a left-wing party with little political power, the ALP under Whitlam rose to prominence. Whitlam instituted several party reforms, emphasizing national rather than local politics and transforming the ALP from a coalition of state parties into a single body. With the election of Whitlam as prime minister on December 2, 1972, the ALP won control of the highest office in the land after Australia had had twenty-three years of conservative leadership under the Australian Liberal Party.

Time in Office

One of Whitlam's main goals as prime minister was to make Australia less economically dependent on other developed nations and to increase Australia's international standing. He also abolished military conscription, released draft dodgers from prison, withdrew all Australian troops from Vietnam, and lowered the voting age to eighteen.

Whitlam's social reforms included making college education free for those who qualified academically, introducing welfare payments for single-parent families and homeless people, abolishing the death penalty for federal crimes, and acknowledging the cultural contributions of Australian Aborigines. His government also ended the last vestiges of the racist "White Australia" policy, reduced government censorship, granted building contracts for urban renewal, initiated reform of divorce laws, appointed more

Inflation and Unemployment in the mid-1970's

The greatest challenge Gough Whitlam faced as prime minister of Australia was a simultaneous increase in inflation and unemployment. In mid-1973, unemployment remained between 1.4 percent and 1.5 percent. In 1974, however, unemployment increased by 0.67 percent between June and August, the highest increase during any two-month period since 1946. By August of 1975, unemployment had reached nearly 5 percent. Inflation rose even more quickly. In March of 1973 the inflation rate was 5.7 percent. By March of 1975 it was 17.6 percent.

Whitlam attempted to deal with unemployment by lowering taxes and increasing government spending—which also increased inflation, so he later reversed this policy. Whitlam also revalued the Australian dollar. He attempted to initiate wage and price controls but failed to win approval for the controls. Whitlam's inability to solve Australia's economic problems was a key factor in the landslide victory of the Australian Liberal Party in 1975.

women to government positions, and instituted equal pay for women.

During his three years in office, Whitlam had difficulty creating an economic policy to deal with high levels of inflation and unemployment. He also failed to control completely the actions of a cabinet filled with ministers with projects of their own. His greatest problem was a Senate dominated by the Australian Liberal Party, which opposed almost all of his policies. The Senate refused to approve legislation necessary to pay for government activities, hoping to force Whitlam to hold new elections. Whitlam refused to hold elections, hoping to force the Senate to approve the legislation.

The stalemate was broken by Sir John Kerr, the governor-general of Australia, in an unprecedented use of the power of his largely ceremonial office. On November 11, 1975, Kerr removed Whitlam from office and appointed opposition leader Malcolm Fraser as prime minister in his place. Whitlam retaliated by leading a vote of "no-confidence" against Fraser in the House of Representatives, hoping to remove him from office. Before the vote could take effect, however, Kerr dissolved both the House of Representatives and the Senate, requiring new elections to be held.

By the time the elections were held on December 13, 1975, the unpopularity of the ALP because of its inability to deal with inflation and unemployment led to its overwhelming defeat. Whitlam soon left politics and began an academic career. He was later appointed to several Australian and international councils.

Bibliography

Walter, James. *The Leader: A Political Biography of Gough Whitlam.* St. Lucia, Queensland, Australia: University of Queensland Press, 1980.

Whitlam, Gough. *The Truth of the Matter.* Ringwood, Victoria, Australia: Penguin Books Australia, 1979.

_____. *The Whitlam Government 1972-1975.* Melbourne, Australia: Viking, 1985.

Rose Secrest

Elie Wiesel

Born: September 30, 1928; Sighet, Transylvania (now Romania)

Jewish author and journalist, winner of 1986 Nobel Peace Prize

Eliezer Wiesel (ay-lee-AY-zur "AY-lee" VEE-sehl) was the only son in a strongly Jewish family. Wiesel's early education revolved around Jewish studies, especially those relating to the Hasidic sect. In 1944, his youth and his education were cut short. World War II was raging, and Nazi Germany had occupied Transylvania. When he was fifteen, Elie and most of his family were sent to Auschwitz concentration camp. Wiesel and his father were separated from his mother and younger sister, who died in the camp. His father died a year later. Young Elie also spent time in the

Elie Wiesel *(The Nobel Foundation)*

Buna, Buchenwald, and Gleiwitz camps. When he was set free at the end of World War II, Wiesel discovered that his two older sisters were alive. He spent the next several years in a French orphanage.

Finding His Voice

Following his release from the French orphanage in 1948, Wiesel began to further his education by studying philosophy, psychology, and literature at the Sorbonne. At the same time, he launched his writing career. He had had aspirations of being a writer for most of his life, having begun writing at the age of ten. As a budding journalist, Wiesel wrote for the French newspaper *L'Arche* and for several French Zionist publications.

Wiesel first focused on topics of interest to the Jewish population in France and in Europe. However, eventually he was sent to cover the beginnings of the new nation of Israel (founded in 1948). There Wiesel wrote extensively on the new nation and the problems it faced. He witnessed many divisions of opinion among the leaders, such as the rift between Israeli president Nahum Goldman and David Ben-Gurion, one of the nation's founders, over the question of whether German money should be accepted to help finance the new country. No amount of dissension could diminish Wiesel's belief in, and emotional attachment to, the new nation.

During this period Wiesel refused to address his experiences in the concentration camps. Upon his release from the camps, Wiesel had begun a self-imposed silence about the subject, which he maintained for ten years. He refused to speak or to write about the year he spent watching those around him die. He saw language as inadequate for explaining the horrors that he had witnessed.

This situation changed, however, following an interview with French Nobel laureate François Mauriac.

Letting His Voice Speak

Wiesel immigrated to the United States in the mid-1950's. Under Mauriac's influence, Wiesel published *Night* (1958), recounting his year in the concentration camps and how he began questioning the justice of God. The work received international acclaim, showing Wiesel that the reading public cared about his experiences and opinions. Wiesel used subsequent works such as *Jews of Silence* (1966), *The Trial of God* (1979), *The Testament* (1981), and *All Rivers Run to the Sea* (1995) to speak directly about his experiences as a Holocaust victim. He questioned how a supposedly civilized world could permit such a tragic event and warned about the possibility that such barbarity could happen again. For his life's work as a writer, teacher, and human rights advocate, Wiesel received many honors: He was appointed chair of the Presidential Commission on the Holocaust (1978) and was awarded the Congressional Gold Medal of Achievement (1985), the Nobel Peace Prize (1986), and more than seventy-five honorary college and university degrees.

Elie Wiesel's writings on the Holocaust and his lifetime of work as a human rights activist brought him the Nobel Peace Prize in 1986. *(Washington Post, D.C. Public Library)*

Wiesel's Experience of Racism

Elie Wiesel was introduced to racism in its deadliest form when he and his family were sent to the Nazi death camps in 1944 merely because they were Jews. Wiesel survived the camps, and he did not allow his memory of the experience to diminish with passing time. He concluded that much of the Holocaust occurred because the most obvious Holocaust victims were members of a minority. For that reason, he thought, individuals and countries refused to act to save those being persecuted and murdered. Confronting racial hatred occupied much of Wiesel's professional and personal adult life. He did not limit his stand against racism to the Jews, but took a strong stand in defense of the defenseless around the world. He spoke out, for example, in support of such diverse minorities as the Soviet Jews, the Miskito Indians of Nicaragua, the missing children of Argentina, the Kurds of Iraq, and the victims of apartheid in South Africa. Elie Wiesel linked the concept of racism to the denial of human rights to any person for any reason.

Author Elie Wiesel speaking at a gathering of Holocaust survivors in Washington, D.C., 1983. *(Bernard Gotfryd/ Archive Photos)*

Bibliography

Brown, Robert M. *Elie Wiesel: Messenger of All Humanity*. South Bend, Ind.: University of Notre Dame Press, 1983.

Sibelman, Simon P. *Silence in the Novels of Elie Wiesel*. New York: St. Martin's Press, 1995.

Stern, Ellen Norman. *Elie Wiesel: A Voice for Humanity*. New York: Jewish Publication Society, 1996.

Wiesel, Elie. *All Rivers Run to the Sea: Memoirs*. New York: Alfred A. Knopf, 1995.

Tom Frazier

Simon Wiesenthal

Born: December 31, 1908; Buczacz, Galicia, Austro-Hungarian Empire (now Buchach, Ukraine)

Austrian-born investigator of Nazi war crimes

Simon Wiesenthal (ZEE-mon VEE-sehn-tahl) was born to a Jewish trader who moved to Buczacz to escape pogroms in Russia and was killed in action in World War I. His mother was later killed by the Nazis. Simon trained as an architect and married Cyla Müller in 1936. They were seized by the Nazis in 1941. When the Americans freed Wiesenthal from the Mauthausen extermination camp in 1945, he weighed less than one hundred pounds. Eleven million others—Jews, gypsies, communists, intellectuals, children, and the elderly and disabled—had been murdered. In the Nazis' attempt to create a "pure" Aryan race, they committed monstrous crimes against humanity. Wiesenthal devoted his life to preserving the memory of the dead and to bringing their murderers to justice.

Methods and Results

Blessed with a phenomenal memory, Wiesenthal would compile and collate factual evidence until he had enough material to make a case against a Nazi murderer, whereupon he would send it to the relevant justice department. If they did not take action, he would call a press conference to bring public pressure to bear on the case.

All of Wiesenthal's work would be done in his small Jewish Documentation Center in Austria; he had never been a fund-raiser and relied mainly on his own intellectual resources. When necessary, however, he quickly mobilized others. In the 1960's, many European countries, including Germany and Austria, had a twenty-year limitation on murder charges. Wiesenthal sought to have the time limit revoked or extended so that charges could still be brought against perpetrators of Nazi genocide. To accomplish this, he polled public figures around the world and published their responses only months before the 1965 expiration (expiry) dates as *Term Expiry? Two Hundred Public Figures Say No.* The book was prefaced with the succinct reply from U.S. senator Robert Kennedy: "Moral duties have no terms."

Over the years, Wiesenthal had both high-profile successes and frustrating failures. In 1960, he played a prominent role in locating Adolf Eichmann. In 1963, Wiesenthal effectively quelled rumors that Ann Frank's *Diary of a Young Girl* (1947) was a forgery by finding Karl Silber-

Simon Wiesenthal *(Library of Congress)*

1573

Simon Wiesenthal before delivering a lecture in Vienna, Austria, in 1965. *(Popperfoto/Archive Photos)*

bauer, the Gestapo officer who arrested Frank. In 1967, Wiesenthal's research resulted in the extradition from Brazil to West Germany of Franz Paul Stangl, the commandant of the Sobibor and Tre-

blinka extermination camps. In 1973, his investigations brought about the extradition from the United States to West Germany of Hermine Braunsteiner-Ryan on charges of particular cru-

---

Wiesenthal's Jewish Documentation Center

When the Allies defeated Nazi Germany in 1945, death-camp survivor Simon Wiesenthal offered his services to the Americans to help track down Nazis who had committed crimes against humanity. He sent volunteers to the displaced persons camps to take detailed statements from people who had suffered or witnessed atrocities. Using the information they collected, Wiesenthal compiled extensive files of places, criminals, and witnesses. With this evidence, Wiesenthal ran his own documentation center in Linz, Austria, from 1947 to 1954; in 1954 he sent his massive collec-

tion of files to the Yad Vashem Historical Archives in Israel.

Wiesenthal kept his file on Adolf Eichmann, however, and eventually found information that facilitated his capture. The Eichmann trial rekindled support for bringing Nazi war criminals to justice, and Wiesenthal opened a new Jewish Documentation Center in Vienna, Austria, on October 1, 1961. There he continued to set straight the historical record about Nazi crimes against humanity and to combat anti-Semitism and neo-Nazism.

The Trial of Adolf Eichmann

After World War II, Adolf Eichmann slipped through several U.S. prisoner-of-war camps without being recognized as one of the chief perpetrators of Nazi genocide. As director of the Nazis' Jewish Desk, he was the logistics expert responsible for the transportation of six million Jews to extermination camps.

Eichmann's wife applied for a death certificate for him in 1947. Simon Wiesenthal produced witnesses who had seen Eichmann alive since his ostensible death, however, so the search for him continued. By 1960, Wiesenthal knew that Eichmann was living in Buenos Aires, Argentina, under the name Ricardo Klement. To assist in his identification, Wiesenthal had Eichmann's four brothers surreptitiously photographed. One of them resembled "Klement" closely.

David Ben-Gurion, prime minister of Israel, had the Israeli secret service abduct Eichmann and bring him to Israel to stand trial. Eichmann was convicted on fifteen counts of crimes against humanity and was hanged on May 31, 1962. The televised trial informed the world of the horrors of the Holocaust and revived efforts to locate and try other Nazi criminals.

elty to women and children in the Majdanek extermination camp.

One of the most infamous Nazis, Josef Mengele, eluded Wiesenthal to the end. The "Angel of Death," who had tortured his victims with senseless so-called medical experiments, was protected by his family's financial resources and died of natural causes in Brazil in 1979. Wiesenthal was also unable definitively to solve the mystery of what happened to the Swedish diplomat Raoul Wallenberg, whose courageous interventions saved thousands of Jews from the Nazis. Wallenberg disappeared in Hungary in January of 1945; several people reported later encountering him in Soviet prisons.

Opposition to Wiesenthal

Wiesenthal's tireless investigations inconvenienced many people, who in turn tried to make life difficult for him. He had to relocate the Jewish Documentation Center when fellow tenants received threatening letters. The center then was guarded by a policeman. Former Nazis and neo-Nazis expressed vehement opposition to Wiesenthal, but he also encountered strong opposition from some Jews. In Wiesenthal's opinion, for example, Bruno Kreisky, Austria's first Jewish chancellor (from 1970 to 1983), let too many former Nazis into public office. Kreisky and Wiesenthal's argument became personal and carried over into the courts. Ironically, Wiesenthal's refusal to condemn another Austrian politician, President Kurt Waldheim (president from 1986 to 1992), brought him into direct conflict with the World Jewish Congress and with the institution that honors his name, the Simon Wiesenthal Center in Los Angeles. Both these organizations accused Waldheim of war crimes. Wiesenthal criticized Waldheim only for withholding evidence that, when brought to light, did not incriminate him.

Moral Considerations

Wiesenthal's memories of those he saw die in the extermination camps were so strong that he never doubted his duty to be deputy for the dead. He was, however, aware that others think differently. His own wife begged him to put the past behind him. Twenty-five years after the Holocaust, Wiesenthal asked intellectuals and religious leaders for their views and published the collected responses to encourage debate. A revised edition of the book, *The Sunflower: On the Possibilities and Limits of Forgiveness*, appeared in 1996.

In the course of tracking down individuals such as Eichmann, Wiesenthal drew attention to a side of human nature that can only be combated if it is acknowledged and comprehended. Thousands of Nazis who participated in routine genocide in the concentration and extermination camps returned to apparently normal civilian lives after the war. Those who were later arrested claimed that they had been merely following orders: Once they put on their uniforms, they ceased to think for themselves. Wiesenthal pointed out that none of them was born a murderer. The Nazis were conditioned to murder under a dictatorship run amok. Mass murder in modern times is organized, industrialized killing, and the victims are not regarded as human. In the extermination camps, they were dehumanized by being sent to the gas chambers naked, starved, and shorn of their hair.

By reminding the world of atrocities committed during the Third Reich, Wiesenthal kept people aware of what happens when tolerance is displaced by prejudice and when people allow the state to define their morality. Wiesenthal did not believe in the concept of collective guilt, only individual guilt. Each person must assume ultimate responsibility for his or her actions.

Bibliography

Levy, Alan. *The Wiesenthal File*. London: Constable, 1993.

Pick, Hella. *Simon Wiesenthal: A Life in Search of Justice*. Boston: Northeastern University Press, 1996.

Wiesenthal, Simon. *Justice not Vengeance*. London: Weidenfeld and Nicolson, 1989.

Jean M. Snook

William II

Born: January 27, 1859; Berlin, Prussia
Died: June 4, 1941; Doorn, the Netherlands

Kaiser (caesar) of Germany (1888-1918)

William II (WIHL-yuhm thuh SEH-kuhnd), born Friedrich Wilhelm Viktor Albert von Hohenzollern (FREED-rihk VIHL-hehlm FIHK-tohr AHL-bayrt fon hoh-ehn-TSOH-lehrn), was the third and last Hohenzollern emperor of Germany. He became well known for his impulsive and erratic public pronouncements. Many historians consider him to be the chief architect of World War I. He married Princess Victoria of Schleswig-Holstein. She died in 1921, and William married Hermine of Ruess in 1922.

Education and Early Career

William was born to Frederick William, crown prince of Prussia, and Princess Victoria, eldest daughter of Queen Victoria of England. From birth, his left arm was withered and shorter than his right. Between the ages of six and fifteen he was in the care of a private tutor. He learned horsemanship and studied the curriculum that had been prescribed for young princes of Prussia since the days of Frederick the Great. In 1874, he was sent to *Gymnasium* (prep school) in Kassel, where he did moderately well, passing his exams before he turned eighteen.

William was then commissioned as a lieutenant in the First Guards Regiment. He took to barracks life quite well, finding welcome relief from the stifling atmosphere of both home and school. However, he soon gained a reputation for being tactless, arrogant, and selfish.

Bismarck's Plan

Otto von Bismarck was the chancellor of Prussia and the main architect of the German Empire. His conservative views often clashed with the views of the crown princess, William's mother. Bismarck feared that when Frederick William took the throne, she would be the power behind it. He suspected that she would try to foster a constitutional monarchy on the English model and thus would undo Bismarck's achievements. Bismarck actively put Prince William in the thick of German diplomacy. In 1884, when in his mid-twenties, William was sent to Russia to attend the coming-of-age ceremony of the future Czar Nicolas. He had barely returned when he was sent to Russia again. Later that year, Bismarck saw to it

William II *(Library of Congress)*

In the years before World War I, Kaiser William II (left) observes German army maneuvers with visiting British military man Winston Churchill. *(Library of Congress)*

Ascension to the Throne

In 1887, Prince Frederick William was diagnosed with advanced cancer of the throat. Soon afterward, Kaiser William I declared that his grandson William, not the crown prince, be authorized to sign state papers when the kaiser was unable to do so: The young prince was being trained for the throne. In March of 1888, Kaiser William I died. He was succeeded by Frederick William, seriously ill with cancer. In June of 1888, Fredrick William died, and his son became Kaiser William II (in German, Wilhelm II). At first William II was content to keep Chancellor Bismarck in office, but a clash between the young emperor and the old "iron chancellor" was brewing.

Problems began to arise fairly quickly. In May of 1889, the coal miners in the Ruhr region went on strike. They were soon joined by workers from other parts of Germany. The mine owners called for government assistance, and Bismarck provided it in the form of troops to break the strike. William, however, voiced his sympathy with the miners. The final straw was Bismarck's antisocialist legislation. Bismarck insisted that the kaiser approve the package; otherwise, he threatened, there would be social revolution. Kai-

that the young prince was attached to the German foreign office. This situation did not please William's parents, who thought him too immature to be dealing with foreign affairs.

The Hohenzollern Dynasty

The Hohenzollerns ruled the state of Brandenburg since Holy Roman Emperor Sigismund appointed Frederick of Hohenzollern elector (prince) of that state in 1415. In 1701, another Frederick combined the titles of elector of Brandenburg and king of Prussia. His son, Fredrick II (Frederick the Great), increased Prussia's power and prestige in Europe with a series of short, sharp, and successful wars, most notably against the Habsburg rulers of Austria. After the fall of French conquerer Napoleon Bonaparte in 1815, the old Holy Roman Empire was destroyed. Prussia began to take the lead in German affairs. In 1861, William I was crowned king of Prussia. He appointed as his chancellor the brilliant and wily Otto von Bismarck. In 1870, Bismarck was able to engineer a historic compromise that placed the king of Prussia at the head of a united Germany. In 1871, William I of Prussia was crowned William I, kaiser (caesar) of Germany.

The Kaiser's Abdication

By October, 1918, it had become clear to the German General Staff that Germany could no longer continue the war. They had been fighting since 1914. The Germans conveyed a message to U.S. president Woodrow Wilson, asking for an armistice. The American reply stated that the U.S. would not discuss peace with the imperial government of Germany. Many Germans began to think that it was time for the kaiser to surrender his power.

On November 3, 1918, a mutiny broke out among German sailors stationed at Kiel and Hamburg. As the mutiny spread, Kaiser William went to army headquarters at Spa. There the generals told him that even the army was falling apart and that they could no longer guarantee the kaiser's safety. On November 9, 1918, the chancellor, Prince Max of Baden, announced that the kaiser had abdicated and that the crown prince had renounced his rights to the throne. On November 10, Kaiser William fled to exile in the Netherlands, where he remained until his death in 1941.

ser William, however, found a third option: on March 17, 1890, Bismarck resigned. There was now no one in the German government who could stand in the way of the kaiser and his mercurial ideas.

Nowhere was Bismarck's guiding hand missed more than in the arena of foreign affairs. William managed to frighten and antagonize most of his neighbors. First he failed to renew a mutual assurance treaty with Russia. Then he contested French interests in Morocco. Finally he engaged in a naval arms race with Great Britain. Partially as a result of these policies, a series of alliances had formed on the European continent.

World War I

On June 28, 1914, Archduke Francis (Franz) Ferdinand, heir to the throne of the Austro-Hungarian Empire, was assassinated in Sarajevo by a Serbian na-

tionalist. Austria blamed the Serbian government for the assassination and sought support from its main ally, Germany, in pressing its claims against Serbia. The kaiser, horrified by the assassination, was quick to give Austria his unstinting support. Because of the various alliances that had been signed by the nations of Europe, when Austria-

German Kaiser William II (center), flanked by his primary World War I military leaders, Paul von Hindenburg (left) and Erich Ludendorff. *(Library of Congress)*

Hungary declared war on Serbia, Russia declared war on Austria-Hungary. Germany declared war on Russia, and France declared war on both Germany and Austria-Hungary. World War I had begun. At first the war seemed to go well for Germany, but it soon bogged down in a bloody stalemate that lasted until 1918. After the entry of the United States into the war in 1917, it soon became clear that Germany could not win.

Abdication and Exile

In early November, 1918, groups of war-weary civilians and soldiers began to revolt against the government. The army told the kaiser that they could not stop the Allied advance or control the mobs at home. They urged the kaiser to abdicate. On November 9, 1918, Kaiser William II abdicated the German throne. He went into exile in the Netherlands, where he died in 1941.

Whether William was primarily responsible for World War I, as many once believed, is debatable. His approach to foreign policy was undoubtedly a factor. Moreover, the chaos of the decades after World War I—the weakness of the unstable German Weimar Republic, the terror of Nazism, and the horror of World War II (1939-1945)—are all part of the legacy of Kaiser William II.

Bibliography

Balfour, Michael. *The Kaiser and His Times*. Boston: Houghton Mifflin, 1964.

Cowles, Virginia. *The Kaiser*. New York: Harper & Row, 1963.

Wilson, Lawrence. *The Incredible Kaiser*. New York: A. S. Barnes, 1963.

Andrew Trescott

Harold Wilson

Born: March 11, 1916; Huddersfield, Yorkshire, England
Died: May 24, 1995; London, England

Prime minister of Great Britain (1964-1970, 1974-1976)

The son of an industrial chemist, James Harold Wilson (JAYMZ HEH-ruhld WIHL-suhn) was a scholarship student at Wirral Grammar School and then at Jesus College at Oxford University. After graduation, he lectured in economics at Oxford, leaving during World War II to serve first in the Ministry of Labour and finally in charge of the economic and statistical services division of the Ministry of Fuel and Power. Wilson performed so outstandingly that he was mentioned in the official British history of the war. In 1945 Wilson was elected to Parliament as a member of the Labour Party; his political career had begun.

Rising Star of the Labour Party

In 1947 Wilson was appointed president of the Board of Trade and so became a member of the Labour cabinet; he was the youngest cabinet member in the twentieth century and the youngest in British history since William Pitt the Younger. Wilson served in the cabinet until 1951. He became a forceful and articulate spokesman of the Labour Party's positions and adapted well to the growing influence of the mass media, in particular television.

In 1963 the Conservative government of Harold Macmillan was in trouble. The British economy was declining badly, and the British Empire's prestige had slipped internationally. The Labour Party was poised to rally behind its long-time leader, Hugh Gaitskell, when he died after a brief illness in January. In a brief but intense struggle with Labour rivals George Brown and James Callaghan, Wilson emerged as the party's leader and its candidate for prime minister in the next election.

In the spring of 1963, after a cabinet scandal (the Profumo scandal), Harold Macmillian resigned and was replaced as prime minister by Sir Alexander Douglas-Home. Parliamentary elections were held in the fall of 1964 and in October, Labour won a razor-thin four-seat majority in the House of Commons. Harold Wilson was prime minister.

Troubles at Home and Abroad

Despite the narrow majority, the Labour government projected a sense of purpose and direc-

Harold Wilson *(Library of Congress)*

British prime minister Harold Wilson waves to supporters in 1969. *(London Times/Archive Photos)*

heavily against the island nation. For two years, Wilson's government staved off devaluation of the pound through a combination of fiscal austerity and selective higher taxes.

The election of March, 1966, increased Labour's majority in Parliament to ninety-nine seats. At the same time, however, the financial situation worsened. A strike by dockworkers brought the crisis to a head, and in November the cabinet announced that the British pound would be devalued. Inevitable side effects included cuts in health, housing, education, and defense spending.

At the same time, the international arena was offering unique difficulties for Wilson and the British government. Under President Lyndon B. Johnson, the United States was pressing for increased British support, even British troops, in the Vietnam conflict. In Africa,

tion, and it moved to reinvigorate Britain. Unfortunately, the Conservative government had left Britain in a deep economic crisis, especially with the balance of payments (British exports compared with international imports) weighted

The Devaluation of the Pound

When Harold Wilson and the Labour Party took office in the fall of 1964, they found the British economy in terrible shape, with an enormous balance-of-payments deficit, high unemployment, and considerable inflation. The Wilson government undertook a series of fiscal austerity programs to improve the situation, but they did not resolve the economic crisis. The perception of Britain's weakened financial status decreased the value of the pound in the international monetary market. It seemed that at some point the government would have to accept this fact and officially lower the pound's value ("devalue" it). While a weaker pound might spur

exports, easing the balance-of-payments deficit and so helping the economy, the measure was not one that the Labour government wished to take.

However, a series of events, including a serious dock strike, further damaged the British economy and forced their hand. On November 16, 1966, the cabinet devalued the pound by 14.3 percent. Prime Minister Wilson made the official announcement the following Saturday on national television. He stressed the essential stability of the pound and the prospect of greater exports. Nevertheless, the country was shaken, and Labour lost much of its popularity among British voters.

The Election of 1964

In early 1963 Britain learned that John Profumo, a Conservative cabinet member, had shared a mistress with a Soviet military attaché and lied about it to Parliament. By the fall, Prime Minister Harold Macmillian had resigned, to be replaced by Sir Alexander Douglas-Home. Harold Wilson had already captured leadership of the Labour Party and would clearly be its candidate for prime minister in the upcoming election. Through the spring and summer, Wilson and Douglas-Home unofficially campaigned throughout Britain. The date for the election was set for October 15, 1964.

At first, the election was relatively restrained, but as the race tightened, Wilson and the Labour Party increasingly attacked the Conservatives as tired and out of touch. Wilson used techniques then unusual in Britain, including television. In an extremely close election, Labour won a four-seat majority. On Friday, October 16, after accepting Douglas-Home's resignation, Queen Elizabeth II asked Harold Wilson to form the first Labour government in thirteen years.

the colony of Rhodesia was ready to declare its independence from Britain rather than submit to black majority rule. Closer to home, after years of repression of the civil rights of its Catholic population, Northern Ireland had exploded into sectarian violence.

Despite these difficulties, the Wilson government enacted a series of far-reaching reforms that expanded opportunities in higher education, rationalized the laws on homosexuality and divorce, and helped modernize British society. In spite of these gains, the economic downturn led to Labour's defeat in the 1970 election, which brought the Conservative Party under Edward Heath back into power.

Return and Retirement

Under Heath, Britain experienced higher inflation and greater unemployment than had been seen in the Wilson years. As had happened under the Labour government, a strike was the factor that precipitated a new election. In Heath's case, it was a strike by British coal miners. Wilson returned as prime minister in February, 1974, with a minority government and won a majority that October in a subsequent election.

Wilson's government negotiated an end to the coal miners' strike within weeks of its election in February, but the larger economic and international issues were not so easily resolved. Britain's international status continued to decline. At home, the economy remained sluggish. In addition, rogue elements of the British intelligence community were plotting against their own prime minister. On March 16, 1976, Harold Wilson stunned Britain and the world by announcing his resignation. He had served for thirty years in the House of Commons and had been prime minister for eight years, at that time the longest service of any prime minister since World War II.

Despite his troubled tenure in office, Wilson proved to be one of the most effective of modern British prime ministers. He was always a pragmatic leader; one of his best-known quotes is "A week is a long time in politics." Wilson himself made much of many weeks: His government outlawed capital punishment, enacted the Race Relations Act to prohibit discrimination, and in 1975 led a successful referendum campaign that brought Britain into the European Community (EC). Late in his life, his enduring contributions were honored with his elevation as Baron Wilson of Rievaulx.

Bibliography

Childs, David. *Britain Since 1945: A Political History*. London: Ernest Benn, 1979.

Gardiner, Juliet, ed. *The Columbia Companion to British History*. New York: Columbia University Press, 1997.

Gascoigne, Bamber, ed. *Encyclopedia of Britain*. New York: Macmillan, 1993.

Howard, Anthony, and Richard West. *The Making of the Prime Minister*. London: Quality Book Club, 1965.

Kay, Ernest. *Pragmatic Premier: An Intimate Portrait of Harold Wilson*. London: Leslie Frewin, 1967.

Wilson, Harold. *A Personal Record: The Labour Government, 1964-1970*. Boston: Little, Brown, 1971.

Michael Witkoski

Woodrow Wilson

Born: December 28, 1856; Staunton, Virginia
Died: February 3, 1924; Washington, D.C.

President of the United States (1913-1921)

Thomas Woodrow Wilson (TO-muhs WOOD-roh WIHL-suhn) was the first son born to Janet and Joseph Ruggles Wilson, a Presbyterian minister and theologian. The family lived in Georgia at the time of the Civil War, when Wilson was a young child. After attending college, he married Ellen Louise Axson in 1885. She died in 1914. He remarried in 1915, to Edith Bolling Galt, and raised three daughters. The heartfelt warmth of his home life contradicted his proud and aloof public image.

Reluctant Professor

Wilson's career began in law, in an Atlanta-based practice, but he returned to Johns Hopkins University in 1883 to pursue graduate studies in political science. He developed compelling oratorical and writing skills. A political career was set aside, and Wilson instead became a professor at several institutions, including Bryn Mawr College, Wesleyan College, Johns Hopkins University, and Princeton University. In 1890, as Princeton University's president, his impassioned speeches to alumni throughout the country gained him a certain amount of renown and notoriety. In 1910 this familiarity furnished the votes necessary for him to be elected as New Jersey's governor.

The Presidency

In 1912 Wilson, in his mid-fifties, ran for the U.S. presidency on the Democratic ticket and was elected. During his first term, he fought for economic reforms. In 1913 he revived the federal income tax. The National Bank, previously abolished by Andrew Jackson, was reestablished. He also created the country's first centralized financial system by signing the Federal Reserve Act.

The establishment of the Federal Trade Commission followed in 1914.

Wilson professed a nonisolationist foreign policy. He promoted nonviolent solutions regarding territorial disputes. As early as 1913, Wilson sketched an outline for Article X of the Covenant for the League of Nations, which supported political independence and mutual guarantees for territorial rights. During this time, World War I was brewing in Europe, and it began in August, 1914. At the beginning of the war, U.S. public opinion generally disapproved of the United States entering the war.

Woodrow Wilson *(Library of Congress)*

U.S. president Woodrow Wilson appearing before Congress in February, 1917, announcing that the United States was officially breaking relations with Germany. The United States was about to enter World War I. *(National Archives)*

Wilson desired to remain a neutral mediator without involving the United States militarily, yet U.S. policies undeniably leaned toward supporting Britain and France over Germany. Wilson was narrowly reelected for a second term in 1916. His neutrality in foreign policy had cost him some votes. Wilson's domestic policy during his second term emphasized social legislation in-

Princeton University

In 1900 Princeton University was a small, parochial undergraduate university undergoing enormous social reforms, which its current president, Francis Patton was unable to carry out. Woodrow Wilson, a faculty member since 1890, was unanimously chosen as Patton's successor, and he immediately established a graduate school. Wilson eloquently expressed great expectations of raising Princeton to the level of Harvard and Yale. He utilized models of Oxford and Cambridge, designing the "quad plan," in which the financial elite and lower-income students would live together with faculty in "quadrangle colleges." This plan met with opposition at a multitude of levels, including from the alumni whose financial support was required. Wilson's tenacity in advocating this program became a sacred cause, and it was a battle that lost him many long-time friends. The ambitious project never came to fruition, and the ongoing struggle between Wilson and certain faculty members forced the trustees to demanded Wilson's resignation.

The League of Nations

Early in his presidency, Woodrow Wilson suggested the creation of an international legal order to promote peace and security. By 1916 he had begun touting the concept in speeches. He incorporated the Covenant, the basis of the League of Nations, into the Treaty of Versailles in 1919. The league Covenant embodied collective security and arbitration in which countries could communicate and resolve problems without war. As parts of the league, it established the Assembly, a Council consisting of permanent representatives from the Allied powers, a Secretariat, and a permanent Court of International Justice.

Wilson intended the league to provide a flexible set of rules for international law, but the Allies opposed its lack of enforcement ability. There was no interest in a League of Nations that could not guarantee territorial security, and Wilson was forced to make concessions in order keep the league intact. Consequently, most of Wilson's principles were lost in compromises, but the league was established. Based in Geneva, Switzerland, it proved useful in settling minor international disputes. Unfortunately, the league could not stop hostile aggression by major countries and therefore could not prevent World War II. Dissolved in 1946, the League of Nations served as a model for the establishment of the United Nations.

cluding the Child Labor Law, constitutional amendments granting women voting privileges, and prohibiting the manufacture and sale of alcohol (a policy known as Prohibition).

World War I

In January, 1917, Wilson began to speak of war aims, as it was becoming clear that the United States would be entering the war. After three years of hoping for an end to World War I with the United States supplying financial support and peaceful mediation but not military assistance, the United States entered in April, 1917. Secretary of State Robert Lansing supported American intervention partly to protect U.S. investments. Wilson pressed Congress to pass the Selective Service Act, drafting men between twenty-one and thirty years of age into military service.

On November 11, 1918, the fatigued German government conceded defeat. Wilson used the armistice as an opportunity to promote the idea of an international organization of peace, and he released his Fourteen Points proposal. The first

U.S. president Woodrow Wilson (left) in Paris with the French president in 1919. Wilson was in Paris for the post-World War I peace conference. *(Archive Photos)*

thirteen points revolved around practical territorial issues. The fourteenth point described a special association of nations with the purpose of mutual guarantees, political independence, and territorial integrity.

Peace Treaty of Versailles

President Wilson led the U.S. delegation at the Paris peace conference. After arduous negotiations, the peace treaty was signed in the Hall of Mirrors at the palace of Versailles on June 28, 1919. Under Wilson's influence the treaty had a humanitarian appeal, claiming profit for all humankind. (In previous treaties at wars' ends, the winners had generally claimed the spoils.) However, the European Allies held Germany responsible for the war's destruction and wanted Germany to pay for all damages. Consequently, the amnesty clause typical of earlier treaties was removed and replaced with demands that Germany make reparations.

An exhausted Wilson returned from Europe to face the Senate Foreign Affairs Committee hearings regarding U.S. ratification of the treaty. The Senate favored the treaty in general but took issue with the League of Nations, fearing that it would encourage U.S. involvement in foreign affairs. When Wilson realized that Congress would not vote for the League of Nations, he toured the country, attempting to sway public opinion in favor of the league. Wilson's health declined, however—he suffered a stroke in Pueblo, Colorado, in September, 1919, forcing his return to Washington. He was left physically incapacitated. His wife, Edith, took command: For the last several months of Wilson's presidency, she and trusted White House aides largely ran the country. Wilson continued to be involved in all decision making, but he received only the closest friends for personal appearances.

The Ailing President

The public was told that the president suffered from a "nervous breakdown from indigestion and a depleted system." Differences of opinion over treaty ratification caused a deep political rift in Congress, and the treaty was not passed. The United States would not become a member of the League of Nations. Wilson's efforts were later acknowledged when, in 1920, he received the Nobel Peace Prize.

On March 4, 1921, Wilson's second term in office ended. His last speech, given via the radio, was on the eve of Armistice Day, November 11, 1923. This dynamic, spiritual broadcast rekindled his popularity. Less than three months later, on February 3, 1924, Wilson died.

Bibliography

Calhoun, Frederick. *Power and Principle: Armed Intervention in Wilsonian Foreign Policy*. Kent, Ohio: Kent State University Press, 1986.

Clements, K. *Woodrow Wilson, World Statesman*. Boston: Twayne, 1987.

Osborn, George C. *Woodrow Wilson, the Early Years*. Baton Rouge: Louisiana State University Press, 1968.

Schulte Nordholt, Jan. *Woodrow Wilson: A Life For World Peace*. Berkeley: University of California Press, 1991.

Wilkinson Bragdon, H. *Woodrow Wilson, the Academic Years*. Cambridge, Mass.: Harvard University Press, 1967.

Nancy Campbell

Isoroku Yamamoto

Born: April 4, 1884; Nagaoka, Niigata Prefecture, Japan
Died: April 18, 1943; Solomon Islands

Japanese admiral, commander of the Japanese fleet during World War II

Isoroku Yamamoto (ee-soh-roh-kew yah-mah-moh-toh) was the son of a former samurai and itinerant scholar and his second wife. He attended the Nagaoka middle and high schools, where he learned English. He graduated in 1905 from the Eta Jima Naval Academy. Yamamoto was married in 1918 and had four children, two boys (Yoshimasa and Tadao) and two girls (Sumiko and Masako).

Diplomat and Aviation Pioneer

Yamamoto was wounded while serving in the Russo-Japanese War (1904-1905). He went on to serve in a variety of posts, including naval attaché to the United States and executive officer of the Kasumigaura Aviation Corps, where he learned to fly an airplane. He also studied at Harvard University in the United States, where he learned firsthand about the industrial power and natural resources available to that country.

During the 1930's, the Japanese army began its conquest of China. This action caused friction between Japan and the United States. In late 1936, Yamamoto was appointed to be vice minister of the navy. During his term, he opposed army aggression in China and the signing of an alliance with Nazi Germany and fascist Italy. He tried to promote a settlement with the United States.

Chief of the Combined Fleet

In August of 1939, Admiral Yamamoto was appointed to the post of chief of the combined fleet, a position which put him in overall command of the ships of the Japanese navy. Since it became clear to him that war with the United States was becoming unavoidable, Yamamoto set about to prepare the fleet.

In December, 1941, the Japanese bombed the U.S. naval base at Pearl Harbor in Hawaii, and Japan went to war against the United States. At first the war went well for Japan. In June of 1942, however, the Japanese attempted to destroy the American forces at Midway Island but were caught by surprise by waiting American carriers. Four of the Japanese aircraft carriers were sunk. These ships and their pilots could not be replaced.

In July, 1942, the Americans landed on the island of Guadalcanal. After the Americans captured the island, Yamamoto decided to make an

Isoroku Yamamoto *(Library of Congress)*

U.S. warships during the Japanese surprise attack on Pearl Harbor on December 7, 1941. From left to right are the *West Virginia*, the *Tennessee*, and the *Arizona*. *(National Archives)*

The Attack on Pearl Harbor

In order for Japan to continue its war effort in China, it needed to obtain resources from Southeast Asia, especially oil and rubber. After seeing the British attack and sink several Italian battleships in the Italians' own port of Taranto, Isoroku Yamamoto wondered if a similar strike might be successful against the U.S. forces stationed at Pearl Harbor in Hawaii. Yamamoto was chief of Japan's combined fleet, and his staff began to plan for such an attack.

On December 7, 1941, a force of Japanese dive, torpedo, and horizontal bombers attacked the American fleet stationed at Pearl Harbor. They also attacked the Army air forces protecting the harbor. The Americans at Pearl Harbor were caught totally by surprise. Outraged, the U.S. government immediately declared war on Japan. The Japanese sank or seriously damaged eighteen ships and destroyed 188 airplanes, most of which were on the ground. However, the Japanese failed to damage the American aircraft carriers or their submarines. Furthermore, the port facilities, airfields, and oil storage depots were also untouched. Many of the ships that were sunk were refloated and took part in battles later in the war.

inspection tour of the South Pacific area. On April 17, 1943, he set out for the island of Bougainville, one of the Solomon Islands. There his twin-engine transport plane was intercepted by a group of American fighters. It was shot down and Yamamoto was killed.

Warnings Ignored

Yamamoto is remembered for planning the attack on Pearl Harbor, but he was also a pioneer of naval aviation; the U.S. armed forces adopted many of his ideas. Yamamoto understood the United States better than most in Japan did. He warned Japanese leaders that going to war with the United States would end in disaster for Japan, but his warnings went unheeded.

Bibliography

Fuchida, Mitsuo, and Okumiya, Masatake. *Midway: The Battle That Doomed Japan*. Annapolis, Md.: United States Naval Institute, 1955.

Hoyt, Edwin P. *Yamamoto: The Man Who Planned Pearl Harbor*. New York: McGraw Hill, 1990.

Lord, Walter. *Day of Infamy*. New York: Holt, Rinehart and Winston, 1957.

Andrew Trescott

Japanese admiral Isoroku Yamamoto in Tokyo, 1934. *(Archive Photos)*

Ahmed Zaki Yamani

Born: 1930; Mecca, Saudi Arabia

Minister of petroleum and mineral resources of Saudi Arabia (1962-1986)

The son of a *qadhi* (religious judge) in Mecca, Saudi Arabia, Ahmed Zaki Yamani (A-mehd ZAH-kee yah-MAH-nee) received an international education. After completing studies at the University of Cairo, in Egypt, he attended Harvard Law School, from which he graduated in 1956. In 1958 the Saudi royal family named Yamani legal adviser to the Council of Ministers. In 1960 Yamani was raised to the council itself as minister of state. In 1962 he was given the post with which he was most closely associated

and through which he exerted the greatest influence—minister of petroleum and mineral resources.

Architect of the Oil Embargo

Yamani established himself as a hardworking, competent minister whose fundamental concern was to safeguard Saudi Arabia's position and revenues in the global petroleum market. Using a variety of tactics, ranging from long, patient negotiations to abrupt displays of impatience, Yamani dominated the Organization of Petroleum Exporting Countries (OPEC) until his dismissal from office in 1986.

In 1973, following increasing tension between Islamic nations and the United States, largely because of American support of Israel, Yamani successfully organized and coordinated an oil embargo that drastically reduced the flow of foreign oil into the United States. The results were dramatic, including long lines at American gas stations, severe regional shortages, and mandatory rationing of gasoline. Crude oil prices soared to record levels, increasing by as much as 70 percent. Throughout the 1970's, under Yamani's direction, OPEC kept oil prices under control, believing that long-run profits were preferable to short-term gains. Yamani sought to match OPEC price increases to economic growth in Western nations. The policy benefited all OPEC members, especially Saudi Arabia.

A Witness to Violence

In March, 1975, Yamani witnessed the assassination of Saudi crown prince Faisal. Yamani and Faisal had been close since Yamani had been named to the Council of Ministers, and in many ways the prince was Yamani's mentor. His murder was a great shock and personal loss.

Ahmed Zaki Yamani *(Library of Congress)*

Saudi oil minister Ahmed Zaki Yamani in his office in 1981. *(Svenskt Pressefoto/Archive Photos)*

In December of the same year, while Yamani was in Vienna, Austria, for an OPEC meeting, he was kidnapped with eleven other oil ministers by Ilich Ramirez Sanchez, better known as Carlos, one of the world's foremost terrorists. Yamani and the other ministers were flown from airport to airport throughout the Middle East and North Africa until Viennese radio read a statement from

OPEC

The Organization of Petroleum Exporting Countries, better known as OPEC, was founded in 1960 in Baghdad, Iraq, to give countries with oil reserves greater control over their most valuable natural resource. Since many of these countries were in the Middle East, it was natural that many OPEC members were Arabic nations. However, OPEC also included countries such as Venezuela, Indonesia, Libya, Nigeria, and Ecuador.

It was not until 1973 that OPEC exercised the considerable power it possessed by taking control of the oil production in its various states. This control dramatically increased world oil prices. At this same time, Islamic oil-producing states imposed an oil embargo on the United States. The combined result of these two actions was a disruption in the economies in Europe, the United States, and Japan. There was a cutback in oil consumption and a resulting decline in oil prices. Iraq's 1990 invasion of Kuwait and the resulting Persian Gulf War in 1991 again caused a fluctuation in the price of oil, but the period after the war saw production levels and prices stabilizing.

the terrorists. The ministers were freed unharmed, but Yamani was subsequently accompanied by personal bodyguards.

Iran Spoils the Plan

In 1979, the Iranian revolution overthrew that nation's ruler, the shah, replacing the monarchy with a fundamentalist Islamic government under the guidance of Ayatollah Khomeini. A serious division appeared in the once-solid OPEC front. Hostile to the Saudi monarchy, and soon embroiled in a long war with its neighbor Iraq, Iran desperately needed oil revenues. It ignored OPEC's price guidelines. As Iran's production fell because of the war and the chaos left by the revolution, other countries took advantage of higher prices. Yamani and OPEC had lost control.

By the mid-1980's, Yamani had fashioned a counter move—the unrestrained production and distribution of oil by OPEC members. The result was a sharp decline in oil prices around the world. Iran was hard hit, but Western Europe, the United States, and Japan felt economic disruption as well. Yamani soon urged OPEC nations to moderate their actions, bring production under more control, and allow the world market to stabilize. However, the Saudi economy was hurt by falling oil production. In October, 1986, King Fahd of Saudi Arabia relieved Sheik Ahmed Zaki Yamani of his ministerial position.

Bibliography

Ahrari, Mohammed E. *OPEC: The Falling Giant*. Lexington: University Press of Kentucky, 1986.

Shwadran, Benjamin. *Middle East Oil Crises Since 1973*. New York: Westview Press, 1986.

Skeet, Ian. *OPEC: Twenty-five Years of Prices and Politics*. Cambridge, England: Cambridge University Press, 1988.

Yergin, Daniel. *The Prize: The Epic Quest for Oil, Money, and Power*. New York: Simon & Schuster, 1991.

Michael Witkoski

Boris Yeltsin

Born: February 1, 1931; Butka, Sverdlovsk region, U.S.S.R.

President of Russia (took office 1991)

Boris Nikolayevich Yeltsin (bur-YEES nyih-kuh-LAH-yeh-vyihch YEHLT-syihn) was born in the town of Butka, in the Soviet Union's Sverdlovsk region, in 1931. He joined the Communist Party of the Soviet Union (CPSU) in 1961. Yeltsin rose steadily through the ranks and became first secretary of Sverdlovsk's CPSU regional committee in 1976. In 1986 Soviet leader Mikhail Gorbachev elevated Yeltsin to the CPSU's top body, the Politburo.

Radical in the Politburo

Gorbachev's selection of Yeltsin for the Politburo position was part of his larger attempt to place more liberal (reformist) allies in positions of authority. Gorbachev had concluded that his country had been severely weakened by the unrelenting international competition of the Cold War. He sought to modify long-standing economic and social policies as a way of reversing the Soviet Union's decline. Gorbachev clearly hoped that Yeltsin and the other reformers would support his various reform efforts.

This Yeltsin did. He took a vigorous and public stand against conservatives in the Politburo and elsewhere who opposed liberalization. Soon, however, Yeltsin was criticizing Gorbachev himself for being too timid in pursuing reform. Events came to a head at a Central Committee meeting in late 1987, when Yeltsin accused the Soviet leadership of hypocrisy and foot-dragging. Shortly thereafter, Yeltsin was dismissed from the Politburo.

In March, 1989, Gorbachev allowed semifree elections to be held for the first time in Soviet history, and in those elections Yeltsin was overwhelmingly elected to the Soviet parliament. In addition to countrywide liberalization, popular forces were pressing for a decentralization of power from Moscow to the regional governments. Concurrent with this, Yeltsin came to be associated less with the goal of reforming the Soviet Union and more with the objective of gaining greater freedom for the Russian Soviet Federated Soviet Republic (RSFSR), the largest of the fifteen constituent republics of the Soviet Union. By the late 1980's, similar independence drives were gaining ground in most of the Soviet republics.

Boris Yeltsin *(Imapress/Archive Photos)*

Russian president Boris Yeltsin (left) in Paris with French premier François Mitterrand. *(Archive Photos/Imapress)*

Leader of the Second Russian Revolution

In the face of mounting public pressure, political intransigence, and worsening economic conditions, Gorbachev's reforms became increasingly desperate. Again hoping to defuse popular dissatisfaction and to propel like-minded allies to power, Gorbachev authorized semidemocratic elections in the country's republics in March, 1990. Again, one of the main beneficiaries of those elections was Yeltsin, who secured a seat in the RSFSR's parliament, which in turn elected him parliamentary leader.

Yeltsin had become Gorbachev's most potent rival. As the leader of the Russian parliament, Yeltsin had a constituency that included more than half of the Soviet Union's population, and his authority extended across three quarters of the country's territory. Several months after attaining the RSFSR's top political position, Yeltsin dramatically relinquished his membership in the Communist Party. As a political maverick frequently at odds with Gorbachev, Yeltsin enjoyed the support of most of the

The Attempted Coup of 1991

In August, 1991, a small group of conservative Communist Party and military leaders attempted a coup against Soviet leader Mikhail Gorbachev. They hoped to preserve the Soviet Union, which they believed Gorbachev had endangered with his reforms.

On August 18, the coup leaders demanded that Gorbachev turn power over to them. When he refused, they placed him under house arrest and assumed "emergency executive powers." Early in the morning of August 19, the Soviet press agency stated that Gorbachev had an "illness" and announced that Vice President Gennady Yanayev had assumed presidential powers.

Yanayev led an eight-member "State Committee for the State of Emergency in the USSR," which began issuing decrees that suspended various civil freedoms.

Boris Yeltsin, who inexplicably had not been detained by the coup plotters, rallied anticoup forces. He proclaimed his own control of the RSFSR and called for general strikes and public resistance. Thousands of Muscovites heeded Yeltsin's call, and they surrounded Yeltsin's "white house" to shield it. Soldiers refused orders to fire on the building, and the coup dissolved after only three days. Yeltsin emerged as the country's liberator.

Yeltzin Reorganizes the Government in 1998

As president of the Russian Federation, Boris Yeltsin frequently altered the makeup of the country's executive leadership. In this way he was able to keep political challengers at bay and to create scapegoats for policy failures. Yeltsin's largest reorganization occurred in the spring of 1998, when he dismissed Prime Minister Victor Chernomyrdin and the entire cabinet. Yeltsin was responding to mounting criticism from the public, the press, and the parliament stemming from the country's worsening financial and social situation. The communist-dominated parliament twice voted against Sergei Kirienko, Yeltsin's choice for prime minister. When Yeltsin put forth the same nomination a third time, the parliament chose to confirm Kirienko rather than permit Yeltsin to dissolve the parliament. Yeltsin then appointed a cabinet that included both old and new faces.

country's liberals, capitalists, and national liberationists. His mandate was strengthened in June, 1991, when in free elections Russian voters decisively elected him to the newly created Russian presidency.

Gorbachev had been trying to occupy the middle of the political spectrum, but the rush of events in the late 1980's polarized society. The two main groups were old-guard communists who wanted to preserve the union and the political system, and liberal reformers who sought varying degrees of capitalism, democracy, and decentralization of power. Yeltsin became the standard-bearer for the latter group.

The climactic clash between these two groups occurred in August, 1991, when a small group of communists and conservative military leaders placed Gorbachev under house arrest and attempted to seize control of the government. Yeltsin instantly became the focal point of the anti-coup forces, and after three days the coup attempt collapsed. From that point onward, Yeltsin was seen as the country's liberator—the new leader for the reform movement begun by Gorbachev six years earlier. Gorbachev never recovered politically from the coup. Moreover, the attempted coup precipitated the final unraveling of the Soviet Union. Within four months, all fifteen republics declared their independence.

President of the Russian Federation

The RSFSR was renamed the Russian Federation after the collapse of the Soviet Union. Yeltsin now led a country that possessed the world's second-largest nuclear arsenal, held one of the five permanent seats on the U.N. Security Council, and otherwise represented the "successor" to the Soviet Union.

Nothwithstanding the Soviet Union's collapse, Yeltsin could not entirely escape the problems that had earlier beset Gorbachev. Many elites, including a majority of Russia's parliamentary members, opposed Yeltsin's efforts to proceed with economic reforms. The growing tension between Yeltsin and the parliament reached a climax in the fall of 1993, when Yeltsin ordered the military to attack the parliament building. Victorious in the confrontation, Yeltsin wrote a new constitution and ordered new parliamentary elections in December, 1993. The new parliament, however, proved no less ideologically hostile to Yeltsin than the last. The following year, Yeltsin found it necessary to order the army to fight secessionists in Chechnya, one of Russia's many ethnic-based republics.

Yeltsin ran for reelection in the summer of 1996, and he failed to achieve 50 percent in the first electoral round against a dozen other candidates. He faced the Communist Party leader, Gennadi

Boris Yeltsin (center) meeting with his ministers in Moscow in March, 1999, to discuss the crisis in the Yugoslavian province of Kosovo. Yeltsin strongly condemned air strikes launched against Yugoslavian Serbs by North Atlantic Treaty Organization (NATO) forces. *(AP/Wide World Photos)*

Zyuganov, in a run-off election a week later and won that race comfortably. Although the Russian constitution limits the president to two terms, Yeltsin would not rule out the possibility of running again in 2000. He hinted that his first election had occurred before the current constitution was written and thus did not count toward his two-term limit.

By the late 1990's, Yeltsin had faced a number of serious health problems. He was frequently beset by heart troubles (and was rumored to have had bouts of alcohol abuse), and his tenure was marked by periodic health-related absences, including a long convalescence connected with heart bypass surgery shortly after his 1996 re-election. Regardless of his political and health-related problems, however, Yeltsin uniquely and decisively influenced the fate of the Soviet Union, the development of the Russian Federation, and the end of the Cold War.

Bibliography

Fedorov, Velentin P. *Yeltsin: A Political Portrait.* Bellevue, Wash.: Imperial Publishers, 1996.

Yeltsin, Boris N. *Against the Grain: An Autobiography.* New York: Summit Books, 1990.

_____. *The Struggle for Russia.* New York: Belka, 1995.

Steve D. Boilard

Yuan Shikai

Born: September 16, 1859; Xiangcheng, Henan Province, China
Died: June 6, 1916; Beijing, China

Chinese military leader and head of Chinese government (1912-1916)

Yuan Shikai (yew-AHN SHIHR-KI), also rendered Yüan Shih-kai, was born into an upper-middle-class landlord family that had several members in civil and military positions under the Qing (or Ching, also called Manchu) empire. Although he received a traditional classical education, Yuan had no taste for such studies and failed the civil service examinations. Instead, he began a military career in 1880 by joining the staff of General Wu Chang-ching, a friend of the family.

Military Experiences

In 1882 Yuan was sent with General Wu's troops to Korea, then under Chinese domination. Their task was to put down a violent uprising. Yuan showed great administrative skills, and when General Wu was summoned elsewhere in 1884, Yuan was left in command of the Chinese forces in Korea. In October, 1885, the Chinese government appointed him head of their representatives in Korea.

Rivalry between China and Japan over Korea was one of the several causes of the Sino-Japanese War, which broke out in July, 1894. Leaving Korea, Yuan aided the war effort by helping organize the transportation of supplies. The Chinese forces were badly defeated in the war. In their efforts to improve the effectiveness of the armed forces, the Chinese government chose Yuan to organize and lead China's first modern military force.

Rise to Political Leadership

As was common in Chinese government, Yuan was appointed to other government positions while exercising his military command. He was appointed a provincial judge in July, 1897. In 1898, deep division arose within the national government, as China's young emperor tried to institute modernizing reforms that were opposed by the elderly dowager empress, Tz'u-hsi. One of the reform leaders, Tan Ssu-tung, tried to persuade Yuan to join a plot against the empress. Yuan apparently informed her supporters, who took the emperor prisoner and executed some of the reform leaders, including Tan. Yuan became a favorite of the empress, who appointed him a vice president of the Board of Works and acting governor of Shandong Province in 1899.

Yuan Shikai *(Library of Congress)*

The Boxer Rebellion

In 1898 a loose organization, whose name may be translated as "boxers united in righteousness," developed in China's Shandong Province, primarily among peasants. Deriving their beliefs from martial-arts traditions and superstitions, they thought themselves invulnerable to physical harm. Angered by territorial acquisitions by foreign powers and by activities of Christian missionaries, they conducted a campaign of terrorism which erupted into open warfare in June, 1900. Germany's chief diplomat was murdered, and the diplomatic quarter of Beijing was besieged. The Chinese government, dominated by the empress dowager, came out in support of the Boxers.

In August, a Western military force of about twenty thousand troops fought its way from Tianjin to Beijing and broke the siege. In September, 1901, the Chinese government agreed to a peace treaty that imposed a number of heavy penalties on them, including a monetary indemnity of about $333 million. In later years, much of this money was redirected to support overseas education for Chinese students.

In 1900 China was disrupted by the violence of the Boxer Rebellion. Yuan firmly put down Boxer activities in his area but shrewdly refused to commit his forces to the suicidal fight against the superior foreign forces. This stance won him favor in the eyes of foreign governments, and his military command became the largest and most powerful in China. In 1901 he was appointed

The Boxer Rebellion: An artist's rendition of U.S. Marines fighting against the Boxers outside Beijing. *(National Archives)*

The Dismissal of the Government in 1914

From the moment Yuan Shikai became provisional president of China in 1912, a critical question was whether he would support constitutional government and democracy. He quickly demonstrated that he would not. He refused to move the national capital to Nanjing. When the first premier, Yuan's longtime friend Tang Shao-yi, showed signs of independence, Yuan dismissed him in June, 1912. When the legislature rejected Yuan's new cabinet nominees in July, 1912, they were deluged with threats of violence on one hand and bribes on the other. Yuan also negotiated loans with foreign financiers without any legislative approval or involvement.

Following the electoral victory of the Kuomintang (KMT) in January, 1913, Yuan arranged the murder of KMT legislative leader Sung Chiao-jen. Resentment against the foreign loans and political violence led to military uprisings against Yuan in July, 1913, but he quelled them effectively. On November 4, 1913, Yuan outlawed the KMT and banned its members from the legislature. Lacking a quorum, the legislature could not function, and Yuan dissolved it on January 10, 1914. His hand-picked political council approved a constitution granting the president virtually unlimited powers.

high commissioner of military and foreign affairs for North China, one of the most powerful positions in the government.

To upgrade China's entire military establishment, Yuan organized a land army of five divisions, known as the Peiyang ("North Sea") Army, using modern training techniques. He maintained strict discipline but demonstrated concern for the welfare of the troops and was a popular commander. He developed a network of protégés within the army and civilian administration. Yuan's rise aroused jealousy among the ethnic Manchus, who dominated the government. Beginning in 1907, they progressively reduced his authority, until by January, 1909, he was removed from all official positions.

Revolution and Republic

In October, 1911, efforts to overthrow the monarchy erupted into open revolution in central China. The Manchu leaders tried to suppress the revolt by sending part of the Peiyang Army, headed by Yuan's supporters, and begged Yuan to resume command. He agreed only after exacting promises of political reforms. In late October,

1911, he was appointed prime minister and commander of the antirevolutionary forces. In mid-November he was able to dismiss most of the Manchu leadership and replace them with his own men in top government positions. His troops engaged in sporadic fighting against the rebels, but his personal ambitions required rebel support rather than their defeat.

Sun Yat-sen, who was more popular than Yuan, was chosen by the rebel legislature as provisional president on December 29, 1911. However, his wish to avert civil war led Sun to relinquish the presidency in favor of Yuan Shikai on condition that the Qing (Manchu) royal family would abdicate and a republic would be formed with its headquarters in Nanjing, far from Yuan's center of power. Further, Yuan was to accept the terms of a constitution drafted by the provisional legislature. On February 12, 1912, the royal family abdicated. The legislature elected Yuan as provisional president on February 15.

President of the Chinese Republic

Yuan soon demonstrated his intention to rule in the manner of the emperors. He refused to move his operations from Beijing to Nanjing. In national elections in early 1913, Sun Yat-sen's newly organized political party, the Kuomintang (KMT), won a majority of legislative seats. In a series of sweeping moves, Yuan arranged for the murder of their parliamentary leader, banned the organization, removed from office three provincial governors associated with it, and dissolved the national legislature itself.

The outbreak of World War I in August, 1914, gave Japan an opportunity to extend its influence in China. The Japanese seized former German-dominated areas and forced Yuan to accept other arrangements that increased Japan's power. These developments were extremely unpopular in China. Yuan was also trying to have himself officially installed as emperor, a title that he claimed at the beginning of 1916. This move aroused bitter opposition, much of it within the military. Yuan gave up this ambition in March, 1916. He died only three months later of uremia.

A Traditional Chinese Ruler

Yuan Shikai had no use for Western ideas and institutions such as democracy and representative government. He was, however, a capable administrator who helped develop a number of modernizing reforms in Chinese government, particularly in improving the educational system. After his death, China's central government became very weak, and power gravitated to regional warlords.

Bibliography

Chen, Jerome. *Yuan Shih-kai, 1859-1916.* Stanford, Calif.: Stanford University Press, 1961.

MacKinnon, Stephen R. *Power and Politics in Late Imperial China: Yuan Shi-kai in Beijing and Tianjin, 1901-1908.* Berkeley: University of California Press, 1980.

Young, Ernest P. *The Presidency of Yuan Shih-k'ai.* Ann Arbor: University of Michigan Press, 1977.

Paul B. Trescott

Sa'd Zaghlūl

Born: July, 1857; Ibyānah, Egypt
Died: August 23, 1927; Cairo, Egypt

Egyptian nationalist leader, prime minister of Egypt (1924)

Sa'd Zaghlūl Pasha ibn Ibrāhīm (sah-AHD zag-LEWL PAH-shah IHB-uhn ih-brah-HIHM) was the son of well-to-do peasants living in the Nile Delta region. He was unlike most prominent Egyptians of his time in that his ancestors were not descended from Turkish conquerors but were pure Egyptians. He was educated at the Muslim University of Al-Azhar in Cairo, where he specialized in Islamic law, philosophy, and theology. It was there that he came under the influence of the Islamic reformers Jamāl al-Dīn al-Afghānī and Muḥammad 'Abduh. Zaghlūl went on to the Egyptian School of Law and worked as a legal advocate and journalist.

Minister and Legislator

Zaghlūl was appointed a judge in the Court of Appeals in 1892. In 1895, he married the daughter of the Egyptian prime minister, and he was made head of the newly created Ministry of Education in 1906. Soon after, Zaghlūl helped form the Ḥizb al-Ummah ("People's Party"), which cooperated with the British. (The British had occupied Egypt since 1882.) As head of the Ministry of Justice in 1910-1912, he made many reforms in the Egyptian legal system. After resigning this post, Zaghlūl was elected to the Legislative Assembly and soon became its vice president. During this time he became a stronger advocate of Egyptian independence from the British.

When World War I broke out in 1914, the British declared Egypt a British protectorate. Martial law was declared, and the Legislative Assembly was dissolved. All overt political activity came to an end, and restrictions were placed on personal freedom. During the war the relationship between the British and the Egyptians deteriorated. Many Egyptians believed that the British intended to make Egypt a permanent colony. Zaghlūl and other members of the former Legislative Assembly spent this time forming activist groups throughout Egypt hoping to produce political agitation with the ultimate goal of full independence from the British.

Sa'd Zaghlūl *(Corbis/Bettmann-UPI)*

Demand for Independence

On November 13, 1918, two days after the end of World War I, a delegation led by Zaghlūl met with Sir Reginald Wingate, the British high commissioner of Egypt. They declared themselves to be the representatives of the Egyptian people and demanded that they be allowed to negotiate a treaty with the British government for Egyptian independence. This delegation (*wafd* in Arabic) was the direct ancestor of the Wafd Party, which would dominate Egyptian politics for more than thirty years. When Zaghlūl's demands were refused, the activist groups he had formed during the war spread disorder throughout Egypt. In March of 1919, Zaghlūl and three of his associates were arrested and deported to the island of Malta. The arrest only increased the civic unrest.

The British government replaced Wingate with Edmund Allenby, who released the prisoners in April of 1919. Zaghlūl traveled to Paris to present the case for Egyptian independence to the Paris Peace Conference, which was discussing the settlement of World War I. He had little success, but his release made him a national hero and brought a temporary end to Egypt's disorder. In the fall of 1919 the British sent Lord Milner, the colonial secretary, to Egypt for negotiations. Zaghlūl led a successful boycott of these negotiations, but he met privately with Milner in London in the summer of 1920. The two parties agreed that the protectorate should be replaced with a treaty of alliance, but they failed to reach a formal agreement.

In 1921 an Egyptian government formed by ʿAdlī Pasha Yakan, a rival of Zaghlūl, attempted to negotiate a treaty with the British, but Zaghlūl's popularity with the people enabled him to prevent this from happening. Zaghlūl was again arrested and deported for his disruptive activities in 1921 and was not released until 1923. Meanwhile, faced with the impossibility of reaching an agreement, the British granted partial independence to Egypt but retained control of key areas of government.

The New Egypt

Zaghlūl became the first prime minister of Egypt in January of 1924 after the Wafd Party overwhelmingly won elections in late 1923. Despite this victory, Zaghlūl was unable to restore order. Violent conflicts continued between the British and the Egyptians. An additional diffi-

The Wafd Party

The Wafd Party was the most important political party in Egypt during the first half of the twentieth century. Known in full as al-Wafd al-Miṣrī ("the Egyptian Delegation"), the Wafd Party was founded by Saʿd Zaghlūl on November 13, 1918, as a delegation representing the Egyptian people in their negotiations with the occupying British. After the British granted partial independence to Egypt in 1922, the Wafd was reorganized as a formal political party in 1923. Its candidates won 90 percent of the seats in the Egyptian Parliament in the first election, and Zaghlūl became the first prime minister.

Although the Wafd Party was in constant conflict with the kings of Egypt and the occupying British officials, it continued to play a dominant role in Egyptian politics until all political parties were banned in 1953 following the revolution of 1952 led by Gamal Abdel Nasser. The goals of the Wafd Party were complete independence from Britain, a constitutional form of government, protection of the civil rights of Egyptian citizens, and Egyptian control of the Sudan and the Suez Canal. Full independence was achieved in 1936, and Egyptian control of the Suez Canal in 1956. The Sudan became an independent country in 1956.

The Young Modernists in 1900

During the late nineteenth century, a group of young Egyptian intellectuals promoted the modernization of their society. The greatest influences on their thinking were the beliefs of the Muslim politician and journalist Jamāl al-Dīn al-Afghānī, who had left Turkey for Egypt in 1871. The most important of these young modernists was Muḥammad ʿAbduh. ʿAbduh's primary goal was to integrate science, reason, and the modern world with religious faith in order to free Islam from outdated rituals and dogma. As the *muftī*

(Islamic legal counselor) for Egypt beginning in 1899, ʿAbduh was also a strong nationalist who promoted unity among all of Egypt's Muslim and non-Muslim citizens. Among the Egyptians influenced by ʿAbduh were Qasim Amin, who promoted the rights of women, and Saʿd Zaghlūl, who was the assistant editor of the *Egyptian Official Journal* under ʿAbduh. Zaghlūl went on to become one of the strongest proponents of Egyptian nationalism.

culty was the struggle between the Wafd Party and Fuʾād I, the newly created king of Egypt, for political power. When the British commander in chief of the Egyptian army was assassinated in November of 1924, Zaghlūl was forced to resign under pressure from Allenby.

The Wafd Party won elections again in March of 1925, but in the chaos of the continuing struggles among the British, the Wafd Party, and King Fuʾād, the Egyptian parliament was dissolved immediately after it was formed. In May of 1926 the Wafd Party again won elections and was able to form a more stable government. Because of his advanced age and pressure from Lord Lloyd, the new British high commissioner, Zaghlūl agreed to form a coalition government with rival parties. Yakan, now with the newly formed Liberal Constitutionalist Party, became prime minister, while Zaghlūl became the president of the

Chamber of Deputies, an office he held until his death in 1927.

Egypt did not win full independence from the British until 1936. Struggles between the Wafd Party and Egyptian kings continued until Gamal Abdel Nasser overthrew the monarchy in 1952 and then banned all political parties in 1953.

Bibliography

Hourani, Albert. *Arabic Thought in the Liberal Age, 1798-1939.* London: Oxford University Press, 1962.

Kedourie, Elie. *The Chatham House Version and Other Middle-Eastern Studies.* New York: Praeger, 1970.

Sayyid, Afaf Lufti al-. *Egypt and Cromer: A Study in Anglo-Egyptian Relations.* New York: Praeger, 1968.

Rose Secrest

Emiliano Zapata

Born: August 8, 1879; Anenecuilco, Morelos, Mexico
Died: April 10, 1919; Hacienda Chinameca, Morelos, Mexico

Mexican revolutionary leader (1910-1919)

Emiliano Zapata (ay-mee-lee-AH-noh sah-PAH-tah) was a leader of peasant forces during the military phase of the Mexican Revolution (1910-1917). The son of a mestizo peasant, he was orphaned at the age of seventeen and took care of his brothers and sisters. In 1897, when village lands were seized by a wealthy landowner, Zapata took part in a protest and was arrested. He continued to be sympathetic to the plight of his fellow villagers, and in 1909 they elected him president of their board of defense. He tried to protect their legal rights to the land in the courts

Emiliano Zapata *(Library of Congress)*

but failed when well-connected landowners used their influence on the judges. Finally, Zapata and others invaded the haciendas and occupied the land forcibly.

Zapata as Revolutionary Leader

In 1910 the long-term president of Mexico, Porfirio Díaz, was challenged by Francisco Madero, a wealthy landowner from northern Mexico. In a published statement called the Plan of San Luís Potosí, Madero promised, among other goals, to return land to peasants. Zapata believed that Madero would help people like him and his fellow villagers and joined the rebellion. Zapata spoke the language of some of Mexico's Indians and told them that he needed their help to regain their lost lands. In March, 1911, Zapata's army defeated government forces at Cuautla on the road to Mexico City. One week later, President Díaz resigned and left the country. A provisional president took office and called for new elections.

Break with Madero

Francisco Madero won the elections in November, 1911, and became the president of Mexico. Zapata went to Mexico City to meet Madero and to ask him to return land to Indian and peasant communities. Madero told Zapata that his first priority was to disarm all fighters and organize a new government. Disappointed, Zapata broke with Madero and issued his Plan of Ayala, in which he criticized the new president and promised to continue fighting for the return of native lands.

In February, 1913, president Madero was taken prisoner by General Victoriano Huerta and murdered. Huerta hoped to end the revolu-

Bodies of the dead in the streets of Mexico City, casualties of the fighting in 1914 when Emiliano Zapata and Pancho Villa occupied the city. (Library of Congress)

tionary reforms Madero sought, and he named himself president of Mexico. Zapata's troops attacked Huerta's army in the south, while Francisco (Pancho) Villa and Venustiano Carranza attacked in the north. Claiming to uphold the constitution of Mexico, Carranza called his forces the Constitutionalists and defeated Huerta in July, 1914.

The 1914 Occupation of Mexico City

When General Victoriano Huerta resigned as president of Mexico on July 8, 1914, the head of the Constitutionalist forces, Venustiano Carranza, attempted to take control of the government. Representatives from various factions met at Aguascalientes to form a new government. Emiliano Zapata feared that Carranza would not enact land reforms and refused to back him for president. Zapata and Francisco (Pancho) Villa both favored Eulalio Gutiérrez for president. Carranza refused to accept this decision and pulled his troops back to Veracruz in order to establish his own government. In December, 1914, Zapata and Villa marched their separate forces into Mexico City. It was the first time the two revolutionary leaders had met. They celebrated their control of Mexico City in the presidential office. They soon found that they had little in common and went their own ways. The war among the revolutionary factions continued, and despite Zapata's attempts at reform, his Liberation Army of the South was pushed from Mexico City by Carranza's troops.

Opposition to Carranza

Later that year, as Carranza tried to take control of the government, Villa and Zapata joined forces to oppose him, supporting Zapata's Plan of Ayala and land reform. Zapata created agrarian commissions to redistribute lands and established a Rural Loan Bank. Despite these accomplishments, Zapata was isolated after Villa's defeat by Carranza's forces in 1915. Carranza called for a constitutional convention in 1917 that produced a new charter for Mexico. Agrarian reforms were promised, but few were carried out under Carranza. Zapata continued in opposition.

In 1919 Colonel Jesus Guajardo asked Zapata to meet him at the hacienda of Chinameca in the state of Morelos. There, on April 10, 1919, Zapata was ambushed and shot to death. Without Zapata, land distribution ceased to be a priority for the government and peasant communities did not benefit equally from the gains of the Mexican Revolution.

Bibliography

Brunk, Samuel. *Emiliano Zapata: Revolution and Betrayal in Mexico.* Albuquerque: University of New Mexico Press, 1995.

Millon, Robert P. *Zapata: The Ideology of a Peasant Revolutionary.* New York: International Publishers, 1995.

Womack, John. *Zapata and the Mexican Revolution.* New York: Random House, 1970.

James A. Baer

Ernesto Zedillo

Born: December 27, 1951; Mexico City, Mexico

President of Mexico (took office 1994)

Ernesto Zedillo Ponce de León (ehr-NAY-stoh zeh-DEE-yoh PON-thay thay lay-OHN) was born in Mexico City but moved with his family to Mexicali in Baja California. While attending elementary and secondary schools in Mexicali, Zedillo became active in student politics. He helped found the Student Union of the Valley of Mexicali and was a member of the Student Society Committee. Zedillo became president of the student cooperative and editor of the student newspaper. In 1965 his parents sent him back to Mexico City, where he completed his secondary education.

Zedillo witnessed the 1968 student riots in Mexico City. Police shot hundreds of students, and Zedillo, who was questioned by police during the events, must have been angered by the ruling party's response. He would later become a reformer within Mexico's dominant political party, the Institutional Revolutionary Party (or PRI, as it is widely known).

Career as an Economist

In 1969 Zedillo began his studies in economics at the National Polytechnic Institute in Mexico City. While continuing his course of studies, Zedillo took a position with the government in early 1971. He also participated in research at the Institute for Economic Studies, an organization run by the PRI.

Zedillo later entered Yale University in New Haven, Connecticut, as a graduate student in economics and graduated with a Ph.D. He wrote his dissertation on Mexico's public external debt. In 1978 he returned to Mexico and participated in an analysis of the balance of payments of the

Bank of Mexico. During this period Zedillo was becoming well known as an outstanding economic analyst. When Mexico devalued its peso in a desperate attempt to improve its economy in 1982, individuals such as Zedillo who had keen insight into the workings of the economic system were very important. Zedillo became the assistant secretary for planning and budget in 1982. For the next five years he held several posts within the government. He was a quiet man and

Ernesto Zedillo *(Reuters/Win McNamee/Archive Photos)*

1609

he focused on his job, but his reputation was growing among party leaders.

President of Mexico

The PRI's choice for presidential candidate in 1993 was Luis Donaldo Colosio Murrieta. Recent elections had brought much criticism of the party's grip on power, and Colosio was a popular and dynamic leader. Colosio named Zedillo as his campaign manager. When Colosio was assassinated and the party was left without a candi-

date, Zedillo became the replacement, even though few Mexicans were familiar with him and he was not a charismatic figure.

Zedillo won the 1994 election, and he soon faced mounting pressures to reform both the party and Mexico's electoral system. In addition, Zedillo had to deal with an insurrection in the southern state of Chiapas that began as the North American Free Trade Agreement (NAFTA) went into effect in 1994. That same year saw another economic crisis as the peso's value declined. Con-

The Peso Crash of 1995

After Mexico's economy strengthened in the 1980's, many observers thought that the economy could support both economic growth and social development. However, the peso, Mexico's currency, became overvalued, and outstanding bank loans reached record levels. On December 20, 1994, the Mexican government of President Ernesto Zedillo devalued the peso in a sudden move that pushed Mexico into a deep recession.

In early January, 1995, Zedillo's government initiated its first emergency economic plan in an attempt to restore stability to the peso. Investors and businesses failed to respond, however, and the crisis deepened. On February 21, 1995, one day after the Bank of Mexico increased short-term interest rates to 47 percent, Mexico, the United States, and the International Monetary Fund reached an agreement on a new emergency economic plan. The United States pledged twenty billion dollars to Mexico, and the Mexican government instituted a series of economic reforms. The value-added tax was increased from 10 percent to 15 percent, gasoline and electricity prices increased by 35 percent, and public spending was cut by 10 percent. These measures succeeded in stabilizing the Mexican currency, but at a cost to much of the population. Layoffs in industry,

Mexican president Ernesto Zedillo delivering his 1998 state of the nation address before the Mexican Congress. *(AP/Wide World Photos)*

increasing prices and taxes, and a reduction in government spending and services affected many poor Mexicans and put political pressure on Zedillo's government.

fronted with serious military, political, and economic crises, Zedillo sought to bring reform in an orderly process.

Bibliography

Centeno, Miguel Angel. *Democracy Within Reason: Technocratic Revolution in Mexico*. University Park: Pennsylvania State University Press, 1994.

Morris, Stephen D. *Political Reformism in Mexico: An Overview of Contemporary Mexican Politics*. Boulder, Colo.: Lynn Rienner, 1995.

Purcell, Susan Kaufman, and Luis Rubio-Freidberg, eds. *Mexico Under Zedillo*. Boulder, Colo.: Lynn Rienner, 1998.

James A. Baer

Ernesto Zedillo (center) inspecting troops on September 16, 1996, the 186th anniversary of Mexican independence. Mexico's defense minister, Enrique Cervantes, is at left. *(Reuters/Heriberto Rodriguez/Archive Photos)*

Zhao Ziyang

Born: October 17, 1919; Hua County, Henan Province, China

Premier of China (1980-1987) and secretary-general of Chinese Communist Party (1987-1989)

A Chinese statesman and reformer, Zhao Ziyang (JOW DSIH-YAHNG), also spelled Chao Tzu-yang, was the son of a rich farmer and grain merchant. He joined the Chinese Communist League in 1932 and the Chinese Communist Party (CCP) in 1938. During World War II and the Chinese civil war, Zhao worked in central China as a party organizer and propagandist. Before the Communist victory in 1949, he had risen to the position of the party chief of the Nanyang prefecture.

Early Career

In the 1950's and 1960's, Zhao climbed steadily in the Chinese government. In 1965, he was appointed the first secretary of the Guangdong CCP committee at the age of forty-six. His political career underwent a severe trial during the Cultural Revolution of the 1960's, when he was targeted by radical students as one of the top "capitalist roaders" in Guangdong. In 1967, he was dismissed from his post. Personal experiences during this period created in him a fear of disorder as well as misgivings about the dogmatism of the CCP.

Zhao was rehabilitated (forgiven for the errors of his ways and brought back into the party's good graces) even before the end of the Cultural Revolution, however, and in 1975 he was sent to Sichuan, China's most populous province, then devastated by heavy fighting among mass organizations. As the top official in Sichuan, Zhao demonstrated foresight and skill in restoring peace and prosperity.

Reformer

During the post-Mao Zedong economic reforms led by Deng Xiaoping, Zhao distinguished himself as a pragmatic reformer. In 1979, he was elected to the central committee of the CCP, and in 1980 he became a member of the Politburo, the party's policy-making committee. He was appointed vice premier in April, 1980, and in September, 1980, he became premier after a bloodless coup led by Deng.

After his initial successes in rural China, Zhao faced the daunting task of revital-

Zhao Ziyang *(AP/Wide World Photos)*

izing China's industry. After years of operation under bureaucratic control, industry was suffering from a host of problems, including inefficiency and obsolete technology. Beginning in the early 1980's, he tried a number of measures aimed at stimulating economic growth. These measures ranged from greater autonomy to industrial enterprises and a new tax system. He also vigorously promoted foreign trade and foreign investment in China.

Knowing that China's vast bureaucracy was a hindrance to further progress, Zhao attempted to streamline the government; he had the endorsement of Deng. Even his modest reforms invited animosity from the hard-liners in the CCP, however, and corruption threatened to undermine his economic reform. In 1986, after a student demonstra-

China's premier Zhao Ziyang speaking to American and Canadian reporters in Beijing in 1984 before a visit to North America; the Chinese foreign minister, Wu Xuequan is at the left. *(AP/Wide World Photos)*

tion against corruption, Zhao found it necessary to sacrifice his ally Hu Yaobang, then secretary-general of the CCP, to salvage his pragmatic program. In 1987, Zhao reluctantly assumed the po-

Science and Technology in China

Centuries ago, China achieved a high level of science and technology when compared with the rest of the world. The Great Wall of China was built in the fourth and third centuries B.C.E. China also is credited with the inventions of gunpowder, paper, and the printing press. Scientists in ancient China developed extensive knowledge about the universe, and Chinese doctors were conducting brain surgery as early as the third century. Since the nineteenth century, China has been trying to modernize its science and technol-

ogy by learning from the West, a process that has repeatedly been interrupted by domestic turmoil and foreign aggression. By the close of the twentieth century, China had made much progress in these fields. It had developed a modest space program and was building the largest hydraulic power project in the world. China's computer industry, though barely existent in the early 1980's, had become the third largest in the world by the late 1990's.

sition of secretary-general of the party. The premiership was taken by Li Peng, a Russian-educated conservative technocrat.

Zhao's Fall

In April, 1989, a political crisis developed in Beijing when the Chinese people bemoaned the death of Hu Yaobang. Angry students took to the streets in protest of widespread corruption in the Chinese government. Hard-liners in the ruling party labeled the demonstration "political turmoil" and called for a crackdown. Zhao Ziyang rejected taking a hard line against the students and refused to impose martial law in Beijing. He was therefore put under house arrest by the hard-liners. On June 30, 1989, Zhao was stripped of his chairmanships of the CCP and the Central Military Commission. While Jiang Zemin was appointed to the leadership of the CCP, Zhao remained in strict confinement. His short career as a reformer represents both the hope and frustration of China's effort to achieve modernization.

Bibliography

Bartke, Wolfgang. *Who's Who in the People's Republic of China*. Brighton, England: Harvester Press, 1981.

Current Biography. Vol. 45, June, 1984.

The International Year Book and Statesmen's Who's Who. East Grinstead, England: Thomas Skinner, 1984.

Who's Who in China: Current Leaders. Beijing: Foreign Languages Press, 1992.

Peng Deng

Zhou Enlai

Born: March 5, 1898; Huaian, Jiangsu Province, China
Died: January 8, 1976; Beijing, China

Prime minister (1949-1976) and foreign minister (1949-1958) of China

Zhou Enlai (JOW EHN-LI), also written as Chou En-lai, was born in Huaian in Jiangsu Province in 1898. His affluent family background and education at missionary schools set him apart from other early leaders of Chinese communism. They worked to his advantage once he assumed diplomatic duties for Communist China after 1959.

Early Career

Zhou Enlai became active with nationalist groups as a student and spent time in prison after a 1920 protest demonstration. Upon release, he left for France and made contacts with the Comintern (the Communist International), the Russian communist organization that coordinated revolutionaries worldwide. The Comintern was notorious for drastic policy shifts and reprisals against those who defied party discipline. Zhou handled this difficult relationship deftly.

When Zhou returned to China in 1924, he was rewarded for his faithful service with a key appointment at the Whampoa Military Academy. It was here that he developed methods to indoctrinate troops that were later used to train the Red Army. During the period between 1924 and 1934, the Chinese Communist Party (CCP) faced internal dissenters, Nationalist Party (Kuomintang) hostility, and disastrous advice from the Comintern. Zhou proved indispensable at this time, negotiating with an easygoing style when necessary or lashing out ruthlessly against opponents when needed. By 1934, the CCP seemed threatened with annihilation, and the leadership of Zhou helped it survive.

Long March to Liberation

In 1934, the Communists decided to begin a retreat of more than 6,000 miles (9,700 kilometers) from their Jiangxi Province stronghold to the remote caves of Yan'an. Horrible casualties were suffered during the Long March, as it came to be known, and Zhou kept morale as high as possible. He helped the party steer clear of the disastrous Comintern policies of the past and build an independent Chinese Communist movement. He also worked hard to impress the journalist Edgar Snow, who visited Yan'an; Snow's book *Red Star over China* (1973) helped generate admiration for the Chinese Communist movement in the English-speaking world.

Zhou Enlai *(Library of Congress)*

Chinese premier and foreign minister Zhou Enlai leaving a session of the 1954 Geneva Conference, at which he sought to increase China's international prestige and win friends for its communist government. *(Library of Congress)*

From 1937 to 1949, Zhou Enlai was the chief CCP negotiator with the Nationalist Party. He also negotiated with American diplomats and generals from 1941 to 1949. Zhou was successful in buying time to allow the CCP to build up the Red Army for an eventual showdown with the Nationalists. By the time the CCP seized power on the Chinese mainland in 1949, Zhou had emerged as the foremost Communist diplomat.

Triumph and Troubles

Communist China struggled with the problem of potential diplomatic isolation from 1949 to 1955. The Korean War also posed a serious security threat. Zhou worked tirelessly to improve the diplomatic position of Communist China. He kept the shaky Sino-Soviet alliance together, making seven trips to Moscow over eleven years. He visited Eastern Europe and Africa. Zhou first gained world recognition at the Geneva Conference in 1954, and he was then prominent at the highly successful Bandung Conference, held in Indonesia in

The Red Army

The founding of Communist China in 1949 was the result of almost thirty years of armed struggle. The Chinese Red Army played a key role in that struggle, and Zhou Enlai played a major role in making the Red Army an effective and successful fighting force. Zhou began the military phase of his career at the Whampoa Military Academy in the 1920's. He developed techniques of political indoctrination that were used throughout the war with Japan, the civil war, and liberation. The army became a pillar of Communist China and provided stability during the chaos of the Great Proletarian Cultural Revolution in the 1960's. The success of the Red Army was largely attributable to the efforts of Zhou Enlai.

The Geneva Conference

The Geneva Conference of 1954 met to negotiate the diplomatic consequences of the French defeat in Indochina. It was the first major conference that Communist Chinese officials attended. Zhou Enlai was determined that whatever the outcome, the conference could be used to win friends for Communist China. The harsh rhetoric upon which the Chinese had relied during the Korean War was drastically toned down. The militant Vietnamese, led by Ho Chi Minh, settled for a treaty that was very modest in relation to their battlefield triumphs. Vietnam was divided into North Vietnam, under Ho Chi Minh and the communists, and South Vietnam, which quickly became a puppet state dependent on American assistance to survive.

By contrast, the Americans at Geneva appeared to be models of Cold War inflexibility. The dour countenance and pronouncements of John Foster Dulles were in stark contrast to the relaxed demeanor and negotiating methods of Zhou. The Geneva Conference marked the beginning of a period when Communist Chinese prestige and influence gradually rose until the 1960's, when the Sino-Soviet split and internal turmoil undid those gains.

1955. At Bandung, China staked a bold claim to the leadership of the nonaligned nations of the world.

Even when the Sino-Soviet alliance fell apart, Zhou turned a setback into a moral victory. China and Zhou claimed that they, not the Russian "revisionists," were the true heirs of Karl Marx. As the 1960's began, domestic turmoil overshadowed the diplomatic triumphs of Zhou. A series of obscure policy disputes and personality conflicts exploded into the savage spectacle of the Great Proletarian Cultural Revolution. This attempt to revive revolutionary ardor and challenge the Communist bureaucracy resulted in excesses and atrocities that would leave psychological scars for decades to come. Many of Zhou's old colleagues were subjected to public humiliation and sent away for "re-education." Zhou Enlai was one of a handful of senior officials who escaped the Cultural Revolution. His wife was a more vulnerable target. She was perceived as a lover of Western culture and bourgeois fashion. At one state dinner, the Red Guard burst in and confronted Madame Zhou with these charges, but no other incident occurred.

Zhou weathered the chaos personally, but his diplomatic efforts were mostly undone. At one point, almost all China's ambassadors were recalled to Beijing for "re-education." By 1971, communist China was as isolated diplomatically as it had been at any time in its history. When the danger of isolation became apparent to Chairman Mao Zedong in 1971, Zhou once again received the call to use his talents for China.

Within a year, Zhou had succeeded in opening diplomatic negotiations with the United States and established diplomatic relations with Japan. Although events involving the new relationship with the United States received the most publicity, the resumption of relations with Japan was a much more difficult undertaking. Japan had exploited China and waged an especially brutal war there for decades. The Japanese foreign minister offered only a very weak semblance of an apology when he visited Beijing, but Zhou pragmatically accepted it in the interest of ending Chinese isolation.

The death of Zhou Enlai in 1976 and the events surrounding it were almost as important as his life. China was in the grips of the Gang of Four, radicals who held Zhou and his policies in contempt. The government held no formal ceremony or mourning period after his death. The people of China had revered Zhou, however, and spontaneous protests of this unfair treatment contributed to the downfall of the Gang of Four and the beginning of political reforms. Zhou was a dedicated Communist and a skillful diplomat. Much of what is good and much of what is troubling in China today can be traced to his efforts.

Bibliography

Hsu Kai-yu. *Chou En-lai, China's Gray Eminence*. New York: Doubleday, 1968.

Keith, Ronald. *The Diplomacy of Chou En-lai*. New York: St. Martin's Press, 1989.

Wilson, Dick. *Zhou: The Story of Chou En-lai*. New York: Viking, 1981.

Michael Polley

Zhu De

Born: December 12 or 18, 1886; Yilong, Sichuan Province, China
Died: July 6, 1976; Beijing, China

Chinese revolutionary and military leader

Born of poor peasants, Zhu De (JEW DEH), also written Chu Teh, was adopted when he was one year old by a wealthy uncle. He received a classical Confucian education and competed in the Imperial Civil Service Examination in 1905. Later he attended new-style schools to become, after graduation in 1908, a physical education instructor at a local elementary school. A year later he entered Yunnan Military Academy.

From Nationalist to Communist

While in the academy, Zhu joined republican leader Sun Yat-sen's Revolutionary League (Tongmenghui), which later became the Nationalist Party—the Kuomintang (KMT). In 1911 he graduated from the academy and took part in the revolution that overthrew the Qing Dynasty. For the next ten years he served as a middle- to high-ranking officer in armies of the Nationalists and several warlords. At that time Zhu began using guerrilla tactics in fighting bandits, tactics which later were used by the Chinese Communist army.

In 1922, disappointed by the chaotic politics of the new Chinese republic, he traveled to Europe, studying in Berlin and at the University of Göttingen. There he joined the Chinese Communist Party (CCP). Expelled from Germany for his political activities, Zhu returned to China in 1926 by way of Russia, there obtaining some military training for about a year. In August, 1927, he took part in the Communist-led Nanchang Uprising against the Nationalists. The next year he established the famous Fourth Red Army with Mao Zedong in Jiangxi Province. This event is regarded by Communists as marking the birth of the ideal Zhu-Mao leadership alliance, with Zhu as the military leader and Mao as the political leader. It was they who led the Communists to defeat the Nationalists and take over mainland China.

The Long March

From 1928 to 1934 the Chinese Red Army, with Zhu as the commander in chief grew tenfold, from about 10,000 to about 100,000. In October of 1934, the Red Army was forced to retreat from its bases in Jiangxi and to begin the Long March, a journey some have called the most incredible

Zhu De *(National Archives)*

Top-ranking officers of the Chinese army, including Peng Dehuai, far left, and Zhu De, second from left. *(National Archives)*

rived in northern Shanxi Province with only 8,000 survivors of the original group from Jiangxi. (However, they were joined by some 22,000 others from other areas.)

War with Japan

In 1937 the Sino-Japanese War broke out; it lasted until 1945. Upon forming the Anti-Japanese United Front with the Nationalists, the reconstituted Communist Red Army became the Eighth Route Army, with Zhu still as commander in chief. His army fought limited conventional battles but carried out massive

march in world history. They walked more than 6,000 miles (9,700 kilometers)—through eleven provinces, over eighteen mountain ranges, and across twenty-four rivers in southwestern and northwestern China. In October of 1985 they ar-

mobile guerrilla tactics in the fight against the Japanese, expanding the Communists' influence in northern China. One of his most important military works, *On Anti-Japanese Guerrilla Warfare*, was published in 1938. By the time of Japan's

The Fourth Red Army

In 1928, Zhu De led his troops to the Jinggang-shan Mountains in the southwest part of Jiangxi Province to meet with Mao Zedong, who had built a Communist base with survivors of the Autumn Harvest Uprising of 1927. They reorganized their troops into the Fourth Army of the Chinese Workers and Peasants' Red Army—the Fourth Red Army. The combined forces comprised some ten thousand people, with Zhu as commander and Mao as political commissar. With this army, Zhu and Mao developed and exploited guerrilla tactics and successfully defended their base against several Nationalist

suppression campaigns. In June, 1930, the Fourth Red Army reorganized again as the First Division Red Army, and in 1933 it merged into the First Front Red Army, also known as the Central Red Army. The Fourth Red Army was the core of the Chinese Communist Party's military forces, becoming the People's Liberation Army (PLA) after World War II. Zhu was its commander in chief until the Communist Party took over mainland China in 1949. Zhu, together with two others, Lin Biao and Chen Yi, were made marshals of the People's Republic of China in 1955.

The Cultural Revolution

Initiated and controlled by Mao Zedong, this ideological campaign began on May 16, 1966, when *The Directive of Launching the Great Proletarian Cultural Revolution* was issued by the Central Committee of the Chinese Communist Party (CCP). It ended on October 6, 1976, when Mao's widow Jiang Qing and the other members of the Gang of Four were arrested following Mao's death. One of the goals of the Cultural Revolution was to overthrow revisionist elements or "capitalist roaders" lurking within the ranks of the Communist Party and government. However, almost all leaders except Mao's radical supporters were affected in some degree. Fortunately, in his eighties and having maintained his distance from the CCP's power and ideological struggles, Zhu De survived this disastrous event with little harm to either his health or his reputation.

---

surrender in 1945, at the end of World War II, the Red Army had become a highly effective regular force of approximately 120,000 men, backed by a militia of 2 million, and controlling an area of one million square kilometers and a population of 10 million.

Winning the Civil War

The civil war between the Nationalists and the Communists resumed in 1945. In the first year's fight against the well-armed, numerically superior KMT forces, Zhu commanded the newly renamed People's Liberation Army (PLA) through a strategic withdrawal from cities and communication lines. He then led a counteroffensive, resulting in a brief strategic standoff in 1947, by which time the PLA had expanded to 2.5 million—almost equal to the KMT force in numbers and above them in both morale and mobility. By October, 1948, and under Zhu's overall direction, the PLA had entered the strategic offensive stage. Using conventional warfare, it soon took over most of northern China, including big cities such as Beijing and Tianjin. In April, 1949, the PLA crossed the Yangzte River and occupied Nanjing, the capital city of the Nationalist government. By the end of that year, the Nationalists were totally defeated and driven from the mainland.

An Old Soldier Fades Away

The People's Republic of China (PRC) was proclaimed on October 1, 1949. Zhu retained command of the PLA, now a national armed force of 5 million, until 1954. After that he held no military posts but many senior (though mainly ceremonial) government positions. He was vice president of the PRC, vice chairman of the National Defense Council (until 1959), and chairman of the standing committee of the National People's Congress. He served on the party's Politburo (executive committee) for many years. Never regarded as a contender for political power, he survived numerous ruthless power struggles within the CCP, including the Cultural Revolution of the 1960's. Zhu had several wives during his ninety-year life span and was survived by his last wife, who was also a Red Army veteran and CCP leader.

As the main CCP military leader, Zhu De, along with Mao Zedong, was primarily responsible for the founding of the Chinese Communist armed force, the Red Army (PLA), which was instrumental in bringing victory to the Communist Party in China. Moreover, he elevated guerrilla warfare from a minor supplement of conventional forces to a major strategic concept. As an individual, Zhu was well known for his gentlemanly character, humility, and tenacity.

Bibliography

Shum, Kui-Kwong. *Zhu De (Chu Teh)*. St. Lucia, Queensland, Australia: University of Queensland Press, 1982.

Smedley, Agnes. *The Great Road: The Life and Times of Chu Teh*. New York: Monthly Review Press, 1972.

Snow, Edgar. *Red Star over China*. New York: Grove Press, 1973.

Guoqing Li

Georgy Konstantinovich Zhukov

Born: December 2, 1896; Strelkovka, Russia
Died: June 18, 1974; Moscow, U.S.S.R.

Soviet military leader during World War II

Georgy Konstantinovich Zhukov (gyih-OHR-gyoo-ih kuhn-stuhn-TYEE-nuh-vyihch ZHEW-kof), the son of a peasant shoemaker, was born on a farm outside Moscow. He received a few years of formal education and then was apprenticed in the fur trade in Moscow. Zhukov remained in Moscow until the advent of World War I in 1914.

Early Military Career

At the beginning of World War I, Zhukov joined the Novogorod Dragoons, with whom he won two awards for bravery. The Russian Revolution occurred in 1917. In October, 1918, Zhukov joined the Red Army, and in 1919 he became a Bolshevik Party member. By the end of Russia's civil war (1918-1921), he had risen to squadron commander under Semyon K. Timoshenko, and he was able to study at the prestigious Frunze Military Academy. In the early 1930's, Zhukov became a specialist in tanks and was sent to Germany, Spain, and China to observe battlefield armored tactics.

In 1939 Zhukov gained recognition by defeating the Japanese in a battle on the Mongolian-Manchurian border, and he was made the deputy commander of the Ukrainian Military District under Timoshenko. In 1940 Timoshenko assumed command of Soviet troops involved in the Winter War with Finland, and he made Zhukov his chief of staff. After the Winter War, Zhukov was promoted to commander of the Ukrainian Military District.

World War II

World War II broke out in 1939. By 1940 German troops had swept through Western Europe, and by 1941 they were ready to attack the Soviet Union. On December 11, 1940, Zhukov made his first public address, in which he suggested that the Nazi-Soviet Pact of 1939 would not protect the Soviet Union. Unlike others who had made similar predictions, Zhukov did not suffer negative repercussions; instead, he was promoted to chief of staff of the high command, again under Timoshenko.

When the Germans attacked in 1941, the Soviet Union was unprepared, and the Germans advanced quickly. Zhukov, who had a reputation for being a tough and brilliant commander, was involved in many of the greatest battles on the eastern front. He led the counterattack in the Battle of Stalingrad (1942-1943) and was responsible for organizing the relief of Leningrad in

Georgy Konstantinovich Zhukov *(Archive Photos)*

The Battle of Stalingrad

During the spring and summer of 1942, the army of the Soviet Union suffered severe defeats by the Germans in World War II. In the fall of 1942, however, the tide began to turn. The Germans, overextending themselves, attempted to capture Stalingrad and the Caucasus region, and the Soviets were able to obtain a superiority of forces for the first time. The Germans began the offensive on November 19, 1942. At first they overpowered the Soviet troops in Stalingrad.

Marshal Georgy Konstantinovich Zhukov led the Soviet counteroffensive, ruthlessly attacking the German flanks and encircling their troops until, in February, 1943, the Germans were defeated. Zhukov's troops were then able to regain the Caucasus and end the siege of Leningrad. The Battle of Stalingrad marked a turning point of World War II, signaling the weakening and ultimate defeat of the Germans.

1943. Zhukov was also involved in the Battle of Berlin (1945), and he headed the Allied delegation that received the German surrender at the end of the war. Subsequently, Zhukov was the first commander of the Soviet occupation troops in Berlin. By the end of World War II, Zhukov had attained enormous prestige. Many outsiders assumed that he would become a government minister or even be Joseph Stalin's successor as Soviet leader. Stalin, wary of Zhukov's popularity, instead made him commander of the Odessa Military District.

The Khrushchev Era and Beyond

In 1953 Zhukov became the deputy minister of defense in the first post-Stalin government. Zhukov was influential in the arrests of Lavrenti P. Beria, who had been Stalin's chief of the secret police, and other police officials. When Nikita Khrushchev became leader of the Communist Party, Zhukov, whom Khrushchev had met when posted in the Ukrainian Military District, was promoted to minister of defense. In 1957 Zhukov helped Khrushchev remain in power during an attempt by the Politburo to oust him. Khrushchev, fearing that Zhukov had grown too powerful, denounced him

Three Allied military leaders during World War II: Soviet commander Georgy Konstantinovich Zhukov (seated, left) with American general Dwight D. Eisenhower (center) and British field marshal Bernard Law Montgomery (right). *(Library of Congress)*

and, in October, 1957, dismissed him from the cabinet and sent him to live outside Moscow. Zhukov's achievements during World War II were written out of Soviet history until Khrushchev's fall from power in 1964. After he was restored in 1965, Zhukov was able to publish his memoirs and military history articles that, although subjected to government censorship, gave the public and historians a new perspective on his involvement and on the workings of the Soviet government during World War II.

Bibliography

Erickson, John. *The Road to Stalingrad: Stalin's War with Germany.* Vol. 1. New York: Harper and Row, 1975.

Zhukov, Georgy Konstantinovich. *Marshal Zhukov's Greatest Battles.* Edited by Harrison E. Salisbury, translated by Theodore Shabad. New York: Harper and Row, 1969.

_____. *The Memoirs of Marshal Zhukov.* New York: Delacorte Press, 1970.

Erin K. McClain

Stalingrad, Soviet Union, after German bombing attacks in 1942. Georgy Konstantinovich Zhukov led the Soviet counteroffensive against the Germans in the 1942-1943 Battle of Stalingrad. *(Library of Congress)*

Mohammad Zia-ul-Haq

Born: August 12, 1924; Jullundur, Punjab (now India)
Died: August 17, 1988; near Bahāwalpur, Pakistan

President of Pakistan (1978-1988)

Mohammad Zia-ul-Haq (moo-HAH-muhd ZEE-ah ewl-HAHK) began his military career in 1944 when he joined the British Indian Army. He became an officer in May of 1945 and served in World War II battles in Burma, Malaya, and Indonesia. After the war, he remained in the army of the newly independent nation of Pakistan, taking part in Pakistan's wars against India in 1965 and 1971.

Islamic Leader

In 1976, Zia was promoted to general and appointed chief of the army staff by Prime Minister

Mohammad Zia-ul-Haq *(Corbis/Reuters)*

Zulfikar Ali Bhutto in recognition of his military professionalism, his devotion to Islam, and his complete loyalty to the Bhutto regime. Despite his being rewarded for his loyalty, increasing civil strife led Zia to take over the government of Pakistan in a bloodless coup on July 5, 1977, and declare martial law.

Although Zia claimed that Pakistan would be under martial law only temporarily, he remained in power as chief martial law administrator until 1978 and as president from then until his death in 1988. During these eleven years he imposed measures to promote nationalism and strict adherence to Islam among Pakistan's citizens. Zia banned trade union activities and imposed traditional Islamic penalties such as flogging for crimes such as theft and drinking alcohol. Zia also adhered to Islamic traditions in economics by forbidding banks to pay or collect interest on loans and by imposing a 2 percent tax on each citizen's wealth to go to the needy.

Maintaining Power

Although Zia had promised to hold elections within ninety days of the coup, his investigations of the repressive activities of the Bhutto regime led him to delay the elections for several years. The former prime minister was arrested in September of 1977 and executed in April of 1979 for conspiring to kill a political opponent. Meanwhile, Zia banned political activity in March, 1978. He banned political parties entirely in October, 1979.

Despite his failure to hold the promised elections, Zia was viewed favorably by many of the citizens of Pakistan as well as by the leaders of allied nations. Pakistan's middle class, which had generally felt unrepresented by Bhutto's govern-

Pakistani president Mohammad Zia-ul-Haq (right) meets U.S. national security adviser Zbigniew Brzezinski in 1980. *(AP/Wide World Photos)*

The Coup of 1977

Late at night on July 4, 1977, General Mohammad Zia-ul-Haq met with officers under his command and announced his plan to remove Prime Minister Zulfikar Ali Bhutto from power. Bhutto had been head of the government since 1971. After elections were held in March of 1977, he was accused of electoral fraud. Negotiations between Bhutto's Pakistan People's Party (PPP) and his opponents in the Pakistan National Alliance (PNA) broke down on July 3, 1977, raising the threat of civil war and leading to Zia's decision to take over the government. During the early-morning hours of July 5, 1977, Zia's officers arrested key members of the government and leaders of the PPP and PNA. He detained them at a military base. Bhutto was detained at the Government House in the city of Murree. That evening Zia announced to the nation that he had placed Pakistan under martial law but that free elections would be held within ninety days. Elections were eventually held in 1985.

ment, was more comfortable with Zia's support of traditional Islamic values. Under Zia, Pakistan experienced one of the highest rates of economic growth in a developing nation. Zia was always careful to retain the loyalty of the military. When the Soviet Union invaded Afghanistan in December of 1979, Zia's aid to the Afghans brought him strong support from the United States. Zia was also aided by the fact that some of his opponents lost popularity among many of the citizens of Pakistan when they were held responsible for terrorist activities or accepted support from the government of India.

When elections were finally held in February of 1985, several members of Zia's government were removed from office, but Zia himself remained in power. He ended martial law in December, 1985, resulting in greater freedom of the press and the legalization of political activity. Zia was killed less than three years later in an apparent act of sabotage. Zia and thirty other passengers, including the American ambassador to Pakistan, were killed when the military transport plane they were aboard exploded and crashed a few minutes after takeoff on August 17, 1988.

Bibliography

Arif, Khalid Mahmud. *Working with Zia: Pakistan's Power Politics, 1977-1988*. Karachi, Pakistan: Oxford University Press, 1995.

Burki, Shahid Javed, and Craig Baxter, eds. *Pakistan Under the Military: Eleven Years of Zia-ul-Haq*. Boulder, Colo.: Westview Press, 1991.

Duncan, Emma. *Breaking the Curfew: A Political Journey Through Pakistan*. London: Penguin, 1989.

Rose Secrest

Governments and Leaders

I. TYPES OF GOVERNMENT

When people live together they create societies. For societies to run smoothly and provide for the needs of their people, they must have governments. *Government* refers both to the practice of ruling and leading people and to the institutions that rulers use.

The Evolution of Government

In the long prehistoric age (before 5000 B.C.E.), when virtually everyone hunted, fished, or gathered food crops, governments could be simple. Because the world was sparsely populated, and because hunting-gathering economies did not require exclusive control of territories, societies had relatively few diplomatic and defense requirements. Most decisions related to the provision of food and shelter.

As populations grew, so did the complexity of social organization. Settled agriculture, beginning about ten thousand years ago, provided food surpluses that cushioned the effects of droughts, floods, and other natural disasters. At the same time, irrigation, storage, and distribution of crops required a new level of management. Farming was more efficient when centralized, and more food led to population growth. This in turn enabled people to specialize, with some specialties becoming more valuable to society than others. From the variety of functions in advanced societies—sometimes called civilizations—social classes emerged. Not every ancient civilization valued social classes in the same way, but almost every civilization was composed of a monarch and his or her family (royalty), a group of people who had earned the special favor of monarchs in the past (aristocracy), representatives of God or the gods (priestly classes or clergy), merchants, the military, and the masses. In many ancient societies, there were also slaves. The poorest people and captives taken in war were made slaves. Each group in society had its own abilities, needs, and interests. If society as a whole were to function effectively, someone had to rule.

As more people lived near one another in relative prosperity, conflicts occurred that had not existed among hunting-gathering peoples. If an agricultural city or state (the area governed by a ruler) were to be successful, it had to establish rules to regulate interpersonal relations (laws) and had to provide arbiters (judges, courts) to determine when the rules had been broken. Finally, someone had to be responsible for seeing that the rules were enforced and that judgments were carried out. Even when government succeeded in establishing a domestic policy that enabled its people to live together in relative peace and prosperity, threats from outside the city or state became increasingly common as populations and wealth grew simultaneously. Thus governments also developed a foreign-policy function, necessary to protect the security and possessions of the people of the state.

During the twentieth century, the world's population expanded at an unprecedented rate. Between 1650 and 1900 it had tripled, growing from 545 million people to 1.6 billion. Within the next hundred years it almost quadrupled, growing to more than 6 billion by the year 2000. This relentless growth led to an increased importance in the foreign-policy component of government, as states competed for limited space and finite amounts of the earth's natural resources. The twentieth century's new set of problems and issues led to a wider variety of types of government than had ever existed before.

Three General Approaches to Government

There are three general approaches to government: *authoritarianism*, *anarchism*, and *pluralism*. Each reflects particular views of human nature and of the amount and type of authority needed to rule. A society's form of government arises from the society's, or its leaders', assessments of the nature, limits, and potential of people living together. For example, are its citizens virtuous and likely to do good, or are they sinful and likely to do evil? Are all people equally likely to exhibit virtue or evil, or are some exceptional people better fit to rule over the less virtuous masses? A society's conception of human nature then must be combined with a decision regarding the type and amount of authority that will be necessary to ensure that governing can be performed efficiently and successfully.

That having been said, it must be noted that rarely is an entirely new system of government created by a society's populace at large, a single leader, or a group of leaders. Forms of government, and the basic assumptions about human nature that underlie them, have been evolving for thousands of years. Not everyone in a society is able to be, or is interested in being, a contributor to government. Governments are formed, led, and changed by those who either are already in positions of power or are driven to attain the necessary power to be involved. A form of government may grow from the conscious desires of a society's population, but it may also be imposed from above by a particularly powerful individual or group. For example, when the Bolsheviks (Communists) seized power in Russia in 1917, theirs was supposedly a revolution of and for the workers, the common people, against the autocratic Russian aristocracy. However, Vladimir Ilich Lenin and a tiny minority of Communists actually ruled the country, saying that the Russian people as a whole were not yet ready to govern themselves. Government may also be imposed on a society from the outside following military or political conquest (imperialism).

Regardless of the form of government that a society or country may have, many people living in the countryside, distant from a nation's capital or major cities, may find their actual way of life little affected by their country's government. Throughout the world, many millions of people are still villagers and simple farmers. They live much as their ancestors lived for centuries, little affected by politics, ideologies, even revolutions.

Authoritarianism

Authoritarianism refers to absolute rule by a single person (a *dictatorship*) or small group of people (an *oligarchy*) who assume that the masses are unable to rule effectively or who seek power to control a nation's wealth. Political opposition is not allowed. Based upon some criteria of superiority, authoritarian governments invest rulers with the authority to control every aspect of governance for the public good. All private interests may be subordinated to the interests of the state. Authoritarian states carefully control communications and rely upon military force and secret police to maintain their rule. A more specific political designation is *totalitarianism*, which usually refers to an authoritarian government with exclusive political control. A totalitarian government uses that control to transform every aspect of society. *Communism* (as practiced in the Soviet Union, China, and most Eastern European countries after World War II) and *fascism* (practiced in Italy, Germany, and Spain around World War II) are specific kinds of totalitarian governments that were prominent in the twentieth century. Both wished to organize all aspects of society according to a relatively clear set of political ideas. In the Soviet Union, for instance, there were attempts to abolish marriage, ban the practice of religion, and collectivize agriculture (combine and transfer ownership of agriculture to the state).

Military rule, royal absolutism, and *theocracy* are other kinds of authoritarianism. In the twentieth century, military rulers often overthrew freely elected governments when those governments were ineffective. Between 1960 and 2000, for instance, many civilian African governments were unable to cope successfully with the problems of newly independent countries. Some military leaders, such as Idi Amin (Uganda), Ibrahim Babangida (Nigeria), and Mobutu Sese Seko (Congo, formerly Zaire) seized the government by force, ruled for long periods of time by personal fiat, and enriched themselves in the process. Mobutu, who was finally toppled by rebels in 1996 after thirty years in power, is reported to have deposited more than $5 billion in foreign bank accounts. In some cases, military authoritarianism was intended to be temporary. Jerry Rawlings, for example, seized power in Ghana in 1981 but generally ruled for the good of the country; he returned Ghana to multiparty democracy in 1992.

In Latin America, military rule was often termed *caudillismo* and represented the extension to politics of a country's social system. In this kind of government, a country is ruled as if it were a personal estate. Some caudillos, such as Porfirio Díaz of Mexico, were simply military figures who ruled by force. During World War II, Juan Perón of Argentina fashioned an alliance between the military and the previously unrepresented urban masses, but in fact he retained all real power. On the other hand, some freely elected civilians later used the military and police to rule dictatorially. For instance, Peru's Alberto Fujimori was freely elected in 1990, but by 1997 he was being criticized for assuming near-dictatorial powers in his attempt to crush various terrorist movements.

Royal absolutism (authoritarian rule by a hereditary monarch) and theocracy (rule by the clergy in the name of God) are forms of authoritarianism that had some adherents in the twentieth century, although they were more common in earlier times. For instance, long after the power of most monarchies had been limited by constitutions, Czar Nicholas II (in power from 1894 to 1917) exerted near total control of Russia, and he fully intended to pass this power to his son. Royal absolutists, and those who support them, usually believe that their authority comes from God.

With the decline of religious faith in the nineteenth century, fewer people believed that monarchs truly had divine authority.

Similarly, fewer people in the twentieth century believed that God's laws could be applied directly to earthly governments, so theocratic governments were rare. Toward the end of the century, however, there was a revival of Islamic fundamentalism in northern Africa and southwest Asia. Theocratic governments were installed in the Sudan, Iran, and Afghanistan. In Iran, power was for a time concentrated in the hands of a Shiite Muslim religious leader, or ayatollah, Ruhollah Khomeini (ruler from 1979 to 1989) before it was gradually diffused to members of a revolutionary council. In other countries, such as Sudan in the 1990's, power was shared between religious and military leaders. In Sudan they agreed on a general plan for rebuilding Sudanese society, torn by civil war, according to a strict interpretation of the laws of Islam.

Anarchism

Anarchism, at the other extreme from authoritarianism, is the belief that no person or party has sufficient moral authority to govern others. Anarchists believe that human beings are capable of cooperative, voluntary management of all social problems. Public government is therefore unnecessary, and it is even immoral because it is coercive. The ordinary functions of government should be left to individuals and voluntary private groups. Because government is not a goal for anarchists, they played almost no practical part in ruling countries in the twentieth century. They did, however, influence the development of communism and *syndicalism* in some countries. Syndicalism is a theory of government in which there is no state structure; rather, a federation of worker-led industrial units rules. Relatively small anarchist units such as the Baader-Meinhof Group (also known as the Red Army) carried out terrorist campaigns against various Western governments.

Pluralism

Pluralism is an approach to government that falls between authoritarianism and anarchism. It is based on the belief that some form of government is necessary but that no absolute authority exists for a single person or group to rule. The interests of individuals and private groups should be allowed to compete with one another but not without reference to the larger interests of the state.

Pluralistic governments in the twentieth century were diverse in composition, and they accepted various sources of legitimate power. These sources included rule by hereditary or elected rulers (monarchy, presidency), the elite (aristocracy), the military, the workers (labor), and the masses (democracy). Accordingly, some pluralistic governments were *constitutional monarchies*, in which some functions were performed by kings or queens, while most were carried out by governmental ministers, elected officials, or other groups. In some constitutional monarchies, as in Japan and Great Britain, the monarch's role is largely ceremonial. In others, such as Morocco, the king has broad powers.

The exact balance of power between competing groups was usually determined by a constitution, which established provisions for allowing citizens to choose between politicians with varying points of view. In a two-party system (as in the United States and Great Britain), power usually alternated between politicians who adopted the broad principles of *conservatism* or *liberalism*. In a multiparty system (as in Italy, France, and Germany), the largest political parties were usually associated with ideologies such as conservatism, liberalism, and *socialism*. Others, however, were defined by more narrow interests. Germany's Green Party, for instance, was created in 1980 to unify the efforts of many regional parties whose primary interest was the environment. The two-party system tended to be more stable, though it gave voters fewer choices. In Italy, where there were sometimes ten parties repre-sented in the legislature, voters had many choices. The large number of parties made agreement on policy issues difficult, however, thus leading to many changes of government as coalitions of various parties formed and reformed in pursuit of their objectives. Italy had more than forty changes of government between 1945 and 1994.

Republics and Democracies

The most common forms of pluralistic government in the twentieth century were *republics* and *democracies*. A republic in the twentieth century was a state not ruled by a monarch or divine authority in which the source of authority was the people as a whole. The traditional idea of a republic, as developed by Aristotle (384-322 B.C.E.) and Polybius (c. 200-118 B.C.E.), was that it should be a mixed form of government in which monarchs, aristocrats, and free adult males should all have a hand in governance. This "mixed constitution" of authority would prevent any person or group from ruling selfishly. With the decline of monarchies and aristocracies after the eighteenth century, new ways to balance authority had to be devised. These new approaches led to different interpretations of the nature of a republic. For instance, after World War II, most people of the Republic of China (the island of Taiwan) supported four decades of one-party military rule under Chiang Kai-shek. They did so mainly because they believed Chiang's government was necessary to protect their personal freedoms from the nearby threatening communist government of mainland China. That government called itself the People's Republic of China, though it was a one-party state with virtually no input from its citizens. "People's Republic," in fact, was a name often used by totalitarian communist rulers who claimed to rule for the benefit of the people, though without their direct participation.

A democracy, on the other hand, is a kind of republic in which the government is composed of directly elected representatives. This type of government is not a republic in the ancient sense of the term, yet in the twentieth century democracies did actually have mixed constitutions, as Aristotle and Polybius had advocated long ago. In the United States, for instance, most adults were able to vote for representatives, senators, the president, and many other officials. Officials served in three branches of government—executive, legislative, and judicial—with powers under the Constitution to limit, or "check," the authority of the other branches.

Presidential versus Parliamentary Systems

The two most common ways to organize pluralistic governments in the twentieth century were the *presidential system* and the *parliamentary system*. In the presidential system, used in the United States, France, Mexico, and many countries in Latin America and Africa, the president is elected directly by the people for a specific term of office. The president's position is not dependent upon a party majority. In some cases, as in the United States, the office of the president is strong, and the president is closely involved in day-to-day operations of the government. In other countries, such as France, the president appoints a prime minister to deal with the daily business of government. Thus it is possible that the president could be from one political party, while the majority of representatives are from another party or group of parties. In the parliamentary system, used in Great Britain, Italy, Australia, Canada, New Zealand, Botswana, and some other African countries, the public votes only for legislators or members of parliament. The majority party then chooses the prime minister, who holds office (up to a maximum number of years) as long as the parliament supports his or her policies.

Although many governments have similar features, it is important to remember that no two pluralistic governments are exactly the same. In some the electors have more direct input than in others. In some the president or chancellor is strong, while in others he or she is relatively weak, with the real work being done by a prime minister. In some governments a monarch plays an important role, while in others monarchy has never been a part of the tradition.

Political Ideologies

General attitudes such as *authoritarianism*, *anarchism*, and *pluralism* are only starting points for establishing and maintaining specific governments. Governments base their goals upon differing assessments of society, and they apply differing values as they seek to solve social problems.

For example, various leaders may believe in the general principle of authoritarianism but may establish very different goals for their authoritarian states. Tz'u-hsi, the empress dowager of China (ruling 1875-1889, 1898-1908), ruled autocratically in order to preserve both her own power and the Confucian system of government that had existed for almost two thousand years. Benito Mussolini of Italy, on the other hand, ruled from 1922 to 1943 with a similar absolute authority and personal ambition, but his goal was to destroy outdated political systems and create an altogether new one according to the tenets of fascism. Even totalitarian states that hoped to fashion entirely new orders of society disagreed on the best system of government. During the 1930's and 1940's, totalitarian governments were in power in both the Soviet Union and Nazi Germany. Yet Soviet leader Joseph Stalin and German leader Adolf Hitler were bitter enemies, and they used their absolute power to work toward markedly different goals.

The Need for Ideologies

An *ideology* is a system of political beliefs, values, theories, and goals. Ideologies are necessary because a basic attitude toward government—thinking it to be good, bad, or a necessary evil—is only a starting point for establishing the institutions by which a country is governed. The character and roles that a government takes are shaped by its ideology. General examples of ideologies include *liberalism, communism, fascism, monarchical absolutism, syndicalism,* and *anarchism*.

A single individual, if this person is convinced of his or her own genius and commands enough military force, might establish an authoritarian government. This government might appear to be simply an extension of the basic totalitarian attitude that the masses are unfit to rule and that all power should be vested in the sovereign or in a small group of individuals. However, to govern a territory (as opposed to overthrowing its previous government), the ruler must create institutions that ensure personal and state security, demonstrate authority to rule, and sustain the economic well-being of citizen and state. No ruler can do this alone. Generals, soldiers, and other influential people must be rewarded in some way for the government to retain their support. Economies must be maintained to ensure an orderly citizenry that will not rebel and that will pay taxes. A system for collecting taxes must be established and efficiently administered. All the while, disputes between subjects will require that rules (laws) be established and justice enforced.

In order to translate basic attitudes toward governance into an actual government capable of grappling with social and political problems, people have relied upon ideologies. These comprehensive systems of political beliefs, values, and goals are usually expressed in a number of key texts, which may be written across a long period of time in reaction to specific crises of governance. Among liberalism's important texts, for example, are John Locke's *Two Treatises on Government* (1690) and *A Letter Concerning Toleration* (1689) and Thomas Paine's *Common Sense* (1775); central communist texts include Karl Marx's *Manifesto of the Communist Party* (1848) and *Das Kapital*, the first volume of which appeared in 1867. An ideology performs several functions. First, it offers an explanation for why certain social conditions exist. If people are to live peacefully together in a society, they must know why there is unequal distribution of wealth. There must also be explanations of why racial tension and economic depression exist, of what citizens' rights and responsibilities are in relation to the government, of why they will be asked to wage war and pay taxes, and of what the state will in turn do for them.

Second, an ideology provides a standard by which both conditions and solutions are judged. Class struggle, for instance, may be viewed positively in an ideology such as communism, while it is condemned by fascist ideology. Third, an ideology helps people who are otherwise different to form a sense of political identity. By establishing a coherent worldview with specific reference to government, individuals can act collectively, knowing that everyone shares the same fundamental goals and confidence that political actions will be judged by clearly defined standards. Finally, an ideology promotes a plan of action. In a complex world filled with bewildering problems and complicated by self-interest, people are attracted to ideologies because they provide clear justifications for specific courses of action.

By the beginning of the twentieth century, almost all the lands of the world were governed by European countries or had developed governments based upon European models. For more than four hundred years, Spain, Portugal, Holland, England, France, Denmark, Belgium, Germany, and Italy had systematically explored the earth's surface, establishing trade relations with—and often political control over—distant societies. By the late nineteenth century, almost all primitive civilizations had fallen under the control of Western powers. Some high civilizations, such as the Mughal Empire in India and the Qing Dynasty in China, had managed for a time to resist Western encroachment. However, their governments, rooted in premodern Islamic and Confucian ideologies, were unable to keep pace with the demands of government in a new global, industrial age. Japan was the only major non-Western country successfully to resist Western domination. They succeeded, however, only by adopting a form of liberalism that had emerged in the West.

Dominant Twentieth-Century Ideologies

The twentieth-century world was dominated by three major political ideologies: *liberalism*, *communism*, and *fascism*. Each of these developed from the Western political and economic experience. In addition to these, *monarchical absolutism*, *syndicalism*, and *anarchism* at times played significant roles in determining the nature of some governments. Though twentieth-century models of government were largely Western in nature, every government was unique. None conformed exactly to an extended model or definition, and most incorporated elements of more than one ideology. In practice, no government slavishly adhered to a single ideology. The Soviet Union and the People's Republic of China were the dominant communist powers of the twentieth century, but each departed from the classical communist ideology of Karl Marx and Friedrich Engels in substantive ways. Chinese communism differed significantly from both Marxian communism (which involved Marx's ideas) and Soviet communism (which applied Marx's ideas to the Russian situation), in part because Chinese leaders valued certain goals and methods rooted in their Confucian-based culture.

Monarchical Absolutism

The oldest of the ideologies noted above, *monarchical absolutism*, proved to be the least influential in the twentieth century. Monarchical absolutism was almost at an end in the Western world by 1900. It was still prevalent in Russia, China, and, in simpler forms, in some parts of Africa and Asia that had not yet fallen under direct European, American, or Japanese control. This kind of government had in some form once been almost

universal in civilized states. A monarch (queen, emperor, or czar) ruled with the authority of God or the gods over a society whose character had been fixed by divine decree. Though absolute monarchies often incorporated bureaucracies, cabinets, legislative bodies, and other trappings of more liberal forms of government, their functions remained clearly under the control of the ruler. Monarchical absolutism was the world's principal form of government from the sixteenth through the eighteenth centuries. The rise of science, the Enlightenment, and the general growth of secularism in the West all worked to undermine the notion of divine authority by the nineteenth century. Monarchies did not disappear, but most increasingly incorporated elements of liberalism.

Liberalism

In the nineteenth and twentieth centuries, liberalism was expressed in governments that valued individual rights and freedoms, protected those freedoms with written laws and constitutions, and provided mechanisms for representation and participation of most or all adult citizens. The ideology of liberalism is rooted in the Protestant Reformation of the sixteenth century and in the early political philosophies of Thomas Hobbes and John Locke. All forms of liberalism emphasize individual liberty, and to a greater or lesser extent they accept the idea that human beings are rational and thus capable of making sound political judgments.

Martin Luther's protests against the doctrine and practices of the Catholic Church in the early 1500's were based on the assumption that individuals are both capable of and responsible for making personal judgments about religion based upon their own reading of the Bible. His support for what he called the "priesthood of the believer" affected monarchical absolutism in two ways. First, it undermined the traditional authority of the Roman Catholic Church, which had been seen as the sole mouthpiece of God by most

Christians. This undermining in turn weakened absolute monarchs, who could no longer look to the Roman Catholic Church for support of their claims to rule with the authority of God. Second, once people began to believe that they could determine their spiritual destiny, it was a small step for some to believe that they should determine their political destiny as well.

The first philosophical work to bear the clear stamp of modern liberalism was *Leviathan* (1651), by Thomas Hobbes (1588-1679). In this work Hobbes argued in favor of absolute monarchy. Nevertheless, the explanations, standards, and points of identification that Hobbes employed were clearly of a different kind than those typically used to support absolute monarchy. Rather than viewing monarchs as properly exercising divine authority over people whose status had been fixed at birth, Hobbes insisted that people have a "natural right" to do as they please. Because people with natural rights are always grasping for power, however, conflict will always be present. As a result, Hobbes argued, rational individuals with natural rights should voluntarily enter into a "social contract" with a sovereign, granting almost absolute power in order to avoid chaos and to ensure order.

Liberalism was further developed by John Locke (1632-1704), whose *Two Treatises on Government* (1690) and *A Letter Concerning Toleration* (1689) became landmarks in the codification of the new ideology. Further enhancing Hobbes's notion that people had "natural rights," Locke argued against religious coercion. He drew a distinction between private and public matters. According to Locke, the natural rights of "life, liberty, and property" could best be protected when people voluntarily join to create a government whose purpose is to protect those rights. When a government violates these rights, the people have a right to overthrow it. Following the Glorious Revolution of 1688 in which the absolutist James II was driven from the throne, Britain effectively developed the first constitutional mon-

archy: The office of the monarch was retained, but with specific privileges and limitations defined by a constitution.

The American (1775-1783), French (1789-1799), and Latin American (1808-1831) revolutions built upon the example of the Glorious Revolution in Britain. Though rooted in specific economic and political grievances, these were also ideological revolutions. Writings such as Thomas Paine's *Common Sense* (1775) and *The Rights of Man* (1791, 1792), the Continental Congress's *Declaration of Independence* (1776), and the French Assembly's *Declaration of the Rights of Man and of Citizens* (1788) clearly incorporated the essential elements of Lockean liberalism. In overthrowing national monarchies, the United States and France founded governments based upon individual freedoms, human rights, and the concept of a social contract, in which government operated on behalf of citizens and in agreement with their wishes. Though French political reforms were fitfully applied in the nineteenth century, the United States successfully rejected the traditional monarchical model of government and established a genuine democracy in which most white males participated both in selecting the government and in shaping its ideas. Between 1808 and 1831, nominally liberal independence movements in Argentina (1816), Mexico (1821), Peru (1821), Bolivia (1825), Venezuela (1830), and Ecuador (1830) quickly yielded to *caudillismo*, a typically nineteenth-century form of totalitarian government in which a military dictator ruled countries as if they were personal estates. Liberal challenges to dictatorship occasionally were successful, but they never permanently succeeded in reforming societies with huge gulfs between rich and poor. Political turmoil was endemic throughout the region, which never escaped its economic dependence upon Europe and especially the United States.

Throughout the nineteenth century, the influence of liberalism continued to grow in the Western world. It almost always stressed the value of the individual, promoted representative government, and emphasized the importance of clearly defined protections such as legal codes and written constitutions. Instead of remaining a simple political ideology of individual rights, it came to encompass both freedom of competition in the economic sphere and the freedom of whole nationalities to choose their own governments. Early in the eighteenth century, liberal economists began arguing against the restrictive economic practices that governments used as tools of diplomacy (mercantilism). Instead, they said, everyone would benefit from the free pursuit of their own economic interests. Governments should remove high tariffs and other forms of regulation so that private individuals would be free to compete in a private sphere of activity. *Laissez-faire*, which may be translated as "let it be"—or, let people do as they choose—became the motto of economic liberals. The person most responsible for defining this form of economic liberalism (*capitalism*) as a key component of liberal ideology was a Scotsman, Adam Smith (1723-1790). His *Inquiry into the Nature and Causes of the Wealth of Nations* (1776) suggested that governmental controls were inhibiting the efficiency and growth of economies because only a few people were able to take advantage of economic opportunities under the restrictive mercantile system. Instead, economic restrictions should be removed so that everyone would have access to opportunity. Self-interest would encourage everyone to attempt to make a profit. In a free economic system this could be done only by producing better or cheaper goods—which in turn would benefit the whole society. The "invisible hand" of supply-and-demand would supplant government policy in determining how an economy should be run.

Nationalism

In the wake of the Napoleonic Wars (1799-1815), *nationalism* emerged as one of the dominant forces of the nineteenth and twentieth cen-

turies. Nationalism was often a key component of liberal thought. Nationalism entails a belief that the culture of one's own nation—its history, art, music, and social values—is of supreme importance and is worthy of devotion and loyalty. Because nationalism emphasizes the strength of shared culture, history, and values, it often includes an emphasis on the ideas that ethnic groups are entitled to be self-governing and that national boundaries should coincide with ethnic ones. With a heightened consciousness of shared cultural values, peoples throughout the world began to reject the claims of dynastic rulers who suggested that their authority was rooted in God's will or in the essence of a royal bloodline.

Although nationalism was a component in many different political ideologies, including the fascism of Mussolini's Italy and Hitler's Germany, it became most closely associated with the rising tide of liberalism. If people are rational, are born free, and are the source of governmental authority (through the social contract), it was a small step to argue that they have the collective right of self-government as well. Autocratic multinational entities such as Austria-Hungary, Russia, and the Ottoman Empire began to disintegrate as local charismatic leaders and patriotic groups led movements of independence or national unity in Greece (1829), Belgium (1839), Montenegro (1858), Italy (1861), Germany (1871), Romania (1878), Serbia (1878), Bulgaria (1878), Norway (1905), and Albania (1913). In the twentieth century, similar movements led to the independence of virtually all former European, American, and Japanese colonies.

Constitutional Monarchism

During the nineteenth century, the United States and most European countries became more liberal. Even autocratic governments in Germany and Austria-Hungary were infused with certain liberal elements, though the power of the emperors and the aristocracy remained strong. Although most nations outside the Western Hemisphere retained hereditary rulers, their powers were to a greater or lesser degree being curbed by written constitutions that guaranteed individual liberties and vested ultimate authority in the citizens of the state. In Western Europe, the balance of competing ideological systems finally tipped in favor of the authority of the people. *Constitutional monarchism* predominated and came to be viewed as a subdivision of liberalism. Countries such as Great Britain, France, Sweden, Denmark, Belgium, and Italy retained much of the outward form of the more autocratic monarchies of Russia, Austria-Hungary, and Germany, but in fact they were politically closer to the liberal democracy of the United States. For example, although the United States was governed by a presidential democracy and Great Britain by a constitutional monarchy, both clearly adhered to the general principles of liberalism and thus were able to cooperate effectively throughout most of the twentieth century.

Conservatism

Though the nineteenth century is often seen as an age of liberalism, a strong strain of *conservatism* was also evident in some politicians everywhere. A view opposing liberalism was necessary if multiparty, pluralistic systems were to give citizens a genuine political choice. Whereas liberalism was based upon the concept that human beings have natural rights and that society can be improved, conservatism started from the presumption that human beings are deeply flawed. This view accorded well with the traditions of the Christian church in Europe, which included as a cornerstone the idea of Original Sin—that human beings are born with a sinful nature. The most prominent early exponent of conservatism was the Irish politician Edmund Burke (1729-1797). During the early years of the French Revolution, he wrote what is usually considered the textbook of modern conservatism, *Reflections on the Revolution in France* (1790). In this work he expounded the main principles

adopted by most conservative parties throughout the twentieth century.

Burke supported representative government but not democracy. Democracy is dangerous, he believed, because it is based upon passions rather than evaluation of long-term interests. Instead, Burke believed that the governance of a country is best served by the "true natural aristocracy." In the eighteenth and nineteenth centuries, this phrase usually—but not always—meant the hereditary aristocracy. These were members of a class who had been granted royal favors, usually including land and titles, in return for service to the Crown. Across the decades and centuries, the aristocracy was thus privileged with wealth and leisure time, which enabled them to be educated and gave them the opportunity to think in the long term and plan for the broader good.

Increasingly in the nineteenth, and almost always in the twentieth, century the "true natural aristocracy" came to refer to the gifted elite, who—through discipline, education, or wealth—had acquired both the talent for governing wisely and the inclination to govern for the good of the whole people. Burke, and most conservatives following him, took a high view of private property. Property was seen as a stabilizing force that caused people to govern wisely and to avoid rash policies that might lead to its dissipation. Finally, Burke argued that government should not be concentrated in the hands of one office or one person. In the eighteenth century, he supported the traditional privileges of the Church and the family as a check on central control. In the twentieth century, conservatives express this principle in a mistrust of state planning and in support for local solutions to local problems.

Capitalism, Imperialism, and Racism

Though liberal governments were, for many of the world's people, a distinct improvement over absolute monarchies, they never delivered as much as they promised. The authority to rule in the name of "the people" was constantly being compromised by the close association of liberal governments with *capitalism* and *imperialism*. Unregulated capitalism created hardships for the working people of liberal countries; many worked long hours in dangerous, menial jobs for low wages. Countries practicing imperialism (rule over other countries or regions) denied to Africans and Asians the same rights that were guaranteed to their own citizens at home. The so-called natural rights to life, liberty, property, and the pursuit of happiness were widely denied to slaves, former slaves, and immigrant workers in the Western Hemisphere as well as to the colonized peoples of Africa, Asia, Oceania, and the Caribbean (often referred to collectively as people of color). Liberal countries such as Great Britain, the United States, France, and Belgium usually argued that full political rights were an ideal that would emerge naturally with the progress of economic and political liberalism. Many liberal leaders felt that within a capitalist economy, slavery would eventually become unprofitable, a situation that would lead to its formal abolition. Others suggested that "primitive" peoples should be allowed to participate in liberal governance only when they were sufficiently educated.

As the nineteenth century progressed, *racism* (the belief in the superiority of one race over another) as a reason for ruling illiberally began to undermine the notion of the gradual evolution of liberalism. Many liberals, either overtly or implicitly, accepted the idea that Europeans were inherently—because of their race—superior to people of color and therefore were justified in ruling over them. Because of their continuing political weakness into the twentieth century, minorities in the United States and colonized peoples around the world would not substantially influence the formation of governments until the 1940's and 1950's.

Socialism

Exploited white industrial workers were not so easily put off as were people of color. By the late nineteenth century, most enjoyed extensive constitutionally protected rights. From the mid-nineteenth century, too, European and American workers were being better educated in expanding public school systems. These factors helped urban workers to band together to protest the poor working conditions, monopolistic practices, and low wages that characterized western urban society during the Industrial Revolution (roughly 1800-1914). Millions of workers sought economic protection through various kinds of collective organizations. In most cases, they joined labor unions, which operated as one of the private pressure groups within the various pluralistic forms of government. Some, however, were attracted to new ideologies that explained why workers were being exploited and suggested how they might stop it.

Modern socialism began as a protest against the individualism and self-interest fostered by liberalism. It was characterized by a belief that because human beings are social by nature, society would be better and more productive if people cooperated with one another rather than competing for individual advantage. The goal of socialism was a classless society in which the means of producing wealth would be controlled by the state rather than by private individuals or groups. François-Noel Babeuf (1760-1797), who used the pseudonym Gracchus, had advocated a simple form of socialism during the early years of the French Revolution, though it remained untested.

Utopian Socialism

Early in the nineteenth century, socialism split into two main camps. *Utopian socialism* built upon Babeuf's ideas to advocate a series of decentralized societies in which relatively small communities would pattern their economic and social lives on cooperative principles. François Fourier (1772-1837) wrote a number of works between 1808 and 1836 in which he laid out a plan for the ideal community, the phalanstery. It would be composed of about sixteen hundred residents who would produce all that was needed while living in harmony. Because a phalanstery would allow people voluntarily to engage in the work that suited their special interests and talents, all the coercive powers of a government—legislation, police forces, and judicial systems—would be unnecessary. A few attempts were made to implement Fourierism, including Brook Farm in the United States, but none was successful.

British capitalist Robert Owen (1771-1857) published his own vision of a utopian socialist society in *A New View of Society* (1814). According to Owen, the social evils of the time were the result of a defective social and economic system, capitalism, that rewarded greed and selfishness. Owen had established a successful socialistic factory at New Lanark, Scotland, in 1800. Despite this fact, capitalists paid no attention to his plea for factories that were clean and safe, where children would, instead of working, be taught the value of cooperation. In 1830 he established the socialist community of New Harmony on thirty thousand acres of land in Indiana. Within four years it had failed, leaving Owen to support worker cooperatives as a means of preparing society for a more radical form of socialism.

Scientific Socialism

While Fourier and Owen were promoting small and self-sufficient communal enterprises, French nobleman Count Claude-Henri de Saint-Simon (1760-1825) dreamed of refashioning the whole of society on a scientific basis, thus laying the foundation for what is called *scientific socialism*. In the complex industrial world, which requires the coordination of many skills and technologies, the "individual" of whom liberals spoke in fact cannot exist. Capitalism is inefficient, Saint-Simon argued, because it leads to a cycle of surpluses and shortages. Only through the coordination and planning of experts could these inefficiencies be avoided. Auguste Comte (1798-1857), Saint-Simon's disciple, carried these

ideas further. Distrusting democracy, he argued for rule by technical experts. Comte's socialist vision was disturbing to many because it advocated a "religion of humanity" that explicitly rejected what he considered the worn-out role of traditional religion.

Frenchman Louis Blanc was the first to make socialism a political force. Following France's 1848 revolution, he led the provisional government to institute government workshops to provide work for the unemployed. Although the experiment in applied socialism was unsuccessful, and the government was soon returned to the rule of an emperor, Blanc demonstrated that socialistic principles could be implemented at a national level.

Karl Marx and Marxism

The most influential of all socialist thinkers was Karl Marx (1818-1883), whose theories of socialism were both more cohesive than those of his predecessors and more carefully founded on economic research. Marx and his protégé Friedrich Engels (1820-1895) defined the ideals of revolutionary socialism. Engels himself acknowledged the originality of Marx's ideas, but he was more effective than Marx in conveying those ideas to the ordinary reader. Marx's particular brand of socialism served as the foundation for modern *communism*. In the nineteenth century, the terms socialism and communism were often used interchangeably, particularly by opponents. This could be done because, with the exception of a handful of small and unsuccessful experiments, socialism remained an intellectual idea, consisting primarily of the unrealized goal of state control of the means of economic production, and the common denunciation of private property.

Born to a liberal, middle-class Jewish family in Germany, Marx studied to become a professor. When his plans for academic life were thwarted by opposition from the Prussian government, he turned to journalism. He began to see first-hand how great was the gap between rich and poor. He gradually became more radical, believing that the existing political and economic system of Europe was too corrupt to be reformed. When his publications were shut down by the Prussian police in 1843, he fled first to France, then to Belgium. During the European revolutions of 1848 he edited the *Neue Rheinische Zeitung*, which made him famous throughout Germany as a radical reformer. When the autocratic government crushed the revolution in Germany, Marx was forced into exile. He spent the remainder of his life in London.

Marx's general principles of socialism were established in the 1840's, when he began a systematic study of the German philosopher Georg Wilhelm Friedrich Hegel (1770-1831). Marx's early essays (1842-1847) already show the influence of Hegel and Marx's own belief in the central role of economics and radical political action. His only systematic statement of socialist ideology was published on the eve of the 1848 revolution in the pamphlet *Manifesto of the Communist Party* (1848), often referred to as the "Communist Manifesto." His most extensive work, *Das Kapital* (capital), was based on painstaking historical research in the library of the British Museum. It was a careful study of the capitalist system, incorporating an analysis of the reasons for its success, an assessment of its flaws, and a prediction of its demise. The first volume appeared in 1867, but the second and third volumes, edited by Engels, were not published until after Marx's death.

Marx interpreted history as the record of an ongoing struggle between classes (between masters and slaves, lords and serfs, and capitalists and workers) who have very different aims and interests. He considered material production to be of primary importance, because "before men do anything else, they must first produce the means of their subsistence." Until classes are abolished, the struggle will continue. Marx argued that capitalism was efficient but fatally flawed in that it alienated workers (the proletar-iat) from the results of their labors and the means of their livelihood. For people to be free, the means of production must be in the hands of the people. Marx explained the passivity of exploited workers by society's teaching of a false consciousness. Through every phase of social education, workers were taught that equality of opportunity under the guise of capitalism was a blessing, that government interference was wrong, and that human beings were naturally competitive. Marx especially deplored religion, which he called the "opiate of the people," because it made them uncritical of the conditions in which they lived. What the workers needed, according to Marx, was a revolutionary consciousness that would lead the proletariat to revolt against those who controlled the means of production (bourgeoisie).

Marx predicted that a workers' revolution would begin in the most industrialized countries and would eventually sweep away all capitalistic societies. These events would happen according to a revolutionary sequence of events that would begin with a series of economic crises. The more advanced the capitalistic economy, the more frequent would become the recessions, depressions, and other fluctuations in the economic cycle. These crises would lead to poverty and misery among the proletariat. The pitiful condition of the workers would lead them to develop a revolutionary class consciousness, and they would realize the flaws in the capitalistic system. Poverty and revolutionary consciousness together would provide class solidarity, which would enable the proletariat, through strikes or civil war, to seize the government. They would then establish a "dictatorship of the proletariat" in which the institutions of the state (courts, police, schools) were carefully guarded against the capitalist reaction. According to Marx, forms of coercion would be necessary only until capitalistic attitudes died away. Then the state would "wither away" in the face of the creation of a universal working class.

Marx's Communist Society

The final stage in Marx's revolutionary sequence was the establishment of a communist society. Marx was vague about its exact nature. Unlike the utopian socialists, he refused to create what he called "recipes for the kitchens of the future." Generally, Marx envisioned a democratic society in which the means of production were publicly owned, production was carefully planned, and distribution of goods and services was based upon the rule, "from each according to his ability, to each according to his need."

Marx did not live to see his judgments and theories put to the test, but his ideas were at the heart of all the vital socialist political movements that flourished between the time of his death in 1883 and the outbreak of World War I in 1914. By the time Vladimir Ilich Lenin led Russia's Bolsheviks in the first communist revolution (1917), Marx's thought had already been interpreted and refashioned in many ways.

Revisionist Marxism

Around 1900, Marx's revolutionary sequence seemed stalled at the second stage, in which the workers were impoverished and in misery. Many socialists tried to answer the question, Why had the workers not developed a revolutionary consciousness? The main critique of Marx's thought came from Eduard Bernstein (1850-1932), whose school of thought became known as *revisionist Marxism*. Bernstein had been a member of the German Social Democratic Party before being forced to flee Germany in 1878. In exile, he had conversations with Marx and Engels. He also observed the course of historical developments and noted the example of English Fabian socialists, who supported a program of gradual reforms. In response to these developments, Bernstein wrote a critique of Marxism entitled *Evolutionary Socialism* (1899). He claimed that Marx had paid too little attention to the ethics of his system and that by focusing on distant goals Marx had himself fallen into a "utopian" trap.

Bernstein also noted that the relationship between the proletariat and the capitalist system had not always developed in the way that Marx had predicted. For instance, workers had shown solidarity in the creation of labor unions, particularly in Germany, and by the 1890's they were able to organize and actually send their own members to the Reichstag (parliament). Marx's prediction that wealth would become concentrated in fewer and fewer hands also appeared to be false, as the success of trade unions had helped bring about higher wages and better working conditions. It appeared to Bernstein, as it had to some early socialist leaders who had opposed Marx in the 1850's and 1860's, that workers might actually be able to use established political systems in order to better their conditions. If this could be done, then violent revolution could be avoided.

Bernstein's revisionism formed the basis of the pluralistic socialist parties—social democratic parties—that flourished in most European countries in the twentieth century. Rather than replacing capitalism and representative governments with a revolutionary state-directed economy and a one-party system, the goal of social democratic parties was to educate the public about the advantages of adopting socialist principles. As a result, British Labour, German Social Democrats, and French Socialists all developed as mainstream parties. They accepted the principle of opposition politics—that political parties of differing viewpoints compete for votes and voluntarily relinquish power when voted out.

Marxist-Leninism and Twentieth-Century Communism

Other socialists, however, including Lenin, interpreted Marx's writings very differently. In what is now termed *Marxist-Leninism*, it was argued that the concentration of capital that naturally occurred in the economic system of capitalism would inevitably lead to imperialism. As luxury industries came to replace truly productive ones, the "labor aristocracy" of skilled workers would be "bribed" by imperial profits to lead unskilled workers into gradual social reform rather than revolution.

Whereas Marx had concluded that communism would arise spontaneously with the collapse of capitalism, Lenin argued that the split between labor leaders and common workers would require that a small party provide leadership in the revolutionary stage. The party's "dictatorship of the proletariat" would lead the way in the destruction of capitalism. Once this phase of socialism (the "lower phase") had achieved its purpose, then the higher form of communism could emerge, in which there would be no class distinctions and the state, unnecessary, would wither away. Marxist-Leninism was the basis of most revolutionary socialist and communist movements in the twentieth century.

Anarchism

Frustrated and dissatisfied with the repression of autocratic regimes, the slow pace of liberal reform, and the political weakness of socialism, some activists turned to other political ideologies around the beginning of the twentieth century. Modern *anarchism* had originated with William Godwin's *Enquiry Concerning Political Justice* (1793), which argued that rational and social human beings could achieve social harmony through discussion and voluntary cooperation. The French economist Pierre-Joseph Proudhon (1809-1865) took this idea a step further, arguing that governments actually were "the scourge of God." He proposed that economies could be driven by nonprofit cooperative banks, which would provide interest-free capital to citizens.

By the late nineteenth century, Russians Mikhail Bakunin (1814-1876) and Peter Kropotkin (1842-1921) had developed anarchism into an actual political force, urging "direct action" by workers to overthrow the state. Though anarchists joined Marxists and other socialist groups in opposition to autocratic and liberal governments, they refused to form political parties and

therefore were unsuccessful in reforming the political landscape. Though failing to topple any governments, they were responsible for temporary disruptions by assassinating Czar Alexander II of Russia (1881), King Humbert of Italy (1900), Empress Elizabeth of Austria (1898), President William McKinley of the United States (1901), and President Marie-François-Sadi Carnot of France (1894).

Syndicalism

Syndicalism, an ideology with links to both socialism and anarchism, also flourished in the two decades prior to World War I. Building on the ideas of Proudhon and Jérôme-Adolphe Blanqui (1798-1854), who first publicly advocated a dictatorship of the proletariat, French labor organizers gradually developed a unique political ideology that clearly emerged in the 1890's. Fernand Pelloutier (1867-1901), a disillusioned Marxist and secretary of the *Fédération des Bourses du Travail*, helped fashion the original ideas of others into a theory of government in which a federation of industrial units, representing the various activities of a worker-controlled economy, would rule. Like most socialists, syndicalists agreed with Marx's analysis of the class struggle and with the necessity of communal ownership of the means of production. Unlike socialists, however, they opposed any kind of state structure, believing that it would necessarily become an instrument of class domination. Like anarchists, they rejected political parties. Syndicalists preferred strikes, industrial sabotage, and violence as the best means for effecting change, but they believed that rule by workers was necessary to provide for larger common needs such as defense.

The most famous text of syndicalism is Georges Sorel's *Reflections on Violence* (1908), in which he introduced the idea that "social myths" could stir the passions and thus promote positive change. This appeal to passion rather than reason was later incorporated as an element of Mussolini's fascism in Italy. Syndicalism was strongest in France, though it also exerted considerable political influence in Italy, Spain, Mexico, and Argentina prior to World War I. In 1908 in the United States, the Industrial Workers of the World (the IWW, or the "Wobblies") split into two factions: The socialists followed Eugene V. Debs, and the anarcho-socialists adopted a kind of syndicalism that preferred strong trade-union centralization rather than the smaller worker-units typical of French syndicalism. Though syndicalism lost much of its force after World War I, with many adherents adopting either communism or fascism, it continued to exercise a significant influence on those ideologies. Left-wing trade union activity owed much to syndicalist ideas, as did anarchist opposition to the communists in Spain in the 1930's.

World War I and Coalition Governments

World War I (1914-1918) dramatically altered the political landscape of the twentieth century. In the two decades prior to 1914, various forms of liberalism and traditional autocratic rule defined the nature of most governments. Autocratic monarchies were everywhere in retreat, and liberal governments had yet to prove themselves in a major crisis. Socialists and syndicalists were beginning to exert considerable influence on politics in many countries, but they had yet to gain control of a government and thus to test their theories in practice.

The tremendous loss of life and economic devastation of World War I rocked the foundations of European governments. In many countries, the war ushered in a relatively new kind of governmental organization—the coalition. In almost every country fighting in the war, coalition or unity governments temporarily bridged gulfs between conservatives, liberals, laborites, and socialists, demonstrating that it was possible for politicians with widely varying ideologies to cooperate when necessary. In France, veteran socialist leader Jean Jaurès led socialists in support of the war before being assassinated. All but a

handful of German socialists supported the German government, even supporting the military dictatorship in the last years of the war. The Labour movement in Great Britain accepted state direction under a coalition government led by Liberal David Lloyd George.

Developments in the 1920's and 1930's

By the early 1920's, several new developments were affecting the application of ideology to the practice of government. First, in the victorious countries of Western Europe, and to a lesser extent in the United States, government intervention in society became accepted. This was so even among most liberals and conservatives who had previously opposed it. One factor in this shift came from World War I: If the government could conscript (draft) millions of men to fight and die on behalf of the country, it seemed right to most politicians that the government should in some way be responsible for them.

In a second trend, immediately following the war, Europe as a whole moved toward more liberal forms of government. By the 1920's, populations in the old dynastic monarchies of Germany, Austria-Hungary, and the Ottoman Empire had established more liberal forms of government. The new nation-states that had been carved from the defeated empires in eastern Europe and the Balkan peninsula were uniformly committed to forms of representative government. Finally, and most dramatically, the pressures of the war had helped Lenin and the Bolsheviks topple the czarist autocracy in Russia and establish the modern world's first communist government in 1917.

The combination of these developments in many ways defined politics around the world during the twentieth century. Autocratic monarchies, which had been the predominant governments of the previous three hundred years, virtually disappeared. Control of most of the peoples of the world was left to supposedly liberal governments. In contrast stood the newly minted Soviet Union, which hoped to lead a worldwide communist revolution. Soviet leaders sought to impose a "modern" totalitarianism that would transform every aspect of life. Most constitutional liberals feared communism, and most countries defined their political systems to some degree in terms of opposition to communism and ways to resist it.

The Great Depression began in 1929, and its effects were devastating in Europe and the United States. Millions of people were unemployed, and they soon believed they had no hope of getting a job. National economies seemed to hover on the brink of collapse. For many people, neither liberal nor communist ideology adequately explained why the world economy was stagnating in the 1920's and 1930's. Neither Western governments nor the Soviet Union seemed to have answers for the era's pressing economic and diplomatic problems. In Europe and parts of Latin America, a new kind of conservatism known as fascism sought to build upon a narrow sense of national identity as a means of attaining support for a new kind of totalitarianism.

Fascism

Fascism developed in direct opposition to what were perceived as the weaknesses of liberalism and communism. Fascism held that the other ideologies presented flawed estimates of human nature. According to fascist ideology, the values of the Enlightenment—humanism, rationalism, secularism, progressivism, and universalism—were not to be esteemed. Fascism was conservative in that it accepted the flawed nature of individual human beings and was therefore skeptical of progressive ideas that sounded good in theory but would not work in practice.

However, fascism rejected the notion of many conservatives that power should not be centralized. Fascists took Burke's "true natural aristocracy" to a higher level. They argued not only against democracy's elevation of the common man but also specifically for the rule of "great men" whose actions are bold and creative. Swiss sociologist Roberto Michels (1876-1936), for instance, wrote of the "iron law of oligarchy." He argued that successful organizations and societies have always been ruled by a small elite (an oligarchy) and that no well-meaning plans of either liberals or socialists could change that "iron law." German philosopher Friedrich Nietzsche (1844-1900) had earlier written that the outstanding achievements of humankind were—and naturally should be—the work of the *Ubermensch* (superman) who could disregard the pressures of the crowd.

Fascists were intensely anticommunist, and they rejected liberalism as an outworn creed. Liberalism had arisen, according to Mussolini, as a necessary reaction to royal absolutism, but it had outlived its usefulness. Fascist movements began in almost every European and Latin American country. Under the charismatic leadership of Mussolini, Adolf Hitler, Francisco Franco, and Juan Perón, fascists had control of governments in Italy (1922-1943), Germany (1933-1945), Spain (1936-1975), and Argentina (1946-1955).

Government at the Century's End

By 1994, almost one hundred new nations had become independent of European and American rule. Nearly all of their governments were significantly influenced by the tenets of liberalism, communism, or fascism. Yet by the final decade of the century, old ideologies and political designations were fragmenting and being redefined.

Just as, earlier in history, tribal rulers, god-kings, decentralized feudal emperors, and hereditary absolutist monarchs had in turn given way to one another, fascism, communism, and other forms of authoritarian government were on the decline. Between 1989 and 1992, communist regimes in eight countries in Eastern Europe gave way to more liberal multiparty governments. The most dramatic of these events were the breakup of the Soviet Union into fifteen independent ethnic republics and the splintering of Yugoslavia into five. These events demonstrated not only the strength of liberalism but also the power of nationalism. Between 1989 and 1994, thirty-five African nations rejected one-party governments, mostly authoritarian in nature, for multiparty or no-party systems.

Liberal governments, too, were in transition. In 1990, West Germany and East Germany, divided since 1945, were reunited under a liberal government, leading to a dramatic reevaluation of political goals. In Canada, 1993 saw the election of fifty-four members of the separatist Bloc Québécois to the House of Commons, making it the largest opposition party. In 1995, the people of Quebec narrowly defeated a separatist resolution, by a vote of 50.5 percent opposed to 49.4 percent in favor). In the Northwest Territories, plans were moving forward to establish Nunavut, a new territory to be governed by the Inuit (Eskimo) population. In Canada's 1997 general election there were five official parties, each owing its success to regional voting. Also in 1997, Britain's Conservative Party lost its first national election since 1976, and the Labour Party came to power. In twenty years, however, the Labour Party of Tony Blair had almost totally shorn its ties to the socialism of the 1970's. It had become a centrist liberal party.

With the fall of the Soviet Union and its satellite states in the early 1990's, the foreign-policy goals of many countries were dramatically altered. During the Cold War era (1947-1990), most countries had found it necessary to side with either the United States (and democratic liberalism) or the Soviet Union (and communism). In the 1990's political parties reevaluated their foreign-policy goals.

The last half of the twentieth century also saw dramatic shifts in the world economy that forced politicians to rethink their attitudes toward trade and other global issues. Formerly poor countries such as Japan, Korea, China, Taiwan, Brazil, South Africa, Botswana, Libya, Saudi Arabia, and Mexico successfully dealt with many of their social problems and found places in the international economy. Most African, South Asian, and Latin American countries still struggled with basic issues such as population growth, disease, and literacy.

Instead of focusing on defense and military issues, which seemed paramount throughout much of the twentieth century, many politicians in the 1990's turned their attention to questions of sovereignty, the environment, technology, and global trade. Such issues had scarcely been visible at mid-century, when major concerns were the destruction of fascism and the threat of the global expansion of communism.

John Powell

II. POLITICAL LEADERS AND TYPES OF GOVERNMENT

Notes on Classifications

The list that follows is a categorization of the political leaders covered by the *Biographical Encyclopedia of 20th-Century World Leaders*. When using this list for research, the reader should keep two important factors in mind. First, labels such as socialist, communist, and fascist can only approximately characterize various governments as they actually exist. For instance, though governments in the Soviet Union, China, and Albania all had a common goal—state ownership of the principal means of economic production, according to which they can all be called "communist"—there were a number of differences that significantly separated their political systems.

Second, characterizing individuals as communists, fascists, or socialists is even more problematic. Political designations vary according to the particular historical circumstance of the countries involved. Moreover, they are considerably affected by the unpredictability of human nature. Political ideology affects the decisions of political leaders, but so do ambition, greed, love, lust, and a host of other factors not directly related to politics. Thus it is not unusual for political leaders to change ideologies or to behave in ways that sometimes seem to betray the ideologies they profess. As a result, political figures in the following list may be found under more than one category.

The individuals listed under "Leaders of Independence and Liberation Movements" often did not actually govern the lands that they were instrumental in freeing, and thus they cannot be assigned to a specific form of government. Also, rulers listed under "One-Party Indigenous States" tended to be authoritarian, although they cloaked their authoritarianism in the traditions of the people. Many African rulers, for instance, explicitly rejected European models of government that had been involved in imperial control,

and they tried to return to a form of consensus government rooted in the African past. These governments almost universally failed, except insofar as they sometimes brought a kind of discipline that comes with most forms of authoritarian governments.

Multiparty Liberal Governments

Constitutional or Liberal Monarchists
Abdul Rahman
Akihito
Bhumibol Adulyadej
Edward VII
Edward VIII
Elizabeth II
Faisal I
George V
George VI
Hassan II
Hirohito
Juan Carlos I
Muhammad V

Conservatives, Nationalists, Rightists
Konrad Adenauer
Oscar Arias Sánchez
Stanley Baldwin
Arthur Balfour
Edmund Barton
Menachem Begin
Richard Bedford Bennett
Theobald von Bethmann Hollweg
Benazir Bhutto
Zulfikar Ali Bhutto
Robert Laird Borden
Louis Botha
Lucien Bouchard
Stanley Bruce
George Bush
Mangosuthu Gatsha Buthelezi
James Callaghan
Neville Chamberlain
Winston Churchill

Joe Clark
Calvin Coolidge
Alfred Deakin
Alcide De Gasperi
F. W. de Klerk
Eamon de Valera
John G. Diefenbaker
Alexander Douglas-Home
Félix Éboué
Anthony Eden
Dwight D. Eisenhower
Arthur William Fadden
Gerald R. Ford
Alberto Fujimori
Charles de Gaulle
Warren G. Harding
Charles James Haughey
Edward Heath
Paul von Hindenburg
Herbert Hoover
William Morris Hughes
Itō Hirobumi
Helmut Kohl
Pierre Laval
Bonar Law
Jean-Marie Le Pen
Harold Macmillan
Datuk Seri Mahathir bin Mohamad
John Major
William Ferguson Massey
Arthur Meighen
Carlos Saúl Menem
Robert Gordon Menzies
Hosni Mubarak
Robert Muldoon
Brian Mulroney
Benjamin Netanyahu
Richard M. Nixon
Franz von Papen
Philippe Pétain
Raymond Poincaré
Georges Pompidou
Ronald Reagan
Theodore Roosevelt

Anwar el-Sadat
Jan Christian Smuts
Gustav Stresemann
Sukarno
William Howard Taft
Margaret Thatcher

Liberals, Democrats, Liberal Democrats, Centrists

Konrad Adenauer
Corazon Aquino
Jean-Bertrand Aristide
H. H. Asquith
Edvard Beneš
David Ben-Gurion
William Jennings Bryan
Henry Campbell-Bannerman
Jimmy Carter
Jean Chrétien
Bill Clinton
Michael Collins
Joseph Cook
William T. Cosgrave
Alfred Deakin
Alcide De Gasperi
José Napoleon Duarte
Alexander Dubček
Matthias Erzberger
Malcolm Fraser
Rajiv Gandhi
Al Gore
John Grey Gorton
Václav Havel
Harold Holt
John Howard
Hayato Ikeda
Lyndon B. Johnson
Constantine Karamanlis
John F. Kennedy
William Lyon Mackenzie King
Juscelino Kubitschek
Robert M. La Follette, Jr.
Wilfrid Laurier
David Lloyd George

Francisco Madero
Makarios III
Nelson Mandela
Tomáš Masaryk
William McMahon
Robert Gordon Menzies
Turgut Özal
Lester B. Pearson
Manuel Quezon
Fidel Ramos
George Houston Reid
Syngman Rhee
Franklin D. Roosevelt
Augusto César Sandino
Eisaku Satō
Eduard Shevardnadze
Joseph Roberts Smallwood
Louis St. Laurent
Sun Yat-sen
Pierre Elliott Trudeau
Harry S Truman
John Napier Turner
Eleuthérios Venizélos
Woodrow Wilson
Boris Yeltsin

Socialists, Social Democrats, Laborites, Radicals

Clement Attlee
David Ben-Gurion
Tony Blair
Léon Blum
Willy Brandt
Karl Hjalmar Branting
Gro Harlem Brundtland
Joseph Benedict Chifley
Georges Clemenceau
John Curtin
Jacques Delors
Milovan Djilas
Tommy Douglas
Abba Eban
Andrew Fisher
Francis Michael Forde

Indira Gandhi
Mikhail Gorbachev
Robert Hawke
Víctor Raúl Haya de la Torre
Édouard Herriot
William Morris Hughes
İsmet İnönü
Rashid Karami
Paul Keating
Aleksandr Fyodorovich Kerensky
Patrice Lumumba
Ramsay MacDonald
Michael Manley
Golda Meir
François Mitterrand
Mohammad Mossadegh
Robert Mugabe
Imre Nagy
Gamal Abdel Nasser
Jawaharlal Nehru
Andreas Papandreou
Shimon Peres
Yitzhak Rabin
Jerry John Rawlings
Gerhard Schröder
James Henry Scullin
Joseph Roberts Smallwood
Paul-Henri Spaak
Lech Wałęsa
Gough Whitlam
Harold Wilson

Wartime Coalitions and National Unity Governments

Léon Blum
Robert Laird Borden
Aristide Briand
William Morris Hughes
David Lloyd George
Ramsay MacDonald
Arthur Meighen
Raymond Poincaré
Josip Broz Tito

Authoritarian Governments

Socialists, Marxists, Communists, People's Democrats

Salvador Allende
Hafez al-Assad
Leonid Ilich Brezhnev
Fidel Castro
Nicolae Ceausescu
Deng Xiaoping
Alexander Dubček
Mikhail Gorbachev
Antonio Gramsci
Andrei Andreyevich Gromyko
Che Guevara
Ho Chi Minh
Erich Honecker
Jiang Qing
Jiang Zemin
János Kádár
Nikita S. Khrushchev
Kim Il Sung
Le Duc Tho
Li Peng
Liu Shaoqi
Georgi M. Malenkov
Mao Zedong
Slobodan Milošević
Vyacheslav Mikhailovich Molotov
Julius Nyerere
Daniel Ortega
Pol Pot
Eduard Shevardnadze
Muhammad Siad Barre
Joseph Stalin
Josip Broz Tito
Leon Trotsky
Walter Ulbricht
Boris Yeltsin

Royal Absolutists

Fahd
Faisal
Francis Ferdinand
Francis Joseph I
Haile Selassie I
Hussein I
Juan Carlos I
Mohammad Reza Pahlavi
Nicholas II
Pu-yi
Norodom Sihanouk
Tz'u-hsi
William II

Fascists

Francisco Franco
Adolf Hitler
Pierre Laval
Benito Mussolini
Juan Perón
Philippe Pétain
Pu-yi
António de Oliveira Salazar

Military Rulers, Warlords, Martial-Law Rulers

Idi Amin
Hafez al-Assad
Muhammad Farah Aydid
Ibrahim Babangida
Fulgencio Batista y Zaldívar
Louis Botha
Houari Boumedienne
Chiang Kai-shek
F. W. de Klerk
Porfirio Díaz
Samuel K. Doe
François Duvalier
Jean-Claude Duvalier
Francisco Franco
Alberto Fujimori
Juvénal Habyarimana
Hirohito
Victoriano Huerta
Ferdinand E. Marcos
Mobutu Sese Seko
Gamal Abdel Nasser
Manuel Noriega

Augusto Pinochet Ugarte
Muammar al-Qaddafi
Jerry John Rawlings
António de Oliveira Salazar
Muhammad Siad Barre
Ian Smith
Anastasio Somoza García
Suharto
Sukarno
Hideki Tojo
Rafael Trujillo
Getúlio Vargas
Pancho Villa
Yuan Shikai
Mohammad Zia-ul-Haq

Leaders of One-Party Indigenous States

Kemal Atatürk
Plutarco Elías Calles
Lázaro Cárdenas
Juvénal Habyarimana
Félix Houphouët-Boigny
İsmet İnönü
Kenneth Kaunda
Jomo Kenyatta
Lee Kuan Yew
Yoweri Kaguta Museveni
Kwame Nkrumah
Milton Obote
Park Chung Hee
Muammar al-Qaddafi
Léopold Senghor
Suharto
Sukarno
William V. S. Tubman
Ernesto Zedillo

Leaders of Theocratic or One-Party Religious States

The Dalai Lama
Ruhollah Khomeini
Hashemi Rafsanjani

Independence and Liberation Movements

Emilio Aguinaldo
Yasir Arafat
Kemal Atatürk
Nnamdi Azikiwe
Surendranath Banerjea
David Ben-Gurion
Michael Collins
Mahatma Gandhi
Ho Chi Minh
Félix Houphouët-Boigny
Mohammed Ali Jinnah
Kenneth Kaunda
Jomo Kenyatta
René Lévesque
Patrice Lumumba
Francisco Madero
Ramón Magsaysay
Makarios III
Nelson Mandela
Julius Nyerere
Syngman Rhee
Augusto César Sandino
Norodom Sihanouk
Bal Gangadhar Tilak
Chaim Weizmann
Sa'd Zaghlūl

BIOGRAPHICAL ENCYCLOPEDIA OF
20th-Century
World Leaders

Leaders by Area of Achievement

Civil Rights

Abernathy, Ralph David, **1:** 4
Buthelezi, Mangosuthu Gatsha, **1:** 237
Dalai Lama, The, **2:** 367
de Klerk, F. W., **2:** 383
Du Bois, W. E. B., **2:** 438
Gandhi, Mahatma, **2:** 540
Garvey, Marcus, **2:** 550
Jackson, Jesse, **3:** 762
King, Martin Luther, Jr., **3:** 856
Lutuli, Albert, **3:** 947
Malcolm X, **3:** 978
Mandela, Nelson, **3:** 985
Mandela, Winnie, **3:** 989
Powell, Adam Clayton, Jr., **4:** 1256
Sakharov, Andrei, **5:** 1367
Tutu, Desmond, **5:** 1518
Wells-Barnett, Ida B., **5:** 1563
White, Walter Francis, **5:** 1565
Wiesel, Elie, **5:** 1570
Wiesenthal, Simon, **5:** 1573

Diplomacy

Albright, Madeleine, **1:** 24
Annan, Kofi, **1:** 38
Arias Sánchez, Oscar, **1:** 49
Asser, Tobias Michael Carel, **1:** 63
Bajer, Fredrik, **1:** 89
Beernaert, Auguste-Marie-François, **1:** 111
Beneš, Edvard, **1:** 118
Bourgeois, Léon, **1:** 172
Boutros-Ghali, Boutros, **1:** 174
Briand, Aristide, **1:** 200
Bülow, Bernhard von, **1:** 224
Bunche, Ralph, **1:** 227
Cassin, René, **1:** 265
Chamberlain, Austen, **1:** 276
Clark, Joe, **1:** 304
Coubertin, Pierre de, **2:** 355

Cremer, William Randal, **2:** 358
Delors, Jacques, **2:** 386
Eban, Abba, **2:** 456
Eden, Anthony, **2:** 463
Erzberger, Matthias, **2:** 484
Evatt, Herbert Vere, **2:** 487
García Robles, Alfonso, **2:** 547
Gobat, Charles Albert, **2:**
Gromyko, Andrei Andreyevich, **2:** 594
Hammarskjöld, Dag, **2:** 621
Harriman, William Averell, **2:** 629
Henderson, Arthur, **2:** 650
Hull, Cordell, **3:** 737
John XXIII, **3:** 779
John Paul II, **3:** 782
Kellogg, Frank B., **3:** 813
Kennan, George F., **3:** 816
Kirkpatrick, Jeane, **3:** 863
Kissinger, Henry A., **3:** 866
La Fontaine, Henri-Marie, **3:** 885
Lange, Christian Lous, **3:** 890
Le Duc Tho, **3:** 906
Litvinov, Maksim Maksimovich, **3:** 926
Myrdal, Alva, **4:** 1122
Nkrumah, Kwame, **4:** 1150
Papen, Franz von, **4:** 1190
Paul VI, **4:** 1202
Pearson, Lester B., **4:** 1205
Peres, Shimon, **4:** 1211
Pérez de Cuéllar, Javier, **4:** 1215
Petty-Fitzmaurice, Henry, **4:** 1234
Pius XI, **4:** 1240
Pius XII, **4:** 1243
Rabin, Yitzhak, **4:** 1272
Renault, Louis, **4:** 1296
Ribbentrop, Joachim von, **4:** 1305
Saavedra Lamas, Carlos, **5:** 1361
Sadat, Anwar el-, **5:** 1363
Shevardnadze, Eduard, **5:** 1392

Leaders by Country

Albania
Teresa, Mother, **5:** 1467

Algeria
Boumedienne, Houari, **1:** 169

Argentina
Menem, Carlos Saúl, **4:** 1062
Perón, Eva, **4:** 1218
Perón, Juan, **4:** 1221
Saavedra Lamas, Carlos, **5:** 1361

Australia
Barton, Edmund, **1:** 102
Bruce, Stanley, **1:** 207
Chifley, Joseph Benedict, **1:** 290
Cook, Joseph, **2:** 343
Curtin, John, **2:** 360
Deakin, Alfred, **2:** 378
Downer, Alexander, **2:** 428
Evatt, Herbert Vere, **2:** 487
Fadden, Arthur William, **2:** 489
Fisher, Andrew, **2:** 504
Forde, Francis Michael, **2:** 509
Fraser, Malcolm, **2:** 524
Gorton, John Grey, **2:** 584
Hawke, Robert, **2:** 642
Holt, Harold, **3:** 709
Howard, John, **3:** 725
Hughes, William Morris, **3:** 733
Keating, Paul, **3:** 810
McMahon, William, **4:** 1054
Menzies, Robert Gordon, **4:** 1065
Reid, George Houston, **4:** 1294
Scullin, James Henry, **5:** 1385
Whitlam, Gough, **5:** 1568

Austria
Francis Ferdinand, **2:** 511
Francis Joseph I, **2:** 514

Waldheim, Kurt, **5:** 1544
Wiesenthal, Simon, **5:** 1573

Belgium
Beernaert, Auguste-Marie-François, **1:** 111
La Fontaine, Henri-Marie, **3:** 885
Spaak, Paul-Henri, **5:** 1426

Brazil
Kubitschek, Juscelino, **3:** 879
Vargas, Getúlio, **5:** 1529

Burma
Thant, U, **5:** 1471

Cambodia
Pol Pot, **4:** 1250
Sihanouk, Norodom, **5:** 1400

Canada
Axworthy, Lloyd, **1:** 76
Bennett, Richard Bedford, **1:** 126
Bennett, W. A. C., **1:** 129
Borden, Robert Laird, **1:** 160
Bouchard, Lucien, **1:** 166
Campbell, Kim, **1:** 250
Carney, Pat, **1:** 259
Chrétien, Jean, **1:** 296
Clark, Joe, **1:** 304
Copps, Sheila, **2:** 349
Diefenbaker, John G., **2:** 404
Douglas, Tommy, **2:** 420
Duplessis, Maurice, **2:** 446
Fry, Hedy, **2:** 527
Gray, Herbert, **2:** 589
King, William Lyon Mackenzie, **3:** 860
Klein, Ralph, **3:** 873
Lévesque, René, **3:** 919
Laurier, Wilfrid, **3:** 894
Manning, Preston, **4:** 1023

Index

In the following index, volume numbers and those page numbers referring to full articles appear in **bold face** type.

Index

Index